Protestant Worship

Protestant Worship

Traditions in Transition

James F. White

Westminster/John Knox Press
Louisville, Kentucky

Scripture quotations are from *The New English Bible.* © The Delegates of the Oxford University Press and The Syndics of the Cambridge University Press 1961, 1970. Used by permission.

Book design by Gene Harris

First edition

Published by Westminster/John Knox Press
Louisville, Kentucky

PRINTED IN THE UNITED STATES OF AMERICA

2   4   6   8   9   7   5   3

Library of Congress Cataloging-in-Publication Data

White, James F.
   Protestant worship : traditions in transition / James F. White. —
1st ed.
         p.   cm.
   Bibliography: p.
   Includes index.

   ISBN 0-664-25037-8
   1. Public worship. 2. Liturgics. I. Title.
BV10.2.W449 1989
264—dc20   89-31883
                                                                CIP

FOR

SUSAN J. WHITE

AS A SIGN

OF LOVE

Contents

Preface

Any book that tries to describe and analyze the worship of roughly a quarter of Christianity is likely to be accused of being overly ambitious or blatantly superficial. These are valid accusations, but I can only plead in self-defense that the benefits to be gained may more than justify such audacity or foolhardiness. I cite two in particular.

There is much to be gained from examining the phenomenon of Protestant worship as a totality. As we shall see, the coherence of the data is far greater than its diversities would seem to indicate. The information, admittedly, is vast—four, almost five centuries and a global setting must be surveyed. Yet an overview can provide perspectives that restricted studies of periods, places, or individual groups cannot permit. This can help us describe the particular vocation of Protestant worship to be that form of worship most responsive to reflecting the varieties of peoples who call themselves Christian.

The other benefit is to try to fit together the individual components of Protestant worship so that the relations of the various traditions to each other become apparent. The various traditions relate to each other in intricate and complicated ways, and these relationships need to be carefully delineated. An organizing principle was suggested to me in a seminary lecture given by the late great church historian, Cyril C. Richardson, many years ago. During thirty years of teaching Christian worship myself, I have found myself frequently returning to Professor Richardson's description of seven Protestant liturgical families. I now find it makes more sense to define those families as traditions, and his seven have grown to nine. (He defined one tradition as "Zwinglian" in addition to "Calvinist," omitted "Pentecostal," and his single "Free Church" seems better defined as three distinct traditions.)

Many limitations are necessary in order to present both the overview and the relationship of the individual components of Protestant worship in a single volume rather than a vast library. The main problem in discussing each tradition is less what to include than what to leave out. I have tried to refer to some of the main studies in the notes and bibliography, but even these have had to be limited. Much also depends upon personal observation of worshiping congregations. Thus the problem of selecting what was most significant has been a constant challenge, and the result must be judged in terms of balance and selectivity. With this in mind, an early decision was made to restrict the study to Europe and North America, while being fully aware that Protestant worship is now a worldwide phenomenon. Even so, the geographical and chronological scope remains vast, and my only hope is to capture the most significant events and tendencies within these cultural limitations.

This work represents the help and cooperation of many groups, institutions, and individuals. I am grateful to hundreds of worshiping congregations who have welcomed me to join them in worship in recent years. Most people do not come to worship with a mental notebook in hand and remain ready to ask questions afterward. But these worshipers have been gracious, always quite willing to explain what it is that makes them feel at home in their kind of worship to the visitor who may not be so accustomed.

These congregations have been my teachers as well as my fellow worshipers. They vary from five persons present in a Pentecostal group in Vermont to fourteen hundred present at a sabbath-day assembly in Michigan, and they range from Europe to many parts of Canada and the United States. They have taught me much about the worship of Almighty God and sharpened my powers of observation in the process. Those who tried to answer my questions about the things they consider holy have taught me even more about the communion of saints.

The opportunity to write this book was provided by the University of Notre Dame in the form of a sabbatical leave. I am especially grateful to my colleagues in the Graduate Program in Liturgical Studies at the University of Notre Dame who have helped shape my thinking: the late Professor Niels K. Rasmussen, O.P., Professor Paul F. Bradshaw, Professor Mark Searle, and Professor Robert F. Taft, S.J. My indebtedness to them for information and insights into the whole discipline of liturgical studies is enormous. My students, too, have daily contributed to my learning. I also wish to thank the Association of Theological Schools for the research grant that made the writing of this book possible. The contributions of the Reverend Canon William M. Jacob and the faculty and students of Lincoln Theological College were enormous. It was vital to me to have a theological library and to be part of a worshiping community while my wife was teaching at that Church of England seminary.

I marvel at the ability of Nancy Kegler, Sherry Reichold, and Cheryl Reed to decipher my corrections and to produce clean copy out of my scribblings. My graduate assistant, Michael Moriarty, has been diligent in ferreting out elusive facts and books and in proof-reading. I am also grateful to the Reverend Stanley R. Hall, Dr. Paul R. Nelson, Dr. Hoyt L. Hickman, Professor Robert D. Hawkins, and Professor William G. Storey for reading and improving various chapters of the book. But most of all I am indebted to my wife, Dr. Susan J. White, for her scholarly skills in checking my data and her editorial ability in improving my expression of information. It is a far better book because of her many contributions.

J. F. W.

University of Notre Dame
May 23, 1989

1

The Study
of Protestant Worship

The study of Protestant worship has usually been conducted by methods derived from the study of Roman Catholic worship. In practice, this has meant that the chief concerns addressed have been liturgical texts, and most of those were for the eucharist. These are properly the staples of Roman Catholic liturgical scholarship, and the methodologies for such research have been carefully developed during the last century and a half. Textual studies, especially of the mass, abound.

The most widely used books on Protestant worship reflect such approaches and concerns. William D. Maxwell's *An Outline of Christian Worship,* first published in 1936 and still in print over fifty years later,[1] relegates noneucharistic worship to a final twenty pages. Bard Thompson's 1961 work on eucharistic rites, *Liturgies of the Western Church,* has been widely used for over a quarter century. More recently, the massive scholarly work *Coena Domini I* and its two projected sequels deal exclusively with eucharistic texts. All these landmark volumes treat primarily the printed texts of the eucharist. A few scholars, particularly Horton Davies,[2] have broken away from this pattern, but basically the paradigm remains: The history of Protestant worship has been largely told in terms of eucharistic texts.

I contend that this gives a distorted image and is totally irrelevant to the worship of most Protestants in America and in many other lands as well. In the first place, most American Protestants do not use printed liturgical texts on any occasion. What is said in worship is either prepared specifically for each occasion (extempore) or is completely spontaneous. There simply are no printed texts to study, and if the words spoken could be recorded they would vary weekly.

More important, even those groups who do use liturgical texts are involved in many forms of participation that are more significant to worshipers than printed words. To confine our attention to printed texts as the sole documentation is to miss much, if not most, of the reality of worship. *The Book of Common Prayer* changed scarcely at all in England after 1662, but Anglican worship was completely transformed in the course of the nineteenth century with regard to architectural setting, music, vestments, and frequency of the eucharist. Study of texts alone would not indicate any change whatsoever. Concentration on published texts has too often blinded us to more important elements of worship. Even the eucharistic prayer, on which so much scholarship has focused in recent years, is a matter of trifling importance for most worshipers.

The eucharist is usually not the most important service for most Protestants, at least not in terms of frequency. Most Protestant worship, historically and at present, has not made the eucharist its central service. Thus the services recorded in *Coena Domini I* may have been used only three or four times a year, and there are groups for whom an annual celebration of the eucharist is sufficient. For major segments of their history, churches that now have weekly celebrations were quite content with only occasional ones. The eucharist is encountered far less frequently than weddings and funerals in many congregations and deserves, just as much as they do, to be called an "occasional" service. To focus solely on the eucharist means to ignore what happens on almost every Sunday during the year. When the eucharist is celebrated, it is often tacked on to the end (or beginning) of the usual Sunday service.

One cannot overestimate the ecstasy and joy that reading the scriptures in the vernacular and preaching the word of God brought to many sixteenth-century Christians as a new and unfamiliar form of communion with God. Such communion was so personal, so intimate, that it often simply made the visible word of the sacraments seem redundant and remote. That was not the intention but frequently the effect of the reformers' work.

We might seriously consider labeling Protestant worship the "non-sacramental alternative." But there is too much variety for such a generic term to be accurate in all instances. We do have to look beyond the sacraments to understand what is central in Protestant worship. The conventional categories for the study of Roman Catholic worship simply are not appropriate.

We need, then, a new approach to the study of Protestant worship, one based on the subject to be studied itself and not borrowed from another tradition. It is, of course, quite possible that a new approach may be needed for the study of Roman Catholic worship too, one not narrowly limited to liturgical texts. But that is not our concern here.

We shall spend little time on liturgical texts, service books, or sacramental theology, the staples of most liturgical scholarship. Eucharistic prayers will scarcely be mentioned. These are not our priorities. Rather, we are trying to delineate the phenomenon of Protestant worship as it happens for ordinary worshipers. Our concern is with the total event of public worship as it occurs in local churches, not as analyzed in textbooks. This I shall try to chronicle and describe.

The role of the historian of worship is to record what practices actually persist and to be descriptive about them. Our function is not to make normative judgments. For example, whatever one believes about the significance of the sacraments in Christian worship is irrelevant to actual practice, which may show them to be of relatively minor importance. The same applies to the observance of a full calendar of the Christian year. Several groups would say they do quite well, thank you, with almost no attention to the traditional yearly cycles. But they have evolved, instead, to their own satisfaction, functional cycles that deserve to be recorded. The description of what actually exists must be independent of any value judgment as to what ought to be present. The impartial historian must consider all things equal. Survival is our only criterion for value.

All normative judgments about worship must be avoided. Attempts to use biblicism as a guideline, as we shall see, tend to be abandoned in the course of time or lead to biblicism of only certain portions of scripture. After all, there is more biblical authority for snake handling (Mark 16:18) than there is for confirmation! Historically, attempts to deduce norms for worship from scripture fail because the Bible was not written for such a purpose.

The historian, then, must be descriptive, not normative. In that way, others are helped to function as liturgical theologians so they may elucidate what the Christian faith is on the basis of what Christians do when they worship. But the diversity of what Christians do when they worship cannot be overlooked. A liturgical theology that gives preferential treatment to some forms over others is highly dubious. If we come to liturgical theology with normative judgments already made in advance, the result will be highly predictable. Any approach that ignores the full spectrum of Protestant worship will be inevitably arbitrary. As broad and comprehensive an approach as possible is necessary to do liturgical theology. The study of Protestant worship is a major and necessary source of data for any serious liturgical theology.

Seven Categories of Worship

How can we adequately describe in concise terms what actually happens in a service of Protestant worship? I shall use seven categories in describing this phenomenon. While these seven certainly do not exhaust all possibilities, they give us a manageable list of points of reference on which to base our studies. The seven categories are:

people, piety, time, place, prayer, preaching, and music. I shall refer
to these seven throughout our study. They may be visualized as in
Diagram 1. "People" comes at the middle and relates both to the
circumstances of worship (on the left) and the acts of worship (on
the right).

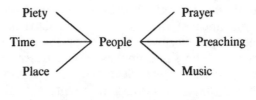

Diagram 1

It should be noted immediately that these categories are hardly the
concerns of most liturgical studies. Nor did I mention the usual
concerns of the liturgical scholar, texts and rubrics, which frequently
mean little to worshipers. People in the pews are often oblivious to
such matters. One does not experience baseball by reading the rules
of the game. Our concern is to examine the experience of the worshiper. These seven categories will help us sort out the evidence.

When we deal with something lasting over a period of time, landmark dates and persons give us our bearings. So we must devote
some space to the temporal references for the phenomenon of Protestant worship. It is not possible to trace all seven categories through
each successive generation for nearly five centuries in the space of a
single volume. I shall concentrate on the originating generation and
times of important liturgical changes.

The sacraments will certainly be mentioned but, since they are not
the chief focus of most Protestant worship, they will not play a
dominant role. The seven categories are present in all the varieties
of Protestant worship except among some Quakers. I shall describe
each of the seven categories briefly to show just what we understand
it to include.

People

The primary ingredient of all worship is people, yet rarely do most
liturgical studies mention the social realities of what was happening
to people in times of liturgical change. *People are the primary liturgical document.* Frequently, the best way to understand varieties of
worship is in terms of people. The people who form Quaker worship
are not the same as for classical Pentecostal worship.

The most important single characteristic of Protestant worship, taken as a whole, is that it comes in varieties, just as do people. Far from prescribing one uniform type of worship in a single language, as did Roman Catholicism for most of this period, Protestant worship early on acknowledged that historical realities have shaped different people in different ways. The Anglican "Articles of Religion" (1563) make it a matter of belief "that Traditions and Ceremonies . . . at all times . . . have been divers, and may be changed according to the diversity of countries, times, and men's manners." We are not dealing with abstract eternal essences, as was the official Roman Catholic view of worship for so long, but with diversity of places, times, and manners, with concrete historical realities that are fluid and changeable. The text and rubrics of the Roman Catholic mass varied little in four hundred years, as one might expect if classical abiding entities are all that matter, even though the realities of Roman Catholic worship did see major changes apart from the stagnation of rites. When one stresses the importance of history, one expects changes in worship.

People change. And those changes are often reflected in the new demands they place on their expression of worship. So we must first ask, What was happening to people that caused their worship needs to change? What social changes necessitated new ways to worship? Why was it so imperative for the reformation of worship to be completed that Puritans went to jail or emigrated to America to accomplish it? How did the American frontier produce a new type of people and, consequently, a new kind of worship?

An important aspect of the role of people in worship has been captured in recent years by the term "participation." Vatican II made famous the phrase "full, conscious, and active participation *(plenam illam, consciam atque actuosam liturgicarum celebrationum participationem).* "[3] These may all be highly desirable characteristics of worship, but they are not specific enough for our needs. What do we mean by "full" participation by people? Does listening to an anthem involve the same degree of participation as singing a hymn? Does listening silently to a sermon involve as much participation as shouting "Amen!" during it? Does liturgical dance involve full participation or discourage it? Or are there "partial" forms of participation?

We must distinguish between passive and active participation. "Passive (or receptive) participation" means people hearing or seeing someone else do something. Liturgical dance by performers alone would be passive. "Active participation" means people doing things themselves: praying, singing, shouting, dancing. Dance by a whole Shaker assembly was active. One of the developments we shall notice is the gradual increase, over the centuries, in the variety of possibilities for active participation in Protestant worship.

The concept of participation changes. In the late medieval West, participation primarily meant seeing, whereas the Reformation understood the term largely to mean hearing. At stake in the Reformation conflict was whether real participation was by eye or by ear.[4] Today, many would probably agree that both are essential to what we call passive participation. But active participation demands an actual commitment of self by being really present. And "real presence is a question of commitment"[5] in the event by doing for oneself one's own worship.

Before we accept too readily the term "conscious," we must realize that there are some important "unconscious" forms of participation for people. These involve simply being there, being a part of the church in a particular time and place. Much of the given of worship never reaches the level of consciousness, yet it forms the worshiper as a part of the church. Since place and time always occur only in relation to other places and times, the uniqueness of each worship event is an unconscious but important kind of participation.

Piety

Our second category, and the one that leads the list of circumstances of worship, is piety, the traditional term for spirituality. We speak of the ways people relate to God and to each other. It is one thing to preach about "Sinners in the Hands of an Angry God" and another to sing "In the Garden." A hellfire deity and a garden-variety God are approached in quite different ways, changing all one does in worship. We are dealing with a highly subjective quality, but that does not make it any less significant. The threescore authors of *The Study of Spirituality*[6] show what a wide variety of ways there are of understanding spirituality, or piety, among scholars.

Yet piety is the essential equipment worshipers bring to church. Subjective as it may be, what one brings to church determines in large measure what one experiences there. Thus if one's piety is largely penitential, all worship will be shaded in that direction. But even that piety can change in time, say to a resurrection piety of rejoicing. One can often find crosscurrents of differing piety within the same congregation.

Time

One of the central facts of Christianity is its territoriality. We can only talk about the church in this place or that. Worship does not exist apart from a place. The same can be said of temporality. We can only discuss worship as it happened at a certain time. The people involved are constantly affected by where and when they worship. Everything we say about worship must be conditioned by these variances of time and place.

For people at worship, the meaning of everything they do is heavily conditioned by the time in which it occurs. Relationships within time are what matter most. Some things derive meaning from being weekly events; others are significant because they occur only occasionally. The location in time dictates very much the expectation worshipers bring to a service and the way they interpret it.

There are four main cycles of liturgical time: daily, weekly, yearly, and lifetime. The daily cycle involves such matters as public, family, or private prayer. What happens on Sundays (or the Sabbath) and the other days of the week determines the weekly cycle. The yearly cycle may concern such matters as the frequency of the Lord's Supper and the various punctuations of time made through the Christian year or the pragmatic year. Both theoretical calendars and actual ones function in every congregation. The lifetime cycle involves important rites of passage. We shall discuss baptism under this heading, although believers' baptism is not so much a rite of passage as the conscious recognition of conversion. Confirmation, marriage, ordination, healing, and Christian burial all derive their chief meaning from the occasion on which they occur in the course of a person's life.

Place

The context of place is also a most important part of the experience of worship. Although the statement about church architecture that "the building will always win" is a bit strong, it is not far from true. The whole space in which things occur shapes their meaning. Frequently, our best documents of past forms of worship are their surviving or depicted architectural settings. Liturgical architecture is an important part of the study of any kind of worship.

We must look at the relationship of the basic spaces for worship: gathering, movement, congregational, choir, baptismal, and altar-table.[7] The relationship of these spaces to each other and to the various liturgical centers—pulpit, font or pool, altar-table, clergy seating—are important indicators of how things work in worship. The designs of liturgical centers tell us much about the importance of what happens at them. Much is determined by relationships: Does the pulpit dominate or the altar-table? Are the people arranged in a long tunnel-like nave away from the action or do they encircle it? We need also to observe the presence or absence of liturgical art in the worship space.

Prayer

We can begin to look at the acts of worship starting with prayer, usually one of the most important aspects of a service. How do the ministers and people speak to God? This basic part of worship can take a wide variety of forms. Indeed, many of the greatest liturgical controversies have been over the form of prayer. Should prayer be fixed in printed books or free in local diversity? Should it be prepared in advance or left to the promptings of the Spirit? Ought Christians pray in everyday language or in a special sacral language from the Elizabethan era?

Similar questions arise as to who voices the prayer for the community. Is it a unison act, a solo performance, or done spontaneously and simultaneously by everyone? Are services devised for lay leadership of prayer? How do weekday prayer services relate to the Sunday gathering of the whole community? Who voices the eucharistic prayer? Both the form and the leadership of prayer supply major cues to discovering how an assembly understands itself as a community.

Preaching

For most Protestants, preaching is the most lengthy portion in the service. At least a third of the time of worship is usually allotted to the sermon, and it frequently occupies half or more of the time that the community is assembled. It is not a coincidence that most Protestant ordained ministers are referred to not as priest, presider, or prayer leader but as preacher. Indeed, in France, *aller à sermon* is the term generally used for going to worship. Homiletics is taught in every Protestant seminary even when liturgics is neglected. This form of communication is of paramount importance for most Protestants.

Having said this, we must recognize that preaching takes a wide variety of forms and serves an assortment of functions. It can focus on bringing unbelievers into the fold or it may be a doctrinal lesson for the faithful. Preaching can be highly exegetical, interpreting the meaning of a biblical text for contemporary life, or it can begin with a topic of human concern and apply religious insights to it. Thus the center of gravity of preaching varies greatly from time to time and place to place. We shall try to indicate the approximate location of that center of gravity in different eras.

Music

Finally, for most congregations, music is an important component of worship. But again this is an elusive matter. Does the music appear as congregational song or as choral music? Is service music present or absent? Does music function as an offering of the choir to God or a proclamation to the people? The forms of music and who are the performers are important considerations. The role of instrumental music, or prohibitions against it, must be considered.

The hymns that are sung most frequently provide some of our best evidence of the types of piety prevalent among the congregation. Not only do hymns give the people words, they may be the only fixed item in the service and so have the additional power of repetition. Thus hymns form one of our best sources for liturgical theology and can be used effectively as a source of theological statements.[8] It is not always easy to find which are the most representative hymns, but the genre certainly has to be recognized as highly significant in shaping and reflecting both piety and belief.

These seven categories—people, piety, time, place, prayer, preaching, and music—will concern us as we investigate the various forms of Protestant worship. Some are more prominent in certain groups than among others at various periods. But except for some Quakers, all are constants to which we shall refer again and again.

Traditions of Protestant Worship

Protestant worship is a vast phenomenon, and we can only approach it in manageable components. The basic organization of our investigation is in terms of what I call "traditions." Traditions seem to be the natural divisions for the material we shall examine. By a "tradition," we mean inherited worship practices and beliefs that show continuity from generation to generation. At stake here is a real but often unarticulated instinct of how worship is done. Children may be the best witnesses to what we mean by tradition, for they soon come to understand what their community does in worship even before they have cognitive terms to label the individual acts. Worship traditions, then, are specific ways of and attitudes toward doing worship that are passed on from generation to generation.

It has been the custom to speak of worship forms using analogies drawn from the biological sciences: taxonomy, evolution or decay, kindred relationships. Worship forms were seen as evolving or decaying as if they were biological species. Frequently, liturgies were classified in terms of families, as if they bore genetic relationships to each other. Thus one could speak of the West Syrian family of liturgies, imposing a biological metaphor on what were actually human artifacts. But things do not beget things, and such analogies are misleading.

I avoid these kinds of analogy in favor of a political one, that of right, center, and left wings. Since political parties and platforms are human constructs, this seems more appropriate. I shall refer to the retention of late-medieval forms as characteristically "right wing" and to moves farther away from medieval worship as "left wing." Our point of reference is what the English of the sixteenth century referred to as "the old religion": in that case, the way things had been before Henry VIII.

The relation of these traditions to one another (just as with political agendas) is a fascinating study because of the inescapable contacts between them, which usually produce oppositions or alliances. What repels at one time may attract at another, and so we see shifting allegiances. An important part of our study will be to see how the various traditions relate to each other across the course of time as well as at their point of origin. None exists in isolation; all are part of the confrontation of ideas and practices just as in the world of politics.

One of the problems of using traditions as our method of sorting out the various forms of Protestant worship is that it is not always easy to mark the edges of a tradition. When did English Puritanism finally move out of the Reformed tradition and become a new tradition? No one can say precisely. Still less can one gauge how distinct American Methodism remained from the Frontier tradition. And in the modern era the edges get increasingly indistinct. The best resolution is to look for the central elements of a tradition, to identify it by its dominant ethos rather than by what is peripheral. These central elements may include the use of service books or their absence, the importance or nonimportance of sacraments, tendencies to uniformity based on codification or lack thereof, autonomy or connectionalism, the varying roles of music and the other arts, ceremonial or its absence, variety and predictability, and various sociological factors. It is only by concern with factors such as these that we can attempt an adequate study.

There are also ethnic and cultural matters of great importance. We shall treat these as matters of "style." Thus lively Presbyterian worship on the American frontier, while still recognizably within the Reformed tradition, could differ greatly from that found in the sedate churches of the East Coast. A single tradition can comprehend a number of styles without totally losing its identity. A black congregation worshiping from the *Lutheran Book of Worship* is within the Lutheran tradition, but its style of music and participation may be quite different from a congregation of Norwegian Americans using the same book. These matters of style are of great interest today for those concerned with making worship more inclusive. How comprehensive of varying styles can a tradition become? We discover each year a bit more about how elastic a tradition can be without stretching beyond its central ethos.

I shall describe nine traditions of Protestant worship, in the belief that most major expressions of Protestant worship in Europe and North America can be classified within one of them. There are, of course, many smaller groups, such as Moravians, Shakers, or Brethren, that are not easy to classify. It seems best to include them within one of the larger classifications with which they seem to have the most in common. Sometimes this may be a bit arbitrary, but the alternative is an endless proliferation of sects.

The nine traditions are Lutheran, Reformed, Anabaptist, Anglican, Separatist and Puritan, Quaker, Methodist, Frontier, and Pentecostal. These can be arranged in a scheme ranging from top to bottom in terms of century of origin and from left to right in terms of decreasing degree of radicalness in the break from the medieval past, as in Diagram 2. These locations left or right refer to the times of origin. Some, such as the Quaker, have been conservative in staying virtually in the same position. Others have at various times moved farther to the left or to the right relative to the medieval background. But they have all maintained roughly the same relationship to one another.

	Left-Wing	*Central*	*Right-Wing*	
16th c.	Anabaptist	Reformed	Anglican	Lutheran
17th c.	Quaker	Puritan		
18th c.		Methodist		
19th c.	Frontier			
20th c.	Pentecostal			

Diagram 2

To make the scheme complete, perhaps Roman Catholic worship since the Council of Trent (1545–1563) should be listed as a tenth western tradition. Even the term "western" is problematical, for some of the liveliest expressions of both Protestant and Roman Catholic worship are found today in Africa or Asia rather than in Europe or North America. But we shall be limiting our investigation to European and North American events.

Our method will be to treat each tradition individually in separate chapters. This will give a vertical or diachronic approach to history instead of a horizontal or synchronic method approach by centuries. Our central thesis is that each tradition has sufficient internal coherence that it can be traced in isolation as it evolves. If this thesis is valid, the vertical method seems more appropriate for dealing with the material. In the final chapter, we shall consider the present relations among various Protestant traditions and the Roman Catholic tradition.

Many of the historical and cultural experiences of the traditions are common. All the earlier ones made their own passages through the era of the Enlightenment, for example, but each reacted in a distinctive way. Therefore it seems best to chronicle these common experiences under the individual tradition rather than under the period. In each instance we shall begin with the origins of a tradition, discuss salient developments in Europe or North America during times of significant change in worship, and conclude with current characteristics.

2

Late Medieval Worship
and Roman Catholic Worship

The immediate source for both Protestant worship and Roman Catholic worship after the Council of Trent (post-Tridentine) is the worship life of late-medieval western Europe. These two mainstreams of present-day Christian worship in the West both derive from a common source, the fifteenth-century church of western Europe. It is necessary to take a quick look at this common heritage before proceeding to trace the distinctive Protestant contributions to Christian worship. Then I shall show how the two streams have related to each other since the sixteenth century. Finally, I shall outline developments in Roman Catholic worship since the Reformation.

The Eve of the Reformation

It is not easy to assess late-medieval worship. Scholars are in wide disagreement about the relative merits of the liturgical life of western Europe at this time in history. Much of this disagreement comes from a discrepancy in objectives, a mismatching of expectations.

Liturgical scholars, on the whole, are rather negative. Joseph Jungmann asserts that "the people were devout and came to worship: but even when they were present at worship, it was still clerical worship. . . . The people were not much more than spectators. This resulted largely from the strangeness of the language which was, and remained, Latin. . . . *The people have become dumb.*"[1] Theodor Klauser speaks of "the generally widespread discontent on the part of Catholics with the discordant, one might even say, chaotic state of liturgical practice, and the similar condition of the liturgical books . . . the immense number of abuses."[2] Herman Wegman is more specific: "The decline in medieval worship must first of all be laid to clericalization and the related individualizing of the piety of the faithful, a piety that grew apart from the liturgy. . . . This liturgy was marked by an excess of feasts, by popular customs, and by details and superstitious practices that overlaid the heart of the faith."[3]

The negative views of these three eminent Roman Catholic liturgical scholars are not duplicated by the modern school of social historians, who, to be sure, are by no means in accord with one another. Efforts to place the Reformation in medieval perspective have had differing results. In an influential essay, Bernd Moeller made a case that "the late fifteenth century in Germany was marked by greater fidelity to the church than in any other medieval epoch"[4] and claimed that precisely because of this "extreme acceleration of medieval ecclesiastical religiosity" the Reformation first broke out in Germany rather than in less devout lands.

This religiosity was expressed in the cult of the saints, particularly in images and sacred objects, and in veneration of the eucharist. "The belief in the objective presence of the divine in material elements could not have been intensified much further."[5] But this very intensity brought about its own demise in the form of popular outburst of iconoclasm by "people who felt themselves fooled by something that they had not taken lightly at all but had in fact believed all too deeply and in spite of the perceived shortcomings of its representatives."[6] Much of the continental Reformation came about, particularly in the cities, from people who felt they had been hoodwinked by discredited objects of piety. The most ardent believers frequently became the most disappointed. And many of these became the most fervent Protestants.

Thus we are left with a mixed bag of continuity and discontinuity. There were mammoth changes in the Reformation era, partly because of the problems of the official liturgy, problems that cause liturgical scholars so much distress. And there were significant changes in popular piety too. Yet the amount of continuity seems increasingly apparent, especially at the level of unofficial popular piety.

Various forms of current popular piety such as the "Modern Devotion," with its stress on the superiority of the interior over against external forms, still resonate in several Protestant traditions. Another feature of the "waning of the Middle Ages" was the concern by lay people to establish endowed preacherships in many German cities, providing, at lay instigation, an antecedent for the Protestant focus on preaching. Poland saw the development over many centuries of a popular tradition of vernacular hymnody, by no means a Reformation monopoly. Beneath many of these developments was a strong penitential piety with its focus on humanity's guilt in the face of God. The Fourth Lateran Council (1215) required the sacrament of penance before receiving communion at Easter, and the association of "penance and communion, and the strong emphasis on moral fitness for communion, form the most positive contribution of the period to eucharistic thought and practice."[7] Certainly it became a lasting part of Protestant piety.

If we look beneath the surface of official rites, we notice many strong currents of popular piety flowing into new channels with much of their original vigor and direction. Some of these have proved ineradicable even in modern-day Protestant worship. The insistence today in many parts of the Reformed tradition on beginning all worship with confession is a good instance of late-medieval penitential piety still flourishing. We shall encounter other examples.

Parallel Development

This was the worship tradition inherited by both Protestant and Roman Catholic reformers in the sixteenth century. Most of the generation of Protestant reformers born in the late fifteenth century were priests, including such leading reformers (in order of birth) as: Archbishop Hermann of Wied (1477), Wolfgang Capito (1478), Andreas Karlstadt (ca.1480), John Oecolampadius (1482), Martin Luther, O.A. (1483), Ulrich Zwingli (1484), Georg Spalatin (1484), Balthasar Hübmaier (1485), Johann Bugenhagen, O.Prem. (1485), Bernardino Ochino, Cap. (1487), Archbishop Thomas Cranmer (1489), Thomas Münzer (1490), Martin Bucer, O.P. (1491), Friedrich Myconius (ca.1491), George Blaurock (1492), Justas Jonas (1493), John Hooper (ca.1495), Menno Simons (1496), Andreas Osiander (1498), Johann Brenz (1499), Bishop John à Lasco (1499), Nicholas Ridley (ca.1500), Peter Martyr (1500), Felix Manz (ca.1500), and last, but not least, John Knox (ca.1505). By contrast, the first-line lay reformers are few, albeit distinguished: Caspar Schwenkfeld (1490), Philipp Melanchthon (1497), Conrad Grebel (1498), Melchior Hoffmann (1500), and possibly John Calvin (1509). These men knew the late-medieval tradition well.

Both sides were to make major modifications during the sixteenth century, but by quite different processes and with very different results. Some things were preserved with tenacity by Protestants, others rejected with vehemence, and yet others modified beyond recognition. The same is true of the Roman Catholic reforms, which by no means coincided with the Protestant reforms. And there were some common concerns, such as the desire for uniformity in liturgical texts, a sixteenth-century agenda made possible by the invention of printing and the resulting possibility of standardization.

The picture is complicated by the fact that there was no uniformity in late-medieval rites. In Luther's Saxony, the wedding rite was still contracted outside the church; in Cranmer's England, the entire service had moved inside ("the body of the church") after the time of Chaucer's Wife of Bath ("husbands at church door I have had five"). So the starting points vary according to both time and place. Medieval liturgical development had taken its own leisurely course; the sixteenth century was to see that change. For many Protestants and all Roman Catholics it meant a sweeping new perspective that liturgy was something changed from the top down, not something percolating up from practices of scattered parishes, dioceses, and religious communities. And there were several drastic changes for Protestants: from passive participation often to active, from worship almost exclusively focused on sacraments to worship only rarely so directed, and from optional preaching to preaching as an essential part of worship.

For over four hundred years, Protestant and Roman Catholic worship evolved in almost airtight isolation from each other. Even the Catholic Revival in the Church of England in the nineteenth century largely took its inspiration from medieval worship, preferring to mimic the fourteenth century rather than contemporary Roman Catholicism. A common heritage became two completely separate histories of development in mutual indifference until the warming trends of the twentieth-century liturgical movement began to melt the barriers. This does not mean that all developments were totally different, merely isolated. For example, both Protestants and Roman Catholics gradually surrendered the medieval practice of baptizing babies by dipping in favor of the more convenient pouring or sprinkling. But it is difficult to find any direct links between parallel developments even when similar in form.

While the medieval inheritance is common property, the post-Tridentine patterns, the time of the Congregation of Rites (a Roman bureaucracy created in 1588 to standardize rites) and the pieties of the baroque period are distinctly not. Both parties had moved beyond the common inheritance of the rites of southern England (Sarum Use) or the standard liturgical textbook of William Durandus (1230–1296), the *Rationale of Divine Offices*. The reformed Roman Catholic liturgical books of this era—the breviary (daily prayers) of 1568, the missal (for the mass) of 1570, the pontifical (bishop's services) of 1596, and the ritual (pastoral rites) of 1614—were not points of contact, not even of conflict. They simply belonged to completely different worlds.

Protestantism could, at times, maintain some medieval practices and pieties with great tenacity while post-Tridentine Roman Catholicism may have wished them away. Infrequent communion, a penitential eucharist, a relish for regional practices, and other medieval characteristics survived in various segments of Protestantism. Luther never could get used to the new concept of a uniform liturgy even for all German-speaking territories. It also meant that some medieval tendencies continued to develop within Protestantism and sometimes reached their logical and inevitable conclusion at the hands of Protestants rather than Roman Catholics. The slowly developing split of Christian initiation so that confirmation was distanced from baptism was made even firmer in Protestantism, where knowledge of the catechism—that is, fundamental doctrines—often became requisite for confirmation. The splintering of initiation had been a long time coming; Martin Bucer (1491–1551) and others made it final.

The splitting of ways between Protestants and Roman Catholics that had begun in 1520 with threats of excommunication and the actual excommunication of Luther (on January 3, 1521) became final in 1570 with the excommunication of Elizabeth I by Pope Pius V with *Regnans in excelsis* (February 25). The two previous popes had made offers to the Queen that would have permitted retention of the *Book of Common Prayer* in exchange for recognition of papal supremacy. But the former Inquisitor General of Christendom, Pius V, finally ended any opportunity for reconciliation, a situation that has continued for over four hundred years.

By 1570, controversies were under way between Protestants of various traditions, and dialogue scarcely existed between Protestants and Roman Catholics. The Roman Catholic tradition and the various Protestant traditions developed in isolation of each other. Only occasionally was the opposite side summoned as a bugaboo if a proposal sounded too "Protestant" (such as using the vernacular) or a practice was deemed too "Catholic" (such as confession to a priest). Each side operated with little direct experience of the worship practices of the other and even less scholarly study.

Both western inheritors of late-medieval worship were going their own ways after 1570, in parallel but completely separate developments. Diagram 3 illustrates the great western liturgical split.

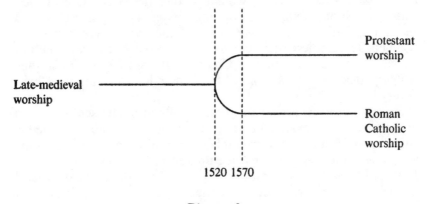

Diagram 3

Roman Catholic Worship Since the Reformation

To make sense of parallel Protestant developments after the six-teenth-century split, we shall trace briefly the independent develop-ment of Roman Catholic liturgical development after the Council of Trent by speaking of five eras: baroque, enlightenment, romantic, liturgical movement, and post-Vatican II.

The Baroque Era

The baroque era of the seventeenth century brought a major dis-juncture between late-medieval worship in the West and subsequent Roman Catholic worship. As Joseph Jungmann states emphatically, "The contrast between the Baroque spirit and that of the traditional liturgy was so great that they were two vastly different worlds."[8] And Anton Baumstark argued that the normal, natural process of hap-hazard liturgical development that had gone on for fifteen hundred years was forever terminated by the efficient bureaucracies of the post-Tridentine era.[9]

A chief feature of the baroque era was the standardization of rites. Although Trent had only mandated reform of the breviary and missal, by 1614 all the liturgical books had been revised. The brevi-ary and missal were imposed on the West, with the exception of a few dioceses and orders. Practices of the Church in Rome came to be normative and the *Roman Ritual* of 1614 eventually replaced most regional practices. The new books were uniform and "non-reformable." To safeguard such standardization, the Congregation of Rites was established in 1588 to exercise central control.

This inaugurated what Theodor Klauser has called the "epoch of rubricism,"[10] or rule by centralized legislation. In the successor Con-gregation's offices today are long shelves holding volumes of inqui-ries decisively answered by Roman authorities over the centuries, ending questions about local options. Even the creative efforts of Jesuit missionaries in remote parts of the earth were eventually doomed. The Chinese rites controversy from the seventeenth century onward ended assimilation of Chinese culture in Roman Catholic worship, dealing a "death blow" to Chinese Roman Catholic Chris-tianity.[11]

It was, however, a time of artistic brilliance. The sculpture and architecture of Giovanni Lorenzo Bernini (1598–1680) and the ar-chitecture of Francesco Borromini (1599–1667) came to adorn Rome and other cities. A new architectural form was developed by the Jesuits at their Il Gesu Church in Rome. Since their rule dispensed them from the obligation of saying the daily office together in church, Jesuits could omit the most used part of parish churches, the choir, which had intervened between the high altar and the congregation. This made the high altar splendidly visible and heightened visual participation by the people. Within a century, Jesuit baroque churches of great magnificence were being built all over the world. By contrast, Wren's Anglican churches were designed as "auditories." Musicians such as Claudio Monteverdi (1567–1643) and others contributed elaborate service music.

The visual brilliance of the period was reflected in new devotions concentrating on what was seen: processions, benediction, and exposition. A variety of new popular cults focused on visual images: the Sacred Heart of Jesus, the Sacred Heart of Mary, Precious Blood. "The Blessed Sacrament and the monstrance have now taken the place of relics and reliquaries and much of the cult of saints has given way to devotion to Our Lady."[12] New feasts focused on the Name of Mary (1683), Mary the Redemption of Captives (1696), the Immaculate Conception (1708), and the Rosary (1716).

The Era of Enlightenment

Roman Catholic worship was not immune to the challenges of the era of enlightenment of the eighteenth century, but the chief result was to make Rome more defensive. Various proposals for liturgical reform were made and rejected. Enlightened monarchs such as Joseph II, Holy Roman Emperor from 1765 to 1790, and his brother, Leopold, Grand Duke of Tuscany from 1765 to 1790, sought to have the state reform the church. Various proposals included a vernacular liturgy, emphasis on preaching, the communion of all worshipers, changes in the ritual and breviary, worship to be made conducive to improved public morality, and restraints on such devotions as pilgrimages, the cult of saints, fasting, and Marian piety.

A landmark for the enlightenment agenda for worship was the Synod of Pistoia held in 1786 under the leadership of Bishop Scipione de' Ricci (1741–1810). It called for one altar per church and one mass each Sunday, opposed Latin for worship, and resisted the cult of the Sacred Heart. The synod's work was thwarted by Rome, and Bishop Ricci resigned in 1790. During this period, Roman Catholic sacramental theology became almost obsessively concerned with the concept of validity (basically, What is the least that can be done still to have a valid sacrament?) and became increasingly resistant to change. In 1661, it was forbidden to translate the mass from Latin.

More freedom was experienced in France, where the National Assembly had refused to publish the decrees of Trent. Gallicanism, as this relative freedom from Roman interference was known, included resistance to liturgical standardization. At the time of the French Revolution, 80 out of 130 dioceses were still using local rites rather than Roman.[13] Considerable experimentation was evident in various French local and regional liturgical books, including the Breviary of Paris (1736) and the Ritual of Alet (1667),[14] and these varieties persisted until the mid-nineteenth century. Archbishop John Carroll (1735–1815) urged in vain a vernacular translation for America.

The Romantic Era

A new era of romanticism became apparent by the second third of the nineteenth century. The guiding light was a revived monasticism. During the fourteen years after 1790, the number of monasteries in France had dropped from over a thousand to less than twenty. In 1833, Prosper Guéranger (1805–1875) reestablished the monastery of Solesmes in France and gave the initial impetus to modern liturgical movement developments. The first century or so of this period was dominated by monks, particularly Lambert Beauduin (1873–1960) in Belgium as promoter, Odo Casel (1886–1948) in Germany as theologian, and Virgil Michel (1890–1938) in America as thinker and editor.

As part of romanticism, much of the program of this period involved the recovery of lost or neglected treasures from the medieval past. The recovery of Gregorian chant with choirs for men only was a (probably misdirected) effort at improving participation. A major reform was accomplished under Pope Pius X (1835–1914), who promoted recovery of frequent communion by the laity.

In a sense, this era ended with the papal letter *Mediator Dei* (Mediator between God and Men) of 1947. Pope Pius XII (1876–1958) grudgingly acknowledged the significance of the calls for liturgical change but condemned many of the aims that were shortly to be made official policy by the Second Vatican Council (1962–1965). His encyclical was a last attempt to hold the line for the old ideals of standardized liturgy, tight restrictions, and fear of too much active lay participation.

The New Liturgical Movement

The era after World War II saw the Roman Catholic Church adopt a new agenda for a new liturgical movement, one largely borrowed from Protestant worship. Indeed, the new movement flourished largely in Protestant countries or among those people who, like Beauduin, had had extensive contacts in such countries. Although liberal Protestants accommodated perhaps too readily to the modern world, Roman Catholicism finally began to overcome its fear of such engagement. Protestants built the first modern church building in 1906, Unity Temple in Oak Park, Illinois, designed by Frank Lloyd Wright (1869–1959). Wright went on to design eighteen Protestant and Orthodox churches and synagogues. Roman Catholics hesitated another two decades before accepting modern architecture, beginning with Notre Dame at Le Raincy near Paris, built in 1923 to the designs of Auguste Perret (1874–1954). But in the years after World War II, leaders such as Maurice Lavanoux (1894–1974) led the Liturgical Arts Society to promote the value of contemporary art forms for liturgical art.[15] Alain Couturier, O.P. (1897–1954), did the same in France.[16] The most pressing issue after the war became that of the vernacular. Colonel John K. Ross-Duggan (1899–1979) in the United States formed the Vernacular Society. An initial victory was the translation of parts of the *Collectio Rituum* (book of pastoral rites) for American use (1954).

Other efforts pointed to greater emphasis on the word of God in worship with increased stress on the importance of preaching. The collapse of efforts to restore the Gregorian chant led to a new interest in vernacular hymnody. There was no mistaking the Protestant direction of many of these reforms, as the opponents of liturgical reform never tired of pointing out. These accusations were undoubtedly a hurdle but did not discourage such courageous leaders of reform as Michael Mathis (1885–1960), H. A. Reinhold (1897–1968), and Reynold Hillenbrand (1905–1979). The agenda for reform was well prepared by 1962.

Post-Vatican II

A fifth era began after Vatican II, that of reformed Roman Catholic worship. In the quarter century after the *Constitution on the Sacred Liturgy* (1963), far more changes happened than in the previous four centuries, and most of them seem to be irrevocable. We can only point out a few highlights here.

Gone, in part, was insistence on absolute uniformity in favor of some fine statements for pluralism and local identity. However, the production of the reformed liturgical books has been a highly centralized and almost exclusively clerical task. At long last, signs of openness to the modern world and its various cultures have been given. The major work, so far, has been the production of the reformed rites and their translation into the various languages of the world. For the people, the crucial change has been the complete shift to the vernacular, thus promoting the "full, conscious, and active participation" that the *Constitution* encouraged. Much has been achieved in making congregational song a popular reality, with an endless variety of hymnals and songbooks provided. Preaching has been made a significant part of Sunday masses.

The work of liturgical revision has produced great changes. The development of a three-year Sunday lectionary has had great ecumenical consequences. A major new approach to initiation is found in the *Rite for the Christian Initiation of Adults* (1972), and significant changes have come about in the rites for infant baptism (1969), funerals (1969 and 1989), weddings (1969), and ordinations (1968). The *Missal* of 1970 included the possibility of four canons for mass and many options and choices. The only clear failure seems to have been the new breviary, the *Liturgy of the Hours* (1971), because it remained tied to monastic patterns. The stage of revision is nearly complete, with publication in English of the bishops' ceremonies and book of blessings under way in 1989.

For the first time in almost four centuries, developments in Roman Catholic worship have been of immense interest to many Protestants. If the postwar period was a time of Protestant ideas coming to the forefront in Roman Catholic thinking, the post-Vatican II era has been a time of Roman Catholic ideas shaping Protestant worship. Protestants have now returned the compliment by borrowing much that is new in Roman Catholic worship. Indeed, new service books from Roman Catholic, Methodist, Lutheran, Reformed, and Anglican traditions seem to be similar recensions of a single text. At times, the Roman Catholic reforms (such as calling the times after Epiphany and Pentecost "Ordinary Time" instead of special seasons) have been more radical than Protestants have cared to undertake; Protestants occasionally seem determined to be the last guardians of some medieval practices. On the other hand, one rarely goes to a Roman Catholic mass without hearing music or hymns long familiar to Protestants.

If we were to picture recent developments, they might be visualized as in Diagram 4.

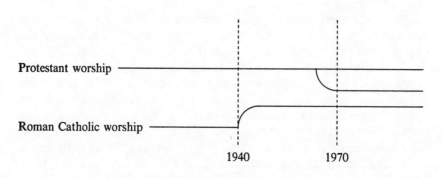

Diagram 4

Developments for many Protestants and Roman Catholics have been proceeding on close but parallel tracks, especially at the end of the time of revision of liturgical books (except among Presbyterians). Of course, many Protestant groups, especially within the Quaker, Frontier, and Pentecostal traditions, seem to be continuing in their own distinctive ways, little affected by recent tendencies among other Protestants and Roman Catholics. Whether these traditions, too, will eventually move in a similar direction is hard to say. It is even harder to predict whether the parallel lines will ever eventually converge. It is also quite possible that at present (1989) the moves of mainline Protestant churches toward assimilating the recent Roman Catholic reforms have come to an end and they are entering an era of neo-Protestant emphasis in worship. We shall return to speculation about the future after examining the origins and developments of the various Protestant traditions of worship in the next nine chapters.

3

Lutheran Worship

Martin Luther (1483–1546) provided the foundation for all Protestant worship with his 1520 treatise *The Babylonian Captivity of the Church,* [1] one of the most radical challenges ever written to the whole system of late-medieval worship and pastoral care. Yet even with such radical origins, *The Babylonian Captivity* ended up being a major force for conservatism. It represents a high degree of stability, undisputed by Protestants (other than Quakers) until the Catholic Revival in the Church of England three hundred years later. And its doctrines are still professed worldwide. It may be the only Reformation document that is simply taken for granted by virtually all Protestants.

The Babylonian Captivity represents a furious attack on the whole late-medieval sacramental system, a system that had slowly evolved over centuries of parish life and had received its theological fine-tuning in the thirteenth century. By no means had all controversy disappeared with that century, and theologians continued to dispute details right up to the onset of the Reformation. But the boundaries of permissible disagreement had become quite clear by the early fifteenth century. John Huss (ca.1369—1415) paid with his life for trespassing beyond those bounds. And Huss's objections were mild compared to Luther's onslaught.

In a single treatise, Luther attacked the whole cradle-to-grave system of sacramental ministration as built on false premises and contrary to the word of God. Only on the sacrament of baptism did he relent in his attack. Thus 1520 marks the first major division in western Christian worship, creating two distinct inheritors of the western tradition, Protestants and Roman Catholics. Any ecumenical discussion today has to begin with the consequences of what Luther said in *The Babylonian Captivity*.

This treatise represents a genuine paradigm shift, for it completely undercuts the ground on which the whole medieval sacramental system stood. It was an intellectual revolution; once the break was made, the pieces never went back together in the same way but demanded a wholly new conceptual framework.[2] The final consequence was to move the central focus of Christian worship for Protestants from worship—which, for lay people, had been almost entirely the sacraments—to one in which the sacraments became occasional intruders on a normal pattern of worship. No greater shift has ever occurred in Christian worship, either East or West.

Yet the same Martin Luther who began this revolution could write in 1523 to the Christians of Leisnig that "the service now in common use everywhere goes back to genuine Christian beginnings"[3] and urge them to respect it. Again, when Luther did publish his own vernacular version of the mass in 1526, he kept a basically conservative shape.[4] And much of his next twenty years were spent defending practices and beliefs that Luther's more impatient followers often felt were more identified with the medieval past than with their own radical thoughts.

Luther's quarrel with existing worship was a lover's quarrel. He was a priest, and the mass and daily office (services of prayers and praise) had been daily experiences throughout his formative years. Whenever possible, Luther sought to preserve the ancient cultus (worship forms). He could quote with approval the saying, "Misuse does not destroy the substance, but confirms its existence."[5] Abuse simply calls for reform. For Luther, a break with the past could be justified only by the highest of authorities, the word of God. Luther is a strange combination of both faithful continuity and radical discontinuity with the past, a tension that has characterized much of Protestant worship ever since. Out of this combination have evolved the various traditions of Protestant worship. As other movements leaned farther and farther to the left, the tension between continuity and discontinuity remained and is present even in contemporary worship discussions.

The obvious place, for a variety of reasons, to begin our discussion of the various traditions is with Lutheran worship. We shall look at Luther's protests, discuss his constructive role in founding the Lutheran tradition, note some of the more prominent Lutheran developments over the next four centuries, and then survey some characteristics of Lutheran worship today.

Luther's Protest

It is significant that Luther is the only person for whom a Protestant worship tradition is named. All others are products of collaborations, but Luther placed such a stamp on Lutheran worship that his mark remains distinctive even today, especially in sacramental theol-

ogy and church music. Evidences remain both of the negative aspects
of protests with which his reform began and his constructive contributions to the tradition named for him.

Three sermons Luther preached in 1519 on penance, baptism, and
the eucharist[6] showed little indication of what was to come. But
things began to erupt in early 1520. In his *A Treatise on the New
Testament, That Is the Holy Mass*[7] Luther began to simmer over the
mass as sacrifice. The full explosion came on October 6 with publication of *The Babylonian Captivity of the Church,* a title itself to be
reckoned with. Essentially, the treatise extends to worship Luther's
overriding concept of salvation as a free gift from God not earned
by human efforts. A more irenic statement of another aspect of the
central doctrine appeared the same year in the treatise *Freedom of
a Christian. The Babylonian Captivity* is such a foundational document, not only for Lutheran worship but for all Protestant worship,
that it must be discussed in some detail. Here sacramental theology
bears a most direct relation to the actual shaping of worship itself.

The Babylonian Captivity brings to a logical conclusion one possible development of the late-medieval concept of the number of sacraments. For most of Christian history, it had not been considered
essential to prove institution by Christ to be necessary for a sacrament, but in the thirteenth century the phrase "instituted by Christ"
became a normal part of the definition of a sacrament, and Luther
is unable to ignore this late addition. When he confronts the sacramental system, he finds that only two or three qualify as sacraments
in having "both the divinely instituted sign and the promise of forgiveness of sins."[8] The word "promise" is the key to Luther's concept
of sacraments, and for him it means a statement found in scripture.
By this standard—one of biblical literalism, to be sure—only baptism
and the eucharist deserve the title "sacrament." A sacrament cannot
be a work of humans; we baptize but it is God who actually baptizes.[9]
According to *The Babylonian Captivity,* both sacraments are God-
given promises to the man or woman of faith. But the Antichrist has
captured the sacraments, and true Christians have been denied freedom just as were captive Jews in Babylon.

Luther's theology of salvation shapes his theology of the sacraments.[10] Since salvation is a divine gift, not a human work, the
sacraments are subject to the same order of salvation. They are signs
and promises of what God does for humans and, like redemption,
can only be received in faith. Above all, the scriptural promise is
expressed as dominical injunctions (commands of Christ), treated as
imperatives: "Do this" and "Go forth therefore and . . . baptize." It
is all a coherent part of Luther's theology of salvation, although flaws
eventually appear for the problem of faith in the case of infant
baptism.

Most of *The Babylonian Captivity* is devoted to spelling out the consequences for individual sacraments. Luther liberates the mass from three captivities by which it has been ensnared. The first is withholding the cup from the laity, a source of agitation by the followers of Huss for over a century. A second and more formidable is the official formula for defining Christ's self-giving in the eucharist by the term "transubstantiation" (the inner reality changes but not the outer); Luther bristles at defining what the church experiences in the eucharist in terms derived from a pagan philosopher (Aristotle). But surely the most dangerous captivity is that which made the mass into a work humans offer to God.

Luther's line of attack on the prevailing concepts of the eucharist as sacrifice became the standard Protestant reaction to this aspect of the mass until the time of John Wesley (1703–1791). However sophisticated the official theology of concepts of sacrifice might be, it was hard for the lay person to think of it other than as a bribe to God.[11] In attacking most concepts of the mass as sacrifice, Luther was challenging not just worship but the accepted basis of the ordained priesthood and, ultimately, church finances.[12]

Sacraments, Luther argued, are based on a divine testament, a word of God that cannot fail. They are a gift offered freely by God, not a sacrifice offered by humans to obtain favor.[13] Sacrifice can only be thought of in terms of responses brought by faith, in offering one's praise, prayer, and body to God. Luther is not as concerned about sacrifice being a repetition of Calvary, thus detracting from its uniqueness, as were later reformers. Rather, he is concerned that sacrifice too easily becomes a form of righteousness based on human activity rather than on God's. Ultimately, worship depends entirely on God's activity, not that of human beings.[14]

The captivity of baptism was less painful, but the Antichrist had often succeeded in making Christians forget the genuine promise to those of faith that salvation is a free and lifelong offer. Over the centuries, the original function of penance had been forgotten, and Luther finally convinces himself that, lacking a material sign, it is not to be numbered among the dominical sacraments even though John 20:22–23 contains words of promise. Short shrift is made of the other four; confirmation, ordination, marriage, and extreme unction are not based on God's own promise and hence cannot be considered sacraments. These services are not to be despised but neither are they grounded on divine promise, since they do not contain the essential words of God needed to make them effectual signs to those who receive them in faith.

Luther's work in *The Babylonian Captivity* both won and lost him friends. Desiderius Erasmus (1466–1536) winced at the radicalness of Luther's statements even though not uncritical of the system himself. The seven sacraments attracted an unlikely champion in King Henry VIII (1491–1547) of England, who wrote a defense that Pope Leo X (1475–1521) declared had been inspired by the Holy Ghost; Henry and his royal descendants were proclaimed "Defenders of the Faith." The treatise won to Luther's side a valuable assistant, the priest Johann Bugenhagen (1485–1558), who was to become the reformer of Denmark and Norway.

If *The Babylonian Captivity* was Luther's bombshell, his other blasts at inherited forms of worship were minor grenades. In August 1521 he refused to continue to celebrate the mass in private.[15] He assaulted the whole monastic system with *On Monastic Vows,* written in late November of that year. But at Christmas, Andreas Karlstadt (ca.1477–1541) took it upon himself to further the work of reformation in Wittenberg in Luther's absence. Drastic changes were made in the mass, eliminating the canon, elevation, and vestments and delivering the bread into communicants' hands.[16] It brought Luther out of hiding at Wartburg Castle to slow things down in order to allay fears among the laity. For the moment, he stopped the reformation of worship in Wittenberg. But others were not deterred, and new vernacular eucharistic rites began to appear: that of Kaspar Kantz in Nördlingen in 1522, the Worms German Mass of 1524, and the Evangelical Mass of Thomas Münzer in 1524 (with other recensions dependent upon it).[17] In various ways, others anticipated some of the reforms that came to be associated with Luther's contributions to Christian worship.

Had Luther's work been solely that of protest, he certainly would not be remembered as the source of a major tradition of Christian worship. It is his constructive accomplishments that make him such an important historical figure, as he moved from diagnosis to prescription. Most of what Luther accomplished in this positive fashion, as well as what he had written in protest, became the basic currency for all Protestant traditions of worship. So we must deal with him both as the founder of the Lutheran tradition and as the prime source for all the other western traditions that built on his constructive efforts.

Luther's Reform

Luther's liturgical reforms were strongly pastoral in the sense that they were conceived of not as scholarly programs but out of the realities of parish life as he knew it. They are truly universal, even though founded upon a particular people, his Saxon neighbors. So it is with the changing role of people in worship that we must begin.

Essentially, Luther was in the process of developing a new theology of the laity. This affected far more than just worship; it inaugurated whole new concepts of the church, of ministry, of secular life, of economics. The Middle Ages had known rigid hierarchical stages of holiness, with clerical and religious communities at the top and lay people in the world at the bottom. But if, as Luther argued, the milkmaid who follows the cow is as holy as the nun in her cloister, there are no ranks of holiness. All Christians are called to minister to one another in whatever station they might find themselves placed. Far from being a leveling down of clerical dignities, this raises laity to the same dignity as clergy and those in religious orders.

In time of need, any Christian could assume the role of clergy. The Christian community that found itself stranded in a wilderness could choose its own minister and be assured that their choice could have as much authority as if ordained by bishops or the pope.[18] In daily life, Christians could and should minister to one another. Even individual Christians could hear each other's confession when no priest was available.

Ordained clergy were not to be dispensed with. As radical sectarians began to illustrate possible implications of his teachings, Luther came to place a more positive value on ordained clergy. They became, for him, far more than just optional or simply a force for decency and order. He came to see ordination as part of Christ's legacy to his church, as part of the divine order. "The public ministry of the Word," he wrote, "ought to be established by holy ordination as the highest and greatest of the functions of the church."[19] Ordination, while not essential to a Christian community, is highly desirable and in accord with God's intention for the church.

Because of Luther's new vision of the laity in the church, baptism acquired new dignity; baptism initiated one into the priesthood of all believers, "For whoever comes out of the water of baptism can boast that he is already a consecrated priest, bishop, and pope."[20] Luther grasped the corporate nature of baptism in inaugurating each Christian's ministry to the community and the community's ministry to that person. He attempted to deal with the problem of infant baptism by claiming it was commanded by God.[21] Through baptism, all became priests and assumed a priestly role in church and society.

The consequences for worship are enormous. The Christian people are no longer simply present in worship for passive participation but to play a priestly role, an essential ingredient of Luther's view of the church and the process of salvation. This necessitates that people fulfill their priesthood in worship by active participation in new ways that make worship accessible to them. Music was one of the means by which all could exercise their priestly ministry, and Lutheran worship became intrinsically musical liturgy. The vernacular allowed people to pray together so all could hear and speak as one body. Luther declared that "a Christian congregation should never gather together without the preaching of God's Word and prayer."[22]

Frequent communion was the most difficult reform for Luther or anyone else to accomplish. For people accustomed to receiving the Lord's Body only a few times a year, to receive it and the cup each week meant a radical shift. In effect, this change remade the laity in the image of priests, who communed and received both elements weekly or daily. To raise the laity to this level of eucharistic piety, formerly expected only of the professionally religious, was no mean task. Furthermore, not only were the laity encouraged to receive at every celebration but, like priests, they were to receive the wine as well as the bread. Thus Luther was reaching back over the four hundred years in which this form of lay participation had disappeared (except for occasional protest movements) in the West.

Although cautious at first, Luther soon realized that little could change the role of the laity without putting the words into a language lay people understood. To be sure, his first liturgical attempt, the *Formula Missae* (Form of the Mass) of 1523, was in Latin.[23] There was some drastic surgery in it, removing most of the canon (eucharistic prayer) but, since the laity had never heard the canon (always recited in silence), few were likely to notice its virtual disappearance. The ceremonial they could observe was little diminished; indeed, the actions of the priest were now more visible to the congregation. Luther's baptismal rite of the same year retained most of the medieval ceremony and would not have been startling to most people, except for the exclusive use of German in it.

Three years seems to be about the right time, whether in the sixteenth century or the twentieth, to learn the defects and strengths of a new service. Three years later, Luther published his final eucharistic and baptismal rites. Even so, the rites were intended for local use rather than to be normative everywhere. His German mass, the *Deutsche Messe* (1526),[24] represents the full use of the vernacular in worship, although Luther could still argue for Latin services in schools. Now the whole service was in a language people could understand and in which they could participate. The canon, that most clerical "abominable concoction drawn from everyone's sewer and cesspool," as Luther called it, had been drastically pruned to eliminate any sense of sacrifice. The chief survivor was Christ's words, the words of institution. Luther, by this choice, concluded the whole medieval trajectory since Ambrose (ca. 339–397). If, after all, the words of institution alone are efficacious, could not the rest be eliminated? Luther had simply brought medieval thinking to its logical conclusion.

Such drastic changes in the roles of Christian people in worship demanded a readjustment in piety. It is one thing to shuffle rites, quite another to reform personal piety. Luther was extremely sensitive to this problem, and part of his genius as a reformer was that he could approach worship reform fully aware of what a Saxon peasant brought to worship and experienced there. Because Luther wished to reshape piety, not destroy it, he was reluctant to make changes that would scandalize the laity.

Thus Luther reacted against Karlstadt's reforms, although some of Karlstadt's practices were eventually to appear in Luther. He was distressed by the suddenness of the reforms of Thomas Münzer (ca.1490–1525) and vehemently decried similar too-rapid shifts in piety. Eventually, tolerance for adiaphora (matters indifferent to effecting salvation) came to be the Lutheran way of dealing with matters that were doctrinally indifferent yet had great popular appeal. Unless a practice communicated something patently false, Luther could accommodate it. And so much ceremonial and liturgical art survived in churches in Lutheran lands, whereas they often were summarily abandoned or destroyed in places reformed by the Reformed and Anglican traditions. Such things as the elevation, vestments, and images tended to remain rather than be abolished. They were firmly lodged in popular piety, and Luther saw no need to trample on them.

Luther dreamed of a kind of "truly evangelical order" for Christians of earnest piety who would not need outward forms and structures at all, those "who profess the gospel with hand and mouth," but he never did pursue such a possibility.[25] These Christians would meet in small groups and were free to use whatever patterns they found helpful. But for most people fixed forms were necessary, and these Luther provided in the "Deutsche Messe."

Luther did not attack the prevailing penitential piety of his time directly. But Lutheran hymnody called attention not to the sinner's misery but to God's greatness and moved toward outpourings of joy on the part of those who had been saved. "Dear Christians, Let Us Now Rejoice," probably Luther's second hymn, sets an enduring theme. Justification by God's free gift plays a significant role in the hymns Luther's congregations sang. Though little is said about sanctification in the confessional documents of doctrinal standards themselves, the hymns were an important tool in shaping people's thinking about living out the Christian life for those who know they have been justified by the righteousness of Christ.[26] These hymns are for those who know the work of Christ has set them free yet for love of Christ are captive to serve all. Such hymns became an important means of reshaping piety away from a penitential model to one that could rejoice in salvation as a free gift. The importance of hymns in reshaping piety among Lutherans cannot be overestimated, especially since they were (and are) often memorized along with the *Small Catechism,* first published in 1529.

In 1528, Luther visited churches in the area around Wittenberg. How much remained to be done to change pastoral realities was a revelation to him. The experience especially strengthened his desire to improve instruction of the people and resulted in the *Small Catechism* and the *Large Catechism* of 1529.[27] Both were important instruments in reshaping piety through instruction. Frequently, answers learned by rote memorization provided people's chief resource in facing life's perplexities. Reinforcing each other, catechism and liturgy became powerful forces in developing a piety based on reformation principles.

At the same time, much traditional piety was maintained and reinforced. Luther wished to retain penance as an important part of lay piety and provided simple forms so that people might confess without cataloging their transgressions by species and number.[28] Luther's own devotion to Mary remained strong and, in its christological dimensions, was encouraged among his followers. Devotion to the other saints, however, was not promoted.

Another of Luther's contributions is what might be called a "baptismal piety." Luther believed that "there is no greater comfort on earth than baptism"[29] and took great consolation in the knowledge of his salvation by reminding himself of his witness: "But I am baptized." God's promise made in baptism was a sure source of confidence, renewed throughout life upon rising each day by anointing oneself with moisture. Because of this form of piety, Luther could assert that it is baptism which "overcomes and takes away sin and daily strengthens the new man, always remains until we pass from this present misery to eternal glory."[30] Lutherans have yet to catch up with the depth of Luther's baptismal piety as a way of life!

The prevailing organization of time on daily, weekly, yearly, and lifetime cycles continued, with certain important exceptions. For schools, daily morning and evening prayer services were encouraged.[31] The weekly emphasis on Sunday was strengthened by the focus on each Lord's Day as a christological event. Events associated with Christ such as the feasts of the Epiphany (January 6) and the Annunciation to Mary (March 25) were retained, with greater emphasis placed on their christological dimension rather than Marian associations.[32] There was a virtual elimination of saints' days in favor of the salvation events of scripture, so fewer festivals were observed. The traditional Sunday epistle and gospel lections were maintained. The greatest change in time was the new emphasis on weekly communion. To a people for whom communion was received once a year, usually at Easter, this must have been an amazing new experience.

The events of the life cycle, expressed in the pastoral offices, brought some change and much continuity. Luther's first baptismal rite of 1523 retained most of the medieval ceremony and added his new prayer over the font, the so-called flood prayer. This linked the present event to the Old Testament events of Noah's flood and the Red Sea crossing.[33] Three years later, Luther produced a revised baptismal rite with significant changes. A number of the ceremonies, such as the blowing on the child, the *ephphatha* (Mark 7:34), two anointings, and the giving of the candle had disappeared. Yet much of the previous rite remained, including the sign of the cross, Luther's flood prayer, the use of Mark 10:13–16 ("Suffer little children"), renunciation of the devil, questions on the creed, dipping (the method Luther preferred), and giving of the white robe.[34]

The change with regard to confirmation was more dramatic, since Luther had made it clear that he did not view confirmation as a sacrament. Luther did not provide a new confirmation rite but went on record in a sermon of March 15, 1523, that he would not be unhappy "if every pastor examines the faith of the children . . . lays hands on them, and confirms them."[35] The result was that confirmation became something of a graduation exercise, in which children publicly show their knowledge of the Christian faith, but in no way was it an act in which God gives new grace. It became a human work, not God's. Thus Luther found one solution for the pressing problem in western Christianity of what to do with confirmation, perhaps not the best possible solution but one that has continued to satisfy much of Protestantism.

Luther's marriage rite is perhaps his most conservative, as marriage rites usually are. His generic Hans and Greta make their vows to each other at the church door in his rite of 1529, "Order of Marriage for Common Pastors."[36] Luther added Matthew 19:6 ("What God has joined together"), which makes it sound like a sacrament, but he declares it is not, even though a "hundred times more spiritual than the monastic estate." The ceremony ends by all processing inside for scripture readings, a sermon, and a blessing.

In the ordination rite, on the other hand, Luther felt free to make major innovations. As early as 1525 he presided at the ordination of George Rörer and, since he did not regard a bishop necessary for ordination, presided in 1542 at the ordination of Nikolaus von Amsdorf (1483–1565) as Lutheran bishop. The most unusual element of Luther's practice was that of having the ordaining pastor recite the Lord's Prayer during the laying on of hands rather than using a conventional ordination prayer.[37]

Luther left no rites for extreme unction, which he did not consider a sacrament. Nor did he provide a burial rite. But Luther gives us some indication of his desires in a 1542 preface to a collection of burial hymns.[38] There it is clear Luther wanted to change the atmosphere of death for Christians from fear to hope. He wished to eliminate requiem masses, vigils, and other acts that focus on something being done for the dead by human agency. Hymnody was a particularly important way to enable the Christian congregation to express its hope in the face of death.

The familiar places of worship remained not greatly changed. The massive iconoclasm of other traditions was not part of the Lutheran program for reformation, and many items that were destroyed in other lands still remain in Lutheran churches in Europe. During Luther's lifetime, there was little need for new church buildings. The first church to be built specifically for Lutheran worship was the Castle Church at Torgau, built in 1544.[39] It is a simple hall-type building designed so all could see and hear what is done at both pulpit and altar-table. The stress on both visibility and audibility was to be prophetic for the future of Lutheran church architecture.

Major changes were made in public prayer. From 1526 on, most prayers were in the vernacular in parish churches and spoken so the congregation could both hear and understand what was said; in some churches, lay people could actively join when prayers were said responsively or in unison or sung together. Prayer could now truly be public. Luther provided an outline in 1526 for a morning and evening service, but it was largely intended for the use of students and seems mostly pedagogic.[40]

One of the greatest changes Luther brought about was in the form and function of preaching as worship. Yngve Brilioth says, "Luther's work is significant in the history of preaching as a new beginning."[41] Luther certainly succeeded in making preaching an essential part of Protestant worship. Preaching had been present among Luther's contemporaries, yet one of his greatest problems was pastors who had no training or experience in preaching. He once lampooned a preacher who had preached on the topic of "blue ducks," yet he could hardly expect those unaccustomed to the art to become instant masters of it.

Luther's chief contribution to improving preaching in worship was by his own example. His sermons dealt with biblical texts in a direct and earthy fashion. They were not studied bits of rhetoric but were folksy and anecdotal, aimed at helping people to visualize the biblical narrative with graphic examples drawn from daily life. They tend to be expository rather than moralistic. George Rörer and others took down the words as Luther preached and frequently rushed the sermons into print. Widely circulated and read, they became examples to follow. In a more deliberate fashion, Luther himself published postils (collections of model sermons) to instruct pastors on homiletics. Many of his sermons must have been recycled by other preachers.

In theory as well as practice, Luther stressed the importance of hearing the word of God expounded "since the preaching and teaching of God's word is the most important part of divine service."[42] All worship was to include preaching, even weddings and other public occasions. Early on, Luther suggested placing the sermon at the beginning of the eucharist, but this was never done.

If Luther shaped the Protestant sermon, his influence in church music is no less outstanding. A fervent lover of music, he found it "one of God's greatest gifts" and relished its use in worship in every possible way. His revised rites for the mass made abundant use of service music. Indeed, he conceived of the entire mass set to music and sung by the congregation, a project realized in the 1978 *Lutheran Book of Worship.* The *Gloria in excelsis* ("Glory to God in the Highest"), *Sanctus* ("Holy, Holy, Holy"), and other bits of service music were soon translated into German paraphrases and placed in the mouths of the people.

The development of a popular hymnody as a constitutive part of worship was particularly important for Luther. As early as 1523, he was using German hymns in church; he wrote two dozen of them himself that year and the next, writing the words (and usually the music) for about thirty-seven hymns in all. Many depend largely on the psalms, but they are produced in bold and vigorous verses, much more forceful than the Victorian translations familiar in England and America.[43]

Luther's work was by no means accomplished alone but done with the help of an able body of lieutenants, most of them priests of the old order. Many of them simply remained in the parishes where they were serving and brought the reformation to their people according to their own abilities. The Lutheran Reformation retained a characteristically medieval stance; it saw no need to impose uniformity through standardization of rites. Just as there had been a variety of rites for services in different dioceses and religious orders (although basically quite similar), Lutherans saw no need to discontinue such local variety. Until recently, Lutheranism has kept this medieval stance despite frequent efforts to achieve a standard service book.

The result was that a series of church orders or agendas were established in various cities and principalities. All of them are based on various combinations of Luther's rites, the prevailing local practices, and the local reformer's own preferences. Luther's work in Wittenberg is the fountainhead of all these church orders, but several common patterns developed, especially those modeled on the work of Andreas Osiander (1498–1552) in Nuremberg in 1524 (Latin) and 1533 (German); the Brunswick Church Order of 1528, of which Bugenhagen was largely the architect; and Mecklenburg, 1552, which Philipp Melanchthon (1497–1560) influenced. From these centers, other cities and areas took their rites. The collection of sixteenth-century orders fills fifteen volumes.[44] Attempts have been made to classify them roughly into three groups: central Saxo-Lutheran (the largest number, including north and central Germany, Denmark, and Sweden), the ultraconservative (Brandenburg and Austria), and a mediating group with Reformed influences (south and west Germany).[45]

Much toleration for existing practices remained when they were not considered detrimental to true doctrine. As Luther remarked, "We, however, take the middle course . . . we are neither papistic nor Karlstadtian, but free and Christian."[46] Conflicts with Calvinists were to solidify Lutheran conservatism, especially on the theology of Christ's presence in the eucharist.

Eventually whole nations were to receive different varieties of Lutheran Reformation. Bugenhagen went to Denmark in 1537 and set about reforming all aspects of church and university life. Since Norway was also linked to Denmark at that time, his work became influential in both kingdoms. In Denmark, he reformed the liturgy somewhat on the pattern used in Brunswick, ordained seven bishops, and reconstituted the university.

The Swedish Reformation was to move in more conservative directions (Finland was also linked to Sweden at this time). The Petri brothers, Laurentius (1499–1573) and Olavus (1493–1552), are the key figures. Both had been trained in Germany and knew the Lutheran developments. Olavus produced the first service book in 1529, and in 1531 his Swedish Mass was accepted. Basically it followed the *Formula Missae* of 1523, with some influences from a Latin mass that Osiander had produced in Nuremberg in 1524. The Swedish church proved itself conservative in many ways, retaining the apostolic succession of bishops, often retaining the use of Latin (or sometimes Latin and Swedish together) and continuing most of the familiar ceremonial. In 1571, Laurentius Petri, who became Archbishop of Uppsala in 1531, produced a Church Order that kept much of the Latin rite but infused it with Protestant reforms. After his death, the *Red Book* of King John III was produced in 1576 but proved unpopular as too Roman.[47] Another approach was tried under King Charles IX in 1600, moving in a Calvinist direction, but this was rejected as too extreme. The result of these lurches right and then left was to make the Church Order of 1571 popular, and thus a basically conservative rite persisted in Sweden and Finland.

The Reformation came somewhat later in Iceland, then under the control of Denmark. Danish church orders were introduced in 1541 in the South Island and ten years later in the North Island. The bishops soon produced local service books, and in 1594 a reformed mass book was published that remained in use for more than two hundred years. Other service books were produced for Lutheran churches in the Baltic states, the Netherlands, and eastern Europe, as Luther's reform spread throughout most of northern Europe.

Developments in Lutheran Worship

After Luther's death in 1546, the Lutheran tradition of worship continued to develop in diverse ways in different lands. Most of the regional churches, however, went through similar experiences, albeit with certain cultural and social differences between them. Obviously, we cannot cover all the significant developments in Lutheran worship in Europe and North America from Luther's day to the present with much detail, but we may be able to sort out dominant tendencies, significant personalities, and important movements.

We shall treat this period in terms of four overlapping periods: the era 1550–1700 as the time of Lutheran orthodoxy, the time from 1650 to 1800 as dominated by pietism, the enlightenment epoch as 1700–1800, and 1800 to 1950 as the time of restorationism. It should be recognized at once that many factors were in operation in each period; these dates only indicate prevalent characteristics.

Lutheran Orthodoxy

The period of Lutheran orthodoxy, 1550–1700, represents the century following Luther's death in which the gains of the Reformation were consolidated and became a way of life despite ongoing theological and military wars. It saw the development of significant theological systems in Protestant versions of scholasticism, the serious study of church history, and the very beginnings of liturgical studies. Many of these changes were reflected in the worshiping life of the Lutheran people of northern Europe.

As the Lutheran reformation spread, new church orders were produced (such as that for Antwerp in 1579),[48] providing standards and forms for the use of congregations. More importantly, the period saw the development of a normative Lutheran piety, a distinctive way of being Christian.[49] Many factors contributed to this, especially the widespread use of Luther's catechisms, which came to be the normative standards for popular belief and which children were expected to assimilate through memory. This was reinforced by preaching and the reiteration of hymns inculcating beliefs and practices. An important part of Lutheran piety was the strong commitment to the doctrine of the real presence of Christ in the eucharist, a belief sharpened by controversy with non-Lutherans.

Other factors contributed to the growth of normative Lutheran forms of worship. The religious wars of the early seventeenth century saw the destruction of many churches as well as the usual losses through decay and fire. A new Lutheran architecture began to develop, appropriating the architectural forms of baroque being developed in southern Europe. A variety of experiments were tried, seeking the most appropriate architectural setting for Lutheran worship. In general, they tended to emphasize the ability of the whole congregation to see and hear all that happened at the altar-table, pulpit, and font. These three items came to be the central focus of buildings, often in the so-called *prinzipalstück* arrangement, in which pulpit, altar-table, and font were located close to each other in front of the congregation. In some cases, the pulpit was directly above the altar-table, with the font in front of both. Almost all possible combinations seem to have been tried.[50] Lutherans came to be fond of a burst of natural light above the altar-table. A normal Lutheran image of a place to worship evolved, one that probably had as much in common with Jesuit baroque as with the spaces built for Protestant worship by other traditions.

The chief liturgical controversy of this period was over which matters were adiaphora and hence to be tolerated without endangering faith.[51] Was it possible to preserve all visual images, ceremonial, and practices that the reformers themselves had not explicitly condemned without endangering true doctrine? What did it mean to be "neither papistic nor Karlstadtian"? Generally, conservatism prevailed and existing churches were not purified of images, although not many were likely to be introduced in new buildings. Much of the old cultus remained, especially those things that emphasized the real presence of Christ in the eucharist.

It is impossible to say exactly how frequently the eucharist was celebrated or how many communicants appeared. Gradually, tying celebrations to the presence of communicants led to less frequent eucharists. The shift to frequent reception of communion had been too radical a change from medieval practice for the laity to become accustomed to it easily. As a result, the first half of the service, the ante-communion, came to be the usual Sunday celebration, the full eucharist becoming the exceptional service despite the expectations of Luther and his contemporaries that a weekly eucharist would be normal. Yet in places such as Leipzig weekly communion was normal for thousands of people, and daily prayer services were well attended until the last decade of the eighteenth century.

Confession was usually linked to announcement of intention to commune. Saturday evening confessional vesper services were observed in some areas and do not seem to have been supplanted by confession to other laity. On the other hand, the practice of confirmation, which Luther had allowed but not advocated, gradually came to be common, partly because of the close connection between church and school. The result was public examination of the children before the congregation with some form of laying on of hands or blessing by the pastor.

This period was marked by continued composition of church music for congregational use, with a number of illustrious composers contributing both service music and hymn tunes. Michael Praetorius (1571–1621), Heinrich Schütz (1585–1672), and others made their marks.[52] Luther's colleagues and successors contributed to the writing of hymns as a way of combining teaching and worship. The output of Lutheran hymn texts during the sixteenth century was prodigious, enough to fill five large volumes.[53] The tradition of Lutheran worship as heavily musical was strongly reinforced and groundwork laid for further development.

Pietism

The period of pietism (1650–1800) reflects a time of disenchantment with conventional church life and an attempt to find deeper roots in a warmly personal religion. It was not a doctrinal rebellion but a desire to find a stronger and more intimate sense of community within existing church structures. Emphasis was placed on small groups, the church within the church, gathered for prayer and discipline. A distinctive piety within a Lutheran ethos developed and came to influence such groups as the Moravians and, through them, Methodism.

Pietism brought new times and places for worship, especially in the small group, the Collegia Pietatis, which met not in opposition to but in addition to the parish community. Under such leaders as Philipp Spener (1635–1705) and August Francke (1663–1727), pietism became a strong force in much of Lutheranism. The small groups, meeting twice weekly for worship (Bible reading and prayer) in private homes in Spener's circle, brought an entirely different scale to the worshiping community, a scale characterized by intimacy. Individuals shepherded one another in reflecting upon and sharing their own relationship with God, and the community exercised pastoral care by stressing a disciplined life. In turn, the spiritual discipline of these small communities served to reinforce the worship life of the larger parish.

The prayer life of individuals and Bible study were central concerns in pietism. A later form of pietism developed in Norway under the leadership of Hans Nielsen Hauge (1771–1824) and was brought to the United States by many Norwegian immigrants. Basically a rebellion against the state church (then under Danish dominance), the Hauge movement, like earlier pietism, placed little emphasis on set liturgical forms and the sacraments.

A major spin-off from Lutheran pietism was the resuscitation of the Unitas Fratrum or Bohemian Brethren, eventually known as Moravian Brethren. This group traced its roots to the Utraquists of Czechoslovakia (who insisted on receiving the wine in communion) of the fifteenth century. A liturgy had been developed by Lukas of Prague (1460–1528) in 1527, and this group had assimilated many Lutheran reforms. A revival of some of this group, nicknamed Moravians or Herrnhuters, came about in the eighteenth century under the direction of Count Nikolaus von Zinzendorf (1700–1760). While preserving the standards of Lutheran orthodox doctrine, this group developed a distinctive piety, reflected in their hymnody and visual arts. Devotional material and hymnody focused on the five wounds of Christ, and eighteenth-century members called themselves "wound worms." Music played a very important role in Moravian worship, both choral and congregational. Distinctive services included a revival of the ancient agape or love feast and Easter morning services. The Moravian Church is the modern descendant and probably belongs most closely in the Lutheran tradition of worship.

Some of the most lasting legacies of pietism have been in hymnody and church music. The greatest of the pietist hymn writers was Paul Gerhardt (1607–1676), remembered for "O Sacred Head, Sore Wounded." Francke contributed "Deck Thyself, My Soul, with Gladness." Building on a great tradition already present in such composers as Dietrich Buxtehude (1637–1707) and Johann Pachelbel (1653–1706), the greatest of all Lutheran musicians was Johann Sebastian Bach (1685–1750). A brilliant musical workman, Bach worked within the calendar and lectionary to produce several series of cantatas based on the gospel lesson for each Sunday and other feasts. Many of his instrumental works were based on Lutheran chorales. Other works include cantatas for concert occasions, the Mass in B Minor, Christmas Oratorio, Magnificat, and St. Matthew and St. John passions. In his own faith, Bach was deeply influenced by pietism, yet he reflects a traditional Lutheran piety.[54]

The Enlightenment

The period of the Enlightenment (1700–1800) brought about great changes in Lutheran worship that are hard to overestimate, however much ignored by liturgical scholars today. The Enlightenment attempted to understand Christianity exclusively in rational terms. God's work was portrayed as that of a watchmaker who contemplates a well-made universe without interfering in its operation. It is natural, given such a disposition, to look at sacraments as unlikely intrusions of divinity into human life. As a result, the Enlightenment tended to suppress what sacramental piety still survived, although without eliminating the practice of sacraments. Curiously, the Enlightenment kept sacraments as biblical commands, and therefore obligatory, but celebrated them infrequently and with little enthusiasm.

Together with the decline in sacramental life went a discarding of much surviving ceremonial, although less so in Sweden, where it had survived relatively intact. Architecturally, the Enlightenment consolidated the move from sacrament churches to preaching churches. Balconies lined church walls to bring a larger number of worshipers close to the pulpit. Indeed, the building Paul Tillich considered the greatest exemplar of Protestant church architecture,[55] the Frauenkirche of Dresden (1726–1738), resembled an opera house and is a graphic portrayal of the triumph of word over sacrament so characteristic of the Enlightenment.

The individualism of pietism was reinforced by the Enlightenment, although the two movements had quite different purposes. The preaching of morality became the characteristic sermon subject of the Enlightenment, and religion was basically seen as an instrument for the improvement of human society. With no expectation of supernatural action, all of worship became largely a means of teaching morality. The message of the eucharist became "be good" rather than "God is good." This represented a major shift in Lutheran worship, one that has not entirely been forgotten. The rupture with the past brought about by the Enlightenment may be even greater than that accomplished in the sixteenth-century Reformation. For many, the Enlightenment still carves an unbridgeable gap between the time of Luther and our times. It was a second revolution in worship, perhaps as profound in its desacralizing of worship as Luther's work had been in resacralizing medieval worship in other forms.

Restorationism

If the Enlightenment created a radical break with the past Lutheranism, the period since 1800 has seen major efforts at restorationism.[56] Some Lutherans have been inclined to confuse the tendencies of the Enlightenment with succumbing to the enticements of the Reformed tradition.[57] The threat of amalgamation was brought to a head in 1817 with the Prussian Union attempt of Frederick William III to combine Lutherans and Reformed in one church. The upshot of this effort was to push many Lutherans toward more awareness of their own Reformation heritage.

In Germany, the work of Theodor Kliefoth (1810–1895), Ludwig Schoeberlein (1813–1881), and Wilhelm Löhe (1808–1872) resulted in a resurgence of the old Lutheran type of service with its basically conservative form derived from the medieval mass and a revival in sacramental life. In Löhe's parish in Neuendettelsau, more frequent eucharists accompanied careful screening of communicants. Löhe's manual was sent to America to be used a model for worship in Lutheran communities in Indiana, Michigan, and Iowa. The architecture of Karl Friedrich Schinkel (1781–1841) provided a romantic revival of medieval forms.[58]

Nikolai F. S. Grundtvig (1783–1872) supplied much of the impulse in Denmark for the recovery of a richer sacramental life.[59] Through his work in recovering elements of Danish heritage and providing for popular education, he recovered affinity for the traditional Lutheran piety of the sixteenth century. The writing of hymns was one of his contributions to Lutheran restoration.

In America, quite different problems arose. In 1748, Henry Melchior Muhlenberg (1711–1787) prepared a handwritten liturgy for Lutherans in Philadelphia. The period that followed saw a variety of liturgical books in use by various emigrant groups. Many Lutherans were attracted to the prevailing revival system in American Protestantism, with its almost complete indifference to historical patterns of worship and sacramental theology. The battle that ensued was a battle, in effect, for the soul of American Lutheranism. Was American Lutheranism to accommodate to the culture or be distinctive?

Further complications came with the arrival in the 1840s of a new influx of Germans. Most possessed an orthodox kind of Lutheran piety, while the later advent of Scandinavians brought large numbers of Norwegian pietists, among others. The history of much of this period is the gradual move from worship in European tongues to English. At the same time, increasing use was made of English hymnody. A series of liturgical books created ever-increasing collaboration among Lutheran bodies, especially centered on the recovery of an authentic Reformation pattern of worship. Landmarks were the "Common Service" of 1888 and the *Common Service Book* of 1917.

The strong Lutheran tradition of church music was maintained and enhanced in a series of hymnbooks, ever-broadening cultural horizons to complement chorale tunes with English church music. The Society of St. James and the Society of St. Ambrose made respective contributions, as did scholars Arthur Karl Piepkorn (1907–1973), Edward Traill Horn (1850–1915), and Paul Strodach (1876–1942). The chief thrust of the period seems to have been the restoration of much sixteenth-century Lutheran practice. Yet, at the same time, a process of assimilation into American Protestantism with its dominant Frontier tradition was continuing. In this period,

American Lutheranism became both more American and more Lutheran, even when this seemed a contradiction.

Present Characteristics of Lutheran Worship

Major changes have occurred in Lutheran worship in every part of the world since the mid-twentieth century. In essence, they have been a move beyond Lutheranism into a new ecumenical era in which the various traditions have changed their identities both by borrowing from others and in developing together new possibilities. The catalyst for all this has been the changes in Roman Catholic worship since Vatican II. Lutherans too have helped themselves to many new Catholic reforms, especially the Sunday lectionary, use of a variety of eucharistic prayers, and revised pastoral rites.

The basic change in Lutheran worship in America was probably a change in people more than anything else. Lutherans were losing their ethnic and cultural identity, a fact illustrated by mergers of most of the Lutheran bodies, leaving only two major groups by 1988. It was still possible to note some distinctive characteristics of parishes predominantly Swedish or Germanic, but even these distinctions were fast eroding. A sure sign of this was the collaboration of a number of Lutheran bodies in the *Service Book and Hymnal* of 1958. An important figure in the development of this book and its predecessor of 1917 was Luther D. Reed (1873–1972). The *Service Book and Hymnal* broke Lutheran precedents by introducing a full eucharistic prayer despite Luther's excision of most of the canon.

This period saw a flourishing of Lutheran commitment to the arts. In the 1950s and 1960s, most of the better examples of church architecture built in America were for Missouri Synod Lutheran congregations, largely guided by the faculty of Concordia Seminary in St. Louis. More recently, composers such as Jan Bender and Paul Mantz have contributed much to congregational, choral, and instrumental music. There seems to have been a move to a much more exegetical style in preaching in recent years, with fuller observance of the Christian year from a richer calendar.

Efforts began in 1966, at the initiative of the Missouri Synod, to produce a common service book, a goal long cherished among American Lutherans. This led to the establishment of the Inter-Lutheran Commission on Worship, which was active until 1978. A series of ten *Contemporary Worship* booklets was produced in order to try out proposed services.[60] The resulting documents then became incorporated in the *Lutheran Book of Worship* of 1978. Later, a Task Force on the Occasional Services was appointed to produce a volume of *Occasional Services,* which appeared in 1982 and included special occasions in the church year, weddings, funerals, and ordinations.[61]

The *Lutheran Book of Worship*[62] provides an interesting way to assess the current status of Lutheran worship in North America. At the last moment, the Missouri Synod withdrew, producing its own book, *Lutheran Worship,*[63] in 1982, thus thwarting the goal of unity. Both books show fidelity to sixteenth-century practice. A large number of Lutheran chorales are represented among the hymn tunes, the normal services are highly musical, with three complete settings for the eucharist, and it is still possible to celebrate the eucharist using only the words of institution instead of a full eucharistic prayer. A new element is emphasis on baptism throughout all services, reflecting that baptismal piety which Luther exhibited so frequently.

On the other hand, the book goes beyond Lutheranism in many important ways. Chief among these is the adoption of the ecumenical lectionary, developed by the Roman Catholic Consilium for the Implementation of the Constitution on the Sacred Liturgy. This has brought three readings into Sunday worship by recovery of an Old Testament lection. A richer calendar forms the basis of the new lectionary, with a fuller cycle of Holy Week celebrations as the most conspicuous example. The practice of initiation places emphasis on baptism rather than on confirmation, with the possibility of future affirmation of what God has done for an individual. Confirmation is in the context of one such baptismal affirmation.

All in all, the new service book represents a shift from restoration of Lutheran practice to acceptance of many practices that are becoming more and more common among other Protestants, such as a common lectionary and more frequent celebrations of the eucharist. While the latter was expected by Luther, it still remains only an occasional service for most Lutheran congregations, with ante-communion as the normal Sunday service. Another new element is the provision of services of revised daily morning and evening prayer, long a minor theme in Lutheran worship.

Many similar currents have been apparent in other Lutheran countries, where liturgical revision has proceeded at varying speeds. Some churches experienced the spate of widespread experimentation common in the United States in the late sixties and early seventies before settling down to consolidate what had been learned from such a euphoric period. The use of musical instruments other than the organ became common, elements of spontaneity were introduced, and more attention was paid to the visual aspects of worship, especially in the form of textile arts. These now seem to have lodged themselves as permanent aspects of Lutheran worship in many countries. Probably no church has made more effort than the Church of Sweden to keep in touch with changes in worship around the world,

Lutheran and non-Lutheran, information carefully reported in several volumes.

At the same time, there has been resistance to change, with some countries reluctant to give up the traditional two-lesson one-year eucharistic lectionary, for example. Other problems have occurred in trying to bring about a common service book for the various Lutheran territorial churches in Germany. Thus the process of liturgical revision, now safely put to rest for another generation in the United States, still goes on in other countries.

The changes in worship have brought about changes in the space for worship. Altar-tables have been moved away from the wall, and in many cases fonts have been given greater prominence. The musical repertoire has broadened considerably. In America, the *Lutheran Book of Worship* makes more use of English hymnody than ever before in a Lutheran hymnal, both in text and tunes. New feasts in the church year, such as Baptism of the Lord or Christ the King, have been welcomed. In turn, other churches have adopted the Lutheran practice of observing Transfiguration on the Sunday before Lent. Lutherans have led in the production of resources for lectionary preaching. Inclusive language continues to trouble many, while the limits to which language about God is subject to change are still being debated, problems shared in common with other traditions. Lutheran worship has kept a distinctive identity, but it is one that has changed much in recent years.

4

Reformed Worship

During the first four days of October 1529 occurred one of the great moments of truth of the Protestant Reformation. To Protestant leaders meeting at Marburg came the clear recognition that they could not agree on all matters of worship, although they could reach unanimity on every other important item. Thus, despite their best efforts, a pattern was established that has ever since been a prominent characteristic of Protestant worship—disparate traditions. Such a development was probably inevitable, but it was not deliberately planned by the movement's leaders. A generation later, by 1563, such variety had been made an article of belief by the twenty-fourth of the Anglican "Articles of Religion." Today, unlike the sixteenth century, diversity does not seem to be the result of failure but is recognized as a positive good in itself; the *Constitution on the Sacred Liturgy* echoes the Thirty-Nine Articles in commending the idea that peoples and attitudes be reflected in worship by "variations and adaptations to different groups, regions, and peoples."[1]

Diversity was not the intention of the nine former Roman Catholic priests and one layman (Melanchthon) who gathered at Marburg in those October days to seek complete agreement. They soon discovered that, although they all came from a single Christian tradition, they were of two different spirits—which Luther pointed out in the candid remark, probably to Martin Bucer, "You have another spirit than we."[2] Luther represented the old learning and piety; Zwingli, Bucer, and Oecolampadius represented the new learning and a new kind of piety. The clash was probably inevitable and certainly not unexpected; Luther had been fulminating for years in a variety of treatises against those whom he chose to call "sacramentarians"[3] over what he regarded as deficient doctrines of Christ's presence in the eucharist.

Zwingli's views had been triggered by a letter written by the Dutch lawyer Cornelius Hoen (?–1524), which was circulated in 1521 but only came to Zwingli's attention in 1524. Zwingli was not the first radical to confront Luther, who had been through much already with Andreas Karlstadt, Thomas Münzer, and the Zwickau prophets. But Zwingli brought a new intellectual challenge, fortified by careful study and considerable skill as a philologist. Despite the differences between those of Luther's spirit and those of Zwingli's spirit, however, the leaders at Marburg were able to agree on fourteen articles, including a common stand in favor of infant baptism.

The crucial issue on the real presence was a single word, the "is" of "This is my body." Ironically, this word probably was not in the Aramaic spoken at the Last Supper, but no one at Marburg was aware of that, of course. The debate, as recorded by various participants and observers, was heated. Luther's focus was on the literal meaning of the words, his concern being with the eucharistic elements. Zwingli believed "is" meant "signifies," as Hoen had suggested. For Zwingli, the center of attention was not "this is" but "do this": what the community does in the Lord's Supper. Luther was traditional in focusing on the elements; Zwingli did indeed represent a new spirit in his focus on the community. What Luther did not appreciate was that Zwingli was stating in a new way the reality of Christ's presence as a transubstantiation of the congregation rather than of the elements.

Luther was right; there was a wide gulf fixed between his view of what God did in the eucharist and what Zwingli saw as the essential means of God's action. With the Colloquy of 1529, the disparity of views became permanent and led to traditions still separate. Accordingly, we move on from the Lutheran tradition to study the origins of the Reformed tradition, its subsequent development, and its present characteristics.

The Origins of Reformed Worship

The Reformed tradition derives from several centers and from the work of a variety of leaders. Such centers as Zurich, Strasbourg, Basel, Berne, and Geneva each made contributions, even though what was communicated to the rest of the world was generally via Zurich and Geneva. We shall begin with the reformation of worship begun in Zurich by Ulrich Zwingli (1484–1531) and continued by his successor, Heinrich Bullinger (1504–1575). The question of whether worship in the Reformed tradition is more indebted to Zurich or to Geneva is not easily resolved; streams from both places flow into the mainstream of Reformed worship. Both Swiss cities were autonomous, and their respective city councils usually could be persuaded to follow the requests of local reformers when sufficient reasons for change were advanced. The magistrates in Zurich favored disputations as means of resolving conflicts, and for these engagements Zwingli was particularly competent.

Zwingli was best known in his role as beloved pastor of the Great Minster, where he had been appointed in 1518. He had demonstrated great devotion to his people when he chose to remain in the city during a plague. Swiss patriotism animated him, and he vigorously protested the use of Swiss men as mercenaries, except in service of the papacy. In 1523, he received a papal pension and commendation for having served as chaplain to papal troops. An important factor in Zwingli's work was his passion for the new learning of the time. He corresponded with Erasmus and was conversant with the scholarship of contemporary humanism. Zwingli was fluent in Greek, and his study of scripture pushed his thinking in directions critical of conventional learning and practices.

Zwingli's reforming career was a short one, less than a decade, but it brought radical transformation to worship. In 1523, a few months before Luther's *Formula Missae,* Zwingli published his first liturgical work, appropriately entitled *An Attack on the Canon of the Mass.* Generally a conservative work, it contained four prayers to replace the canon of the mass: "They are prayed theology"[4] in a most literal sense. Didactic in tone, yet in eloquent Latin, they refer to the whole breadth of salvation history, invoke the Holy Spirit, and inculcate a new eucharistic theology. There is deep devotion to the eucharist evident here, but all in all Zwingli's work often seems to be a reformation directed from the head rather than from the heart, as in Luther. And it cannot be ignored that Reformed worship has always seemed the most cerebral of the western traditions.

Today, it is common to consider purely symbolic interpretation of the eucharistic bread and wine as the legacy of Zwingli. Such an approach to the eucharist prevails in much of American Protestantism and is often labeled as "Zwinglian." But that is far too simplistic an interpretation. Zwingli worked within a sacralized universe. He certainly believed in the presence and activity of God in that world, but the universe of many modern Protestants is that of the eighteenth-century Enlightenment, a universe completely desacralized. To call the Enlightenment position Zwinglian is to miss an important shift that occurred in the eighteenth century. The desacralized worldview of many modern Protestants makes sacraments or any other divine intrusions into the world questionable. The world of Zwingli saw God, far from being absent, as *intervening* in the midst of the worshiping congregation.

Much of the success of Zwingli's reformation is due to his relationship with the people of Zurich. Zwingli's reformation was largely instituted by preaching versed in God's word. In 1525, Zwingli and his partner, the priest Leo Jud (1482–1542), began a daily service of prophesying, a service of the word in which lessons from the Old Testament were read and expounded and the people invited to respond. The burghers of Zurich were being flooded with constant encounter with scripture. Zwingli and his cohorts preached fourteen times a week, as regularly as television news.

The Sunday preaching service seems to have evolved from a late medieval service known as prone, a short unofficial vernacular service used in various areas occasionally before, during, or after mass. Zwingli had used it from 1519 to 1523 as a preparation for the mass. He may have derived his particular version from one published in 1526 by John Ulrich Surgant in Basel in *Manuale Curatorum*. Zwingli's Sunday service contains a curious assortment from late-medieval liturgical piety: the Lord's Prayer, an Ave Maria ("Hail, Mary"), a sermon, a remembrance of those who had died during the previous week, another Lord's Prayer, another Ave Maria, the Apostles' Creed, the Decalogue, and a confession and absolution (as if the mass were to follow).[5] It is a concoction of piety and creedal and ethical instruction. Rejecting the practice of preaching on the gospel appointed for the day, Zwingli began preaching in course: that is, on consecutive biblical lessons. Zwingli's people were being formed with a scriptural piety, especially by heavy exposure to the Old Testament narratives. It is not strange that the sense of covenant community became a major part of their formation or that the Old Testament invectives against idolatry were familiar to their ears.

But side by side with these biblical elements, Zwingli's teaching and practices were introducing a strain that might seem at odds with the biblical revelation: a disregarding of the physical world as a means of conveying the spiritual. Zwingli believed that "it is clear and indisputable that no external element or action can purify the soul,"[6] and thus it was completely consistent to discount the use of physical objects and actions in worship. A sense of the sign value of things in conveying God's grace is altogether lacking. This disjuncture between the physical and spiritual sets Zwingli apart from Luther and Calvin. Essentially it is a matter of piety. If the physical cannot lead one to God, one has drawn a circle around much of the traditional Christian cultus and marked it for destruction.

This is exactly what happened in Zurich in 1524 when the places of worship were altered. But in Zurich it was by no means a frenetic assault on idols after the manner of Karlstadt. In September 1523, Leo Jud had preached against images in churches. Objections were also raised against prayer to the saints, even though the Ave Maria persisted in Zurich's service until 1563. Eventually, there were several disputations before the city council. The people at large seemed to favor the removal of the images from churches, although they did not object to them for private use. Finally, by command of the council, the images were removed in an orderly and systematic fashion from June 20 to July 2, 1524.

Somewhat more surprising was the elimination of music from worship, since Zwingli was an accomplished musician and had composed motets himself.[7] Music was also a subject of disputation and the verdict was guided by unconditional obedience to scripture, which was construed to mean no more music. In 1523 the singing stopped, not to be heard again in Zurich until 1598. Its absence must not have been greatly missed, because in 1527 the council gave orders for the destruction of the pipe organs as well. These took longer to reappear, a new organ not being installed in the Great Minster until 1874. It is possible that the competition between the choirs of the Great Minster and the Fraumünster for musical quality had been less than edifying, but at any rate the cure was drastic. Obedience to scripture was a higher calling. If music had to be discarded for prayer to take place, it was a necessary sacrifice.

The process was not philistinism or indifference to the arts. Zwingli was sensitive to the arts and recognized their power. But if it was not power for the good of the worshiper, it had to go. The result was a consistent austerity. There was directness and honesty in a service spoken in a natural voice and in ordinary bread served on wooden plates as at home. And the elimination of images from the place of worship kept the mind focused on God's word rather than on the skill and imagination of a human artist. Some thought the results 'hideous"; others called it "luminous."

If changes came to the places of worship, the times of worship were altered too. We have mentioned the daily prophesying. In 1525, Zwingli published his second eucharistic liturgy, *Action or Use of the Lord's Supper,* a radically simplified form.[8] The Lord's Supper was to be celebrated only on the great Christian festivals—Christmas, Easter, Pentecost—and on the patronal festival of Zurich, Sts. Felix and Regula (September 11)—days on which the people normally communed. On the other fifty Sundays, when few if any communed, there was to be no eucharist. Men and women were to sit separately and recite the *Gloria in excelsis* and Psalm 113 antiphonally. This was too much active participation for the council, and these items were left to the ministers to recite. There was no avoiding communion, for the bread and wine were carried about to the people in the pews, where each broke off a piece of bread and then drank from the cup.

The life occasions also changed. A new baptismal rite, introduced in 1525, followed the work of Leo Jud and possibly Luther, but confirmation was abolished. Baptism was seen as a seal within the covenant. Zwingli spoke of it as infant dedication, a rationale for infant baptism still widespread among many contemporary Protestants. What is important, as in the eucharist, is the role of the community, for baptism places one in a covenant community and seals such a relationship. A new wedding rite added a long prayer of blessing. Zwingli did not live to complete the other life-cycle rites.

Zwingli had moved to full vernacular for the Sunday service in 1525, and the people were expected to join in prayer, particularly the Ave Maria and Lord's Prayer. Daily prayer as a public service was limited to prophesying, essentially preaching services. Saints' days and fasting were deprecated by Zwingli in favor of this daily discipline of scripture reading and preaching at eight o'clock each morning. Preaching was certainly not in short supply in Zurich but formed a major item in all worship. Most of it seems to have been of an exegetical nature.

Zwingli's reform was cut short by his untimely death on the battlefield in 1531, but he had succeeded in giving a strong orientation to what was to become a distinct tradition in worship. Zwingli always seemed a bit jealous of Luther and, although Zwingli's reformation followed many patterns similar to those of Luther, it is clear that most of the developments in Zurich were the result of Zwingli's own personal reading of scripture, pastoral wisdom, and careful planning of worship. He found aid and encouragement from reformers in other cities, notably Johann Oecolampadius in Basel (after 1523), the pastors of Berne (1528 on), and Martin Bucer in Strasbourg (1523 on). His battles at home with the Anabaptists only served to sharpen his own convictions.

After Zwingli's death in 1531, the creative edge of the Reformed tradition shifted west, particularly to Geneva and Strasbourg. John Calvin (1509–1564), who dominated the second phase in the origins of this tradition, had two men as mentors in the area of worship, William Farel and Martin Bucer.

William Farel (1489–1565) in 1536 persuaded Calvin to remain in Geneva. Farel had been working for reformation there since 1532, having traveled around such centers of the Reformation as Basel and Strasbourg. Farel had begun a reformation at Montbéliard before coming to Geneva and had prepared a liturgy, largely dependent on one already in use in Berne since 1529. He had published his liturgy, "Manner and Fashion," in 1533 and a new edition in 1538, "Order and Manner," for use by the church in Geneva. Calvin knew and used this liturgy in Geneva,[9] and perhaps he had influenced it somewhat. This same liturgy Farel took to use in the church in Neuchâtel, where he settled in 1538.

After his expulsion from Geneva from 1538 to 1541, Calvin worked as a colleague of the former Dominican priest Martin Bucer (1491–1551) in Strasbourg. There he found a well-established tradition of worship among German-speaking Protestants. This had originated in 1524 in the work of a local priest, Theobald Schwarz (1485–1561), and was basically a Germanizing of the Latin mass. The reformation in Strasbourg had soon been taken in hand by Martin Bucer. Bucer was also involved in the attempt to produce a reformed rite for Cologne (1542–1543) and in the 1550 Anglican ordinal and 1552 revision of the *Book of Common Prayer*. He is the one person to have had strong direct influence on the origins of two traditions: the Reformed via Calvin and the Anglican via Cranmer. During his three years in Strasbourg, Calvin used a liturgy that was in many ways a French translation of the one Bucer was using. Upon his return to Geneva, Calvin published a service book in 1542, "Form of Prayers and Ecclesiastical Chants," having produced an earlier version in Strasbourg about 1540. Although he borrowed heavily both from the Strasbourg rite and Farel's, Calvin put his own imprint on all he did in the area of worship.

Calvin's understanding of people is central to his whole approach to worship, and it is best to begin with this aspect of his thought and its consequences. No one had a dimmer view of the prospect of humanity left to itself than Calvin, a view summed up in his view that "no part [of man] is immune from sin and all that proceeds from him is to be imputed to sin."[10] Not only is humanity perverse but also ignorant of its own good. Such perversity and stupidity can be overcome only by God's grace, and God out of mercy has chosen to liberate a select number from the limitations of their humanity. God has gathered all the chosen in the church, where they might be instructed, disciplined, and joined together in praising their Redeemer for gratuitous mercy in choosing them.

But the mercy of God does not end there. The Creator, knowing even better than humans their capacity, "so tempers himself to our capacity," providing for the elect visible means to help them know God's mercies. The institution of sacraments provided those visible signs of God's love whereby God "imparts spiritual things under visible ones."[11] There is a world of difference between Calvin's concept of the importance of signs, for humans to experience God's self giving, and Zwingli's dualism between nature and spirit. Calvin had recovered the biblical mentality that God uses material things to give us spiritual things. And Calvin's theology of signs yields important insights into how human relate to one another and to God.

Calvin saw the necessity of the church as visible embodiment of God's will to save the elect, and he echoed the words of Cyprian (ca. 200–258) as to the necessity of having the church as Mother to have God as Father.[12] The church was essential to salvation, and baptism was the entrance to the church. Calvin mirrored Zwingli's stress on the covenant people and distinguished between the visible church, known to humans, and the true but invisible church, known only to God.

The social context of Calvin's work in Geneva was significant. Geneva had become an independent city, ruled over by several councils. Its location made it an important commercial center with an increasing population. The city councils were reclaiming "ancient liberties" in asserting the city's independence. One could entrust much of the work of the church to respected lay people.

Under Calvin, discipline and instruction pervaded every aspect of public life, including worship. Virtually dictator after 1553, he resolved to make Geneva a city set on a hill for the world to see what a truly reformed city could be. The *Ecclesiastical Ordinances,* drafted in 1541, provided a system of pastoral supervision by elders who had "the oversight of the life of everyone."[13] Parents who failed to raise their children in the faith, along with other transgressors, could be refused communion by a process known as "fencing the tables." This direct connection of worship and morality was to have a long, if not happy, legacy, for it gave worship a social function quite distinct from the glorification of God.

For the people of Geneva, worship was an integral part of the life of a city that was consciously the model for Reformed cities throughout Europe. But to deserve such a historic role, it was felt necessary to use every opportunity to instruct and to reprimand; worship became the chief opportunity for this. Calvin's liturgy of 1542 strongly reflects the moral demands for righteousness. Its opening confession reminds worshipers that they are "incapable of any good and that in our depravity we transgress thy holy commandments without end or ceasing."[14] To remove any doubt, the Ten Commandments were sung, a practice probably originating with Bucer in Strasbourg. At communion, a long list of sins was read and everyone guilty of them categorically excommunicated.

The tone of the service is prolix and verbose, never lacking a chance to instruct, whether in the form of prayer, spoken rubric, or exhortation. In fact, much of the instruction is addressed to the Almighty in the form of prayer intended to be edifying to the congregation. So great was the imperative to teach that each service contains a condensed course in theology and ethics. This became a lasting characteristic of Reformed worship, contributing to its overwhelmingly cerebral character.

Calvin's chief failure in Geneva was to achieve communion "at least once a week," which he greatly desired. But in a situation where all present were virtually obliged to commune or be excommunicated as open sinners, the shift from infrequent to weekly communion was much too radical. Calvin's people were more conservative than he had reckoned, and he could only record his chagrin that this important reform was not accomplished.

He did, however, institute a practice that was to have significant consequences for the whole Reformed tradition and others: a period of preparation before each quarterly celebration. This was announced the previous Sunday to enable "each one to prepare and dispose himself to receive it worthily, and in such reverence as pertains to it."[15] Children and strangers were to receive instruction previously. So the Holy Supper came to be approached after a great deal of self-examination and introspection.

Such an introspective piety came to be characteristic of Reformed churches. If God's decrees were inscrutable, human beings at least could examine themselves to see if there was hope they might be among the elect. Every sign of sin could be relentlessly traced, confessed in private, and forgiven. Thus Reformed piety tended to be highly penitential, with a strong inward focus on human unworthiness. In many ways, it was a genuine survival of much of late-medieval piety, which tended to place the same emphasis on human unworthiness before a just and angry God. Indeed, the Reformed tradition may have succeeded in keeping alive this aspect of medieval Christianity with greater tenacity than any other branch of western Christianity. Calvin's is basically a penitential eucharist, serving the purpose of two sacraments, that of penance and that of eucharist. For him, it seems more a case of being forgiven *in order* to receive the eucharist than being forgiven *through* receiving the eucharist.

Yet there was a joyful aspect to worship in Geneva in the singing of psalms. Unlike the Lutheran tradition, where the singing of hymns was encouraged, or the Zurich Reformation, where no singing at all was allowed, Calvin saw to it that the psalms were put into metrical French by Clément Marot (1497–1544) and others. He encouraged such composers as Claude Goudimel (ca.1510–1572) and Louis Bourgeois (1510–1561) to produce tunes. Some of their compositions such as "Old Hundredth" are still widely used. Visitors to Geneva remarked upon the solemnity and joy that psalm singing gave to services and were impressed by the degree of active participation achieved. Hymns were excluded, as were pipe organs, so that all music was actually congregational song. The congregation also sang the Commandments. All singing was scriptural and essentially confined to the Old Testament.

If music was able to put the joys and sorrows of the psalms into the mouths of the congregation, there was less concern, maybe less need, for the visual aspects of the places of worship. The medieval churches continued in use in Geneva but they were subjected to the same purging of images as in Zurich. A plain table was brought in and communicants sat or knelt about it. Eventually, sitting about the

Lord's Table came to be the distinctive Reformed posture for receiving the Lord's Supper and continues so today in the Netherlands. This practice made it easy to repel the notorious sinner from a seat at the table. Calvin preferred to lead most of the service from the pulpit, and prominent pulpits came to be the distinctive feature of Reformed churches. Calvin also insisted that the baptismal "stones" be placed before the congregation so that the baptism of infants could be a fully congregational event. Usually this meant moving the font to a position near the pulpit and eventually using basins placed in a metal hoop attached to the pulpit. All were to see the actions of worship, however simplified they became. Thus, while ceremonial was limited to what was edifying, a special effort was made to ensure that everything done was both seen and heard by the entire congregation.

Drastic simplification occurred with regard to time. Daily services were not provided, but family prayers were encouraged if not demanded. Saints' days and other festivals were eliminated in favor of an exclusive focus upon Sunday as the weekly occasion for parish worship. Midweek preaching was also provided for the godly. Although Calvin had to settle for quarterly communion, he tried to stagger celebrations among the churches in Geneva, so monthly reception could be achieved. But the quarterly celebrations became important punctuations in the church's year, with days of preparation before them.

The simplification of the church year was characteristic. Calvin wished to model his reform "According to the Custom of the Ancient Church," as the subtitle of his service book proclaimed. It was a printed liturgy with rites for Sunday, the Lord's Supper, baptism, and weddings. Calvin had no scruples about retaining those ceremonies he considered edifying. On the other hand, others, such as the act of laying on of hands at ordination, while undoubtedly biblical, he had no compunctions about rejecting.[16] Calvin was not simply a biblicist but wanted to achieve genuinely patristic worship. The primitive church was his model, not just the church of the New Testament but the church of the Fathers and martyrs.[17]

The services marking the life cycle were simplified. Baptism, as stated, was to be a public rite. It was reshaped by Calvin to form a very simplified rite. Confirmation was abolished but provision was made for young people to "give an account of their faith" before the congregation. This led eventually to a public ceremony of profession of faith as the normative Reformed rite of passage for those coming to maturity in the community of faith. A new marriage rite was provided.[18] Marriage, Calvin argued, was not a sacrament but a good state, just as "farming, building, cobbling, and barbering are lawful ordinances of God, and yet are not sacraments."[19] Extreme unction, in which they "smear with their grease not the sick but half-dead corpses,"[20] was abolished and funerals condemned and abolished altogether in many Reformed churches. Calvin did come close to considering ordination a sacrament.[21]

Public prayer for Calvin tended to be extraordinarily didactic. The opening confession was spoken by the minister, each person "following my words in his heart." Prayers were read by the minister loudly enough to be heard by all present. The tradition of family prayers became a significant part of Reformed worship although exasperatingly hard to document. It persisted far longer than any set liturgies and still thrives in various countries.[22]

Preaching was an inevitable part of the Reformed service. The use of lectionaries was abandoned in favor of continuous reading of books of scripture as preaching pursued its way through each in turn. Biblical texts were expounded and then applied to contemporary life, particularly in terms of doctrine and morals. Calvin's theology was largely an exegetical theology, and many of his later years were spent in producing commentaries on most of the books of the Bible.

Calvin's eucharistic theology stresses the work of the Holy Spirit in raising humans to feed on Christ, although his liturgy does not make this explicit. One feature came to be an earmark of Reformed liturgy, an epiclesis (invocation) of the Holy Spirit, the Collect for Illumination (prayer invoking the Holy Spirit) before the reading of scripture. It found a permanent place in Reformed worship and recently (1972) was adopted in the Methodist tradition. Another characteristic is the reading of 1 Corinthians 11:23–26 ("the Lord Jesus, on the night . . .") as a "warrant" for the eucharist, not as prayer in the medieval or Lutheran traditions but in a somewhat legalistic fashion as God's commandment that justifies the celebration of the Holy Supper.

Geneva became the model for much of Protestant Europe. Calvin and Zwingli's successor, Heinrich Bullinger, were able to reach an accord (eventually accepted by all the Swiss Reformed) on the doctrine of the Lord's Supper in the *Consensus Tigurinus* (Zurich Agreement) published in 1549. Although Calvin saw himself as deliberately mediating between Luther's doctrine of the eucharist and that of Zwingli, he never succeeded in building bridges to Lutheranism (although the effort was made and reciprocated by Melanchthon). After Luther's death, the Lutheran position hardened and the Reformed were treated as radicals more dangerous even than Roman Catholics. Lutherans tended to treat Zwingli's eucharistic doctrine as normative for the Reformed tradition, even though Calvin's doctrine came close to that of Luther except on the matter of communion of the impious.[23] Although the Reformation continued in separate churches in the various Swiss cities and is still organized in separate cantonal churches in Switzerland, common characteristics soon emerged that make it possible to speak of the tradition originating in Zurich, Strasbourg, Basel, Berne, and Geneva as a single tradition, the Reformed.

Geneva became an international city known for hospitality to refugees. The Genevan Academy, founded in 1559 and led by Calvin's successor, Theodore Beza (1519–1605), helped spread Reformed learning. Refugee English Protestants arrived in the 1550s, many of whom returned to form the basis of the Puritan tradition. Calvinism spread over much of western Europe, and worship in Geneva was usually the model adopted.

One of the most significant of these transplants of the Reformed tradition occurred in Scotland, where the priest John Knox (ca.1505–1572) had pioneered the reformation in Scotland after the martyrdom of George Wishart (ca.1513–1546). Knox was imprisoned by the French, fled to England, then left there under Queen Mary for an unsuccessful ministry in Frankfurt. In the process, he had left his mark on the *Book of Common Prayer* of 1552 in his insistence on what came to be called the "black rubric" (instruction printed in black), disclaiming that any adoration of the bread and wine was intended by kneeling at the eucharist. This resurfaced in another form in 1662 and in nineteenth-century Methodist rites in America.

Knox turned up in Geneva for a stay during the late 1550s, pastoring a congregation of fellow exiles and compiling a service book based on Calvin's *The Form of Church Prayers.* This became Knox's *The Forme of Prayers* (1556).[24] The translation from a French-speaking piety into Scottish meant, if anything, an even greater emphasis on didacticism. Knox abolished the traditional Christian year and instituted a reading service prior to the morning service. The year 1564 marks both the final establishment of John Knox's service book as the official formulary of the Kirk (Church of Scotland) and also the death of John Calvin, ending the first phase of Reformed history.

Development of Reformed Worship

As the Reformed tradition of worship continued to be deliberately transplanted from Geneva, it took root in many countries. In general, by the end of the sixteenth century, Reformed churches everywhere had acquired "a fixed Reformed liturgy used without variation or exception not only for the celebration of the sacraments but for ordinary Sunday worship as well."[25] In this space it is impossible to trace the details in each national church, but we shall note a few salient continental leaders and developments and comment in more detail on developments within the Kirk of Scotland and among

American Presbyterians. Some of these developments had parallels in other Reformed churches; others are unique.

The various cantonal churches in Switzerland remained independent of one another, but there was a gradual coalescence in worship practices. Further consolidation of the Reformed tradition was demonstrated in the Second Helvetic Confession (1566), which became the normative doctrinal statement for the Reformed in the Rhine Valley, France, Switzerland, Scotland, Hungary, and Poland. Liturgical and sacramental questions ceased to be central sources of controversy, and the great issues that stirred Reformed souls to dispute, especially in the Netherlands, revolved around predestination and freedom of the will. Among French Huguenots, persecution was endemic until the Edict of Nantes made Protestant worship temporarily safe in 1598. Revocation of the edict in 1685 saw intensified persecution, a time known as the "wilderness" in which worship went underground and was held in barns and desolate places. Not until 1802, after the French Revolution, was Huguenot worship again legal.

A kind of liturgical renascence developed in Neuchâtel, Switzerland, early in the eighteenth century under pastor Jean Frédéric Ostervald (1663–1747). Enamored of Anglican worship, Ostervald sought to recover set liturgical forms for the Reformed and published a liturgy in 1713.[26] This is still in use in the Huguenot Church in Charleston, South Carolina.

By and large, the history in Scotland and North America among Presbyterians is that of a tradition compromised, becoming vulnerable to both political and cultural pressures as it evolved. Presbyterians in Scotland found unity in the 1564 edition of Knox's *The Forme of Prayers,* which the General Assembly in that year required the ministers to use in all worship. It became known as the *Book of Common Order* and set a definite structure for worship, with detailed models for all the prayers, although ministers were free to improvise their own wording. Reformation in Scotland would probably have continued on a slow and uneventful course had it not been for intervention by the English. After the union of the kingdoms in 1603, the idea of national unity was hard to suppress. An attempt was made in 1618 by Bishop William Cowper (?–1619) of Galloway in the form of a compromise between the Knox book and the *Book of Common Prayer.*[27] Coming to nothing, the effort was pursued more forcefully in the 1630s with another version, imposed in 1637.[28] The resentment its introduction provoked showed the attachment of the Scots to their own forms as well as their nationalism.

But other influences were under way in England and had been for a long time. Not all the English felt that the *Book of Common Prayer* was the highest fruit of the Reformation. During the reign of Catholic Queen Mary, a number of the exiles who had spent time in Geneva had become familiar with Reformed worship. Under Elizabeth I (1558–1603), they sought to move the Church of England toward the more radical reforms of Geneva. Although Anglican theology of this period was largely based on Calvin, except on the eucharist, there was royal resistance to capitulating to the Reformed. Reformed practices initiated by Zwingli such as the prophesying services and the abandonment of vestments began to appear clandestinely. Thomas Cartwright (1535–1603), a Cambridge don, was the most conspicuous leader in this attempt to reshape the Anglican tradition. In 1584, a new liturgy based on Knox's service book was put surreptitiously into print, the so-called Waldegrave Book (after the printer), and entitled "A Booke of the Forme of Common Prayers." Two years later it was republished in the Netherlands in Middleburg.[29] Efforts made to get Parliament to approve these Genevan-style books were successfully blocked by Elizabeth.

The closing years of the sixteenth century saw the gradual emergence of a new position in England, neither that of Canterbury nor Geneva but much more radical than either. We shall deal with the Separatist and Puritan tradition at length in chapter 7, but suffice it to say here that it considered both positions too conservative in retaining a number of items not clearly provided for in God's word. Even Calvin had been pragmatic in keeping some ceremonies that were ordained by human beings as long as they promoted decency and good order for the building up of the church. God "did not will in outward discipline and ceremonies to prescribe in detail what we ought to do."[30] But the new radicals were not pragmatists but biblicists.

Like Elijah's cloud the size of a person's hand, this group grew in the next half century to a mighty storm, and under the Puritan Commonwealth the time at last came for a new stage of liturgical change at the hands of the Westminster Assembly of Divines. The abolition of the *Book of Common Prayer* for a period of fifteen years also brought about a surrender of the Scottish *Book of Common Order* in favor of the Westminster Directory, entitled *A Directory for the Public Worship of God Throughout the Three Kingdoms of England, Scotland, and Ireland* and published in 1645.[31] This document, although revolutionary in abolishing the service books that had been an essential part of the Reformed tradition, was destined to become normative for Presbyterians. It professed to "hold forth such things as are of Divine Institution in every Ordinance; and other things we have endeavored to set forth according to the Rules of Christian Prudence, agreeable to the general Rules of the Word of God."[32] The hope was for "a consent of all the Churches" in essentials.

Although the *Directory*'s authority was to be short-lived in England except among the Presbyterian minority, it replaced the *Book of Common Order* in the Kirk of Scotland. A last attempt was made by the English Presbyterian Richard Baxter (1615–1691) to prepare a truly Reformed service book, the so-called Savoy Liturgy of 1661. While the quality of the book was high, the political circumstances were far from expedient and it was never put into use. Baxter's eucharistic rite has been admired today for giving expression to Calvin's theology of the Holy Spirit in the prayer of epiclesis, inclusion of a fraction (breaking of bread) and libation (pouring of wine), and the high doctrine of consecration (setting aside the elements for holy use).[33]

Baxter and others also contributed to a flourishing tradition of family prayers that became one of the treasures of the Reformed tradition. His *The Reformed Pastor*[34] gave counsel on how the minister should encourage such worship. The Kirk developed *The Directory for Family-Worship*[35] in 1647. It called for "secret worship of each person alone, and private worship of families." Family worship includes "prayer and praise" and "reading of the scriptures, with catechising in a plain way." The head of the family is to be responsible, and the elders of the Kirk are to stir up diligence among the various families. Recalcitrant parents are to be "suspended and debarred from the Lord's supper."

Scotch and Scotch-Irish Presbyterians flocked to America during the eighteenth century, but it was not until 1788 that a newly organized national church was able to establish a norm for worship in the form of the first American directory, *The Directory for the Worship of God.* Successive schisms and unions brought further versions of the *Directory.* Two things may be said about these in general: Ultimately all are based on the 1645 Westminster *Directory,* although by 1988 the connection had become rather remote; and they have generally been treated with considerable indifference, more as hortatory guidelines than legal enactments. By mid-nineteenth century, want of uniformity becomes an accurate description of Presbyterian worship.

In America, the Reformed tradition endured a fresh attack, this time from the new Frontier tradition, which I shall describe in detail in chapter 10. The Scots brought with them the tradition of sacramental seasons. The *First Book of Discipline* of 1560 had hinted that four eucharistic celebrations a year were sufficient. The practice of seasons of preparation (foreshadowed in Calvin) eventually developed into important "sacramental seasons" of penance and preparation. Out of such occasions on the American frontier grew the practice of camp meetings, which fostered a new form of ministering ultimately systematized as revivals. Ironically, it was an erstwhile

Presbyterian, Charles G. Finney (1792–1875), who brought revival patterns into the mainstream of Presbyterian church life on the more sedate East Coast. The consequence was a further erosion of historical consciousness among Presbyterians and a discarding of almost everything particularly characteristic of Reformed worship in favor of American revival patterns.

Gradual weakening of some Reformed principles can be seen as early as 1751, when the Synod of New York rejected a challenge against hymnody. By 1843, even the Old School (conservative) wing could publish *Psalms and Hymns,* with uninspired texts taking their place alongside those from scripture.

There were defenders of the Reformed tradition in worship, although by mid-nineteenth century in America and Scotland they were considered eccentrics. In 1855, Charles W. Baird (1828–1887) cautiously hoped for "a formulary of Public Prayer and administration of ordinances [to be] supplied ... while we have little expectation that such a formulary, however perfect, will ever be adopted as a standard of the Church."[36] He makes it clear how few heeded existing *Directories* and pleads only for optional forms. In the Kirk of Scotland, a minister was censured in 1859 for praying from a book in public worship. By 1865, the Church Service Society was founded to promote just such activity.[37]

Among the German Reformed in Pennsylvania, a defense of the very possibility of a Reformed liturgy arose under the leadership of John W. Nevin (1803–1886) and Philip Schaff (1819–1893). Nevin decried the prevailing revivalism in *The Anxious Bench* (1843) and called for the recovery of Calvin's eucharistic theology in *The Mystical Presence* (1846).[38] After much controversy, a liturgy was produced in 1857[39] which was a landmark in restorationism in Reformed circles, although of more interest in the twentieth century than at the time.

These and other developments led to the publication of the *The Book of Common Worship* in 1906, "for voluntary use," and other editions in 1932 and 1946. Similar developments in the Church of Scotland led to a new *Book of Common Order* in 1928. All these volumes represent the stage of recovery of almost lost distinctive Reformed patterns. The very term "Presbyterian liturgies" had seemed self-contradictory to many people in the nineteenth century.

What was this tradition that over a period of three hundred years had become so seriously compromised that by the mid-nineteenth century most Presbyterians doubted there was any distinctive tradition other than the prevailing American pragmatism that they could call their own? We must consider some of the chief factors involved over these three centuries.

For the most part, the Reformed tradition had served highly

literate people. Even today, it attracts largely professional people and tends to the cerebral. The Reformed tradition has placed a high value on an educated ministry and has done more than any other to raise the intellectual standards of theological education in the United States. Yet it has always demanded a ministry of responsible lay people—elders and deacons—who, paradoxically, are ordained laity.

Much of this focus is probably due to the fierce devotion to scripture that has been the dominant factor in Reformed piety. Zwingli, Calvin, and their successors set precedents by doing theology that was basically exegetical and in stressing the primacy of God's word in every endeavor, including worship. A major factor in shaping piety was family worship, which provided a daily pattern of scripture reading, psalmody, and prayer. The durability of this tradition is witnessed to in various ways, especially Victorian novels, but it has largely fallen victim to the complications of modern family life. Various guides and manuals were published over the centuries to instruct the head of the family in presiding over these forms. Some of the best minds of the Reformed tradition devoted their energies to nurturing this kind of worship.[40] At its core seems always to have been the reading of scripture. Prayer was often extemporaneous, but some manuals provided sample prayers.

Another enduring factor has been a heavily penitential atmosphere, which seems to have kept alive a major theme in late-medieval piety. Bucer probably encouraged this as much as anyone by placing the Decalogue—hence, examination of conscience—at the very beginning of worship. It is not insignificant that Presbyterians have been the most adamant of modern liturgical revisers in insisting on beginning worship with confession. More than any other tradition, the Reformed seems to have cultivated a penitential piety.

The didactic and moralistic tendency slackened somewhat during the nineteenth century, when preaching for conversion tended to prevail. An emotional factor became important, and worship often became subservient to the pragmatic purpose of making converts. An earlier shift in piety had come about in the Enlightenment era in desacralizing the sacraments. The Scotch Confession of Faith of 1560 had insisted, "We utterly damn the vanity of them that affirm Sacraments to be nothing else but naked and bare signs."[41] Baxter, a hundred years later, had insisted that the consecrated bread and wine became "sacramentally the body and blood of thy Son Jesus Christ."[42] But the Enlightenment tended to turn the sacraments into moral lessons, and the Reformed tradition largely found this temptation irresistible. In a way, the disciplinary character of the sacramental seasons fed this moralistic tendency by making the Lord's Supper a time for such intensive introspection. Thus emphasis came to be increasingly on human agency in the sacraments rather than divine gift. Zwingli's strong sense of God's activity in forming the community seems to have been as little heeded as Calvin's stress on feeding on Christ.

The importance of the Lord's Day long characterized the Reformed attitude to time, and this was often reflected in sabbatarian laws restricting Sunday activities.[43] The observance of all other holy days, including Christmas, was forbidden in the Scotch *Book of Discipline* of 1560. In modern times in the Netherlands, Good Friday was observed by the celebration of the Lord's Supper. All eucharistic piety focused on the Lord's death rather than the resurrection. It is still unusual to find Easter celebrations of the eucharist because much Reformed piety still sees the eucharist with medieval eyes. Throughout much of Reformed history, variety in the year came through the sacramental seasons and, in America, camp meetings, revivals, and homecomings.[44]

The life cycle saw church celebrations of baptism, public profession of faith, ordinations, and marriage, but public funerals were often discouraged and no forms for funerals are provided in the Christian Reformed Church's current *Psalter Hymnal*[45] formularies. Baptisms were meant to be public and the child was expected at an appropriate age to make a public profession of his or her faith before being considered ready to receive the Lord's Supper. Ordinations were by presbytery (groups of elders) with the laying on of hands reintroduced after a hiatus of this practice in Geneva and Scotland.

These centuries also saw a search for an appropriate Reformed sense of space for worship. Usually this focused on bringing the largest number of people as close as possible to the pulpit. The typical Reformed pulpit was high and embellished with woodwork, pulpit window, sounding board, Bible cushion, and drapes. Until the early nineteenth century, the usual means of communion was by the congregation, gathered about a table or tables and seated on benches. This was given up in the nineteenth century, everywhere but in the Netherlands, in favor of the Puritan pattern of pew communion. Balconies were a common feature of Reformed churches, and various experiments were tried with a variety of central forms—Greek crosses, octagons, squares—in efforts to find the best spatial arrangement for worship.[46]

Such buildings proclaim the centrality of preaching in Reformed worship, and the architecture faithfully replicates the functions of the building. But styles of preaching tended to evolve too, and these changes were mirrored in changes in the design and location of the pulpit. The wineglass pulpit of the eighteenth century reflected a style of preaching largely devoted to exegesis of biblical texts and their application to daily life. Nineteenth-century pulpits tended to be desks set on a platform upon which the preacher or visiting evangelist could roam as he sought to convert souls or reheat the dimmed coals of congregational fervor.

Public prayer was conducted also from the pulpit. Since the *Directory* encouraged extempore prayer according to standard contents but local wording, the congregation's role in prayer became that of passive participants. In many cases, as less and less use was made of the outlines in the *Directory,* public prayer reflected the personality and reading of the preacher. In becoming intensely local, it could lose the perspective of the wider church. Public prayer was complemented by the prayer life of families. When adequate sample prayers and models were followed, this could give a balanced prayer life. The practice also developed of a laity accustomed to praying extemporaneously at home. Frequently, midweek services developed in which small groups met to pray together. Often led by lay people, these provided an important school of prayer for families.

At first, music was limited to psalm tunes for the singing of the psalter. Often this was lined out in the absence of printed music. A small body, the Reformed Presbyterian Church, still insists on the exclusive use of psalms as the only singing permitted in worship; psalms are sung to metrical versions.[47] But hymnody had become acceptable to most Presbyterians about the same time as it did in the Church of England, by the middle of the nineteenth century. Instrumental music became more and more prominent as pipe organs were gradually introduced during the nineteenth century, even in Zurich. Revivalism encouraged the use of choral groups, and eventually these became full-fledged choirs. Although a Presbyterian choir would have seemed a contradiction in terms to John Knox, they had become common by the end of the nineteenth century. This was the antithesis of the restorationism going on in the rediscovery of Reformed liturgies, for it added something the Reformers would not have tolerated: the passive participation of listening to a choir. While recovering its own identity, Reformed worship was at the same time borrowing from other traditions.

Present Characteristics of Reformed Worship

The period since Vatican II has seen a variety of changes in Reformed worship, changes that one writer has called "catching up to Calvin."[48] In general, it has seen both a reassertion of the definite outlines of the Reformed tradition as first delineated in sixteenth-century Switzerland, a position best demonstrated in the scholarly writing of Hughes Oliphant Old[49] but reflected by others as well. This position has been slowly gathering momentum since the writings of Charles W. Baird in the mid-nineteenth century. On the other hand, there has been a strong impulse to absorb the best of the post-Vatican

II reforms, from both Roman Catholics and other Protestants, especially United Methodists. In some respects, these are contrary directions; in others they have much in common. Old, for example, would have scriptural readings done in course; the others prefer the selective readings of the ecumenical lectionary; yet presumably all would choose formalized patterns over a local preacher's favorite texts.

Some of the landmarks of the recent period have been the preparation of directories in 1983 by the newly united Presbyterian Church (U.S.A.) and another that received approval in 1989. The process of liturgical revision had its beginning during Vatican II with *Service for the Lord's Day* (1964) and *The Book of Common Worship: Provisional Services* (1966). These prepared the way for *The Worshipbook: Services* (1970) and *The Worshipbook: Services and Hymns* (1972).[50] *The Worshipbook* led the way in introducing among American Protestants the ecumenical lectionary, the Presbyterian version of the Roman Catholic Sunday Lectionary that went into use in liturgical year 1970. *The Worshipbook* was introduced too early to appropriate more recent liturgical concerns: inclusive language, new approaches to the process of Christian initiation, or a variety of eucharistic prayers. These later concerns are being addressed in a series of Supplemental Liturgical Resources, which began in 1984 with the eucharist and have continued with baptism, marriage, funeral, and daily prayer services.[51] Additional volumes are projected.

A major development has been the encouragement of the eucharist as the normal Lord's Day service, but proponents of weekly communion meet the same resistance Calvin met; the proposal still seems far too radical. One major innovation of the new books that has caught fire is the use of a lectionary. Before 1970 this was rare; since then it has come to be followed in nearly half of Presbyterian congregations. There are several major consequences: Use of the lectionary has encouraged exegetical preaching, brought a larger amount of scripture reading into worship, and led to a much richer observance of the two cycles of the Christian year. Altogether, the rise of the lectionary has probably been the most significant change in the last two decades.

Other reformed bodies have recently produced new liturgies. The Kirk of Scotland has produced a new and greatly revised *The Book of Common Order (1979)* taking account of post-Vatican II developments.[52] There are new services in *Rejoice in the Lord,*[53] the new hymnal (1985) of the Reformed Church in America, and in the new *Psalter Hymnal* of the Christian Reformed Church.[54] The United Reformed Church of England produced its first service book, *A Book of Services,* in 1980.[55] The *Book of Worship: United Church of Christ* (1986) also has reformed roots, especially from the Evangelical and Reformed churches.[56]

Presbyterians, as did many others, went through a euphoric period of experimentation in the late 1960s and early 1970s. Practice tended to produce verbose liturgies, now almost immediately recognizable as dated, but also opened people's eyes to new visual interests, especially in textile arts. This seems to have survived despite a tendency to treat even textiles as a verbal medium. The range of musical expression has been enlarged, with folk song and guitar music taking their places alongside traditional hymnody and organ music. Now that the experimentation of the 1960s can be evaluated, it can be seen that its chief contributions were twofold: in dramatizing the possibility that worship could and ought to change according to cultural shifts and in enlarging the types of expression available.

Recent trends seem to favor more frequent celebrations of the eucharist and a greater variety of special occasions such as Ash Wednesday and Holy Week and other festivals, once foreign but now familiar, such as Transfiguration and Christ the King. Architecturally the freestanding table that is now mandatory among Roman Catholics is again becoming common among Presbyterians. As the process of baptism is being rethought, with provision for yearly baptismal renewals, more prominent fonts are becoming common. The new services stress active participation, with both unison prayers and the possibilities of spontaneous intercessions and thanksgivings. In many congregations, charismatics have brought other kinds of active participation.

Today, many of the legacies of the period of frontier dominance are still apparent, especially in the tendency for each congregation to order its worship to suit itself. Some history is being recycled in attempts to recover the importance of psalmody through new ways of reciting and singing the psalms. Perhaps Presbyterians have still not caught up with Calvin, but efforts are certainly being made to do so, and even to go far beyond what he envisioned.

5

Anabaptist Worship

The failure of agreement on the Lord's Supper at Marburg in 1529 was the most spectacular of the divisions among Protestant reformers. But it was not the only matter on which they were unable to find concord. Already the other sacrament, baptism, had been the occasion of heated and divisive debates, and the ruptures resulting from the disputations on baptism would be just as permanent as those emanating from the disagreement about the Lord's Supper.

Early in the decade, Luther had been troubled by his fellow priest, Thomas Münzer, who had urged the postponement of baptism (although not advocating rebaptism) and had produced his own *Deutsche Evangelische Messe* (German Evangelical Mass)[1] in 1524. The so-called Zwickau prophets or Storchites had begun to have serious doubts about infant baptism as early as 1520. They vigorously expressed these doubts in Wittenberg the following year, thereby provoking Luther to champion infant baptism, but the Peasants' War of 1525 swept away any result from these abortive efforts.

These were but the advance guard of countless movements that were to gather both adherents and opponents during the 1520s and 1530s. Many of these groups eventually vanished; others survived. The Spiritualist Casper Schwenkfeld (1490–1561) and his followers discontinued any outward celebrations of the eucharist in 1526, establishing a resolutely noneucharistic worship. The Lord's Supper was not resumed until 1878 among the small groups of Schwenkfelder churches centered around Philadelphia. Schwenkfeld did not repudiate baptism, even infant baptism, although he stressed its inward dimension.

Another group whose descendants continue today were the early Unitarians of Transylvania, led by Francis Dávid (ca.1510–1579). Himself successively Lutheran and then Reformed, Dávid became convinced that infant baptism was wrong, as indeed was all baptism in the name of the Trinity. Dávid not only opposed infant baptism but prayer to Christ; some of his followers also suspended the Lord's Supper. Eventually infant baptism and the Lord's Supper were restored among these early Unitarians. A later generation, led by Faustus Socinus (1539–1604), again argued against the need for any baptism except for converts, but Socinus's disciples inclined to the baptism of believers by immersion. Unitarianism in England and America continued this sixteenth-century legacy.

The fortunes of a great number of these and other sixteenth-century groups have been chronicled by George Williams, who divides them into three groups: Spiritualists, Evangelical Rationalists, and Anabaptists.[2] Our present concern is with the third segment of the radical or left-wing Reformation, the Anabaptists. Known chiefly today through various Mennonite and Amish churches and the Hutterian Brethren, these groups, once notable for the radicality of their break with medieval worship, are distinguished today more by the tenacity with which they have conserved their early forms of worship through the centuries.

Back to Zurich, then, we must go, to the disputations before the city council in 1523 and 1525 with which the movement known as the Swiss Brethren had its origins. Two priests, Balthasar Hübmaier (ca.1485–1528) and George Blaurock (1492–1529) took the lead in dispute with their fellow clergy, Zwingli and Jud, over the question of infant baptism. The radicals found infant baptism unscriptural and unreasonable; those defending the status quo found it both biblical and rational. In the end, the city council found Zwingli's views more persuasive. Those opposing infant baptism came to be known as "Anabaptists" ("again baptizers") and were hounded out of Zurich under savage persecutions.

We cannot by any means trace all the leaders and movements within Anabaptism. But we shall try to distinguish clear and consistent beliefs and practices with regard to worship and thereby discern a distinctive worship tradition.

The Anabaptist tradition of worship provides our first example of "Free Church" worship. That term is too imprecise for our purposes, but it can be applied in a general way to two other historic types of worshiping communities with different origins and developments from the Anabaptists. For the other varieties of Free Church worship, we shall also use names referring to historical origins: Separatist and Puritan tradition (chapter 7) and Frontier tradition (chapter 10).

Free Church worship, in all three instances, has two distinctive characteristics. First, such worship demands freedom to reform worship exclusively on the basis of scripture without any compulsion to dilute the purity of reformation by compromise with human traditions. Second, the ordering of worship is determined locally by each worshiping community. It is the ultimate form of subsidiarity in liturgical matters. The witness of the Anabaptist movement was that, for both of these possibilities to be realized, the absence of intervention by the civil government was necessary. The brief episode of Anabaptist rule in Münster (1533–1535) only served to confirm this observation.

Early in the Reformation, it became abundantly clear that no consensus on what the scripture says about God's will for worship would be possible. Some groups were prepared to tolerate those human traditions that were not contrary to the clear word of scripture. But the center of Free Church worship is the attempt to model all worship on the revealed word of God in every possible detail. A common assumption was that, just as God had revealed how humans were to act in other spheres of life such as the ethical, God had also prescribed rules for worship. This is biblicism pure and simple, but every religious group in the sixteenth century appealed to biblical authority whenever possible. Free Church worship is simply the most insistent on the sole authority of scripture.

For Free Church worship, a corollary to freedom from state interference in matters of worship is freedom from ecclesiastical intervention beyond the local worshiping community. Thus Free Church worship is basically liturgical congregationalism. This does not mean liturgical chaos; indeed, the degree of predictability is usually almost as high as in other traditions of worship. But it often means that published liturgies are considered superfluous at best and idolatrous at worst. If God's word is clear to anyone who reads, each Christian community can discern what is God's will by itself and must be free to act accordingly. Hence liturgical books, although not totally absent, are an anomaly in Free Church worship.

The Free Church insistence on the freedom to follow God's word and on freedom from outside intervention certainly characterizes Anabaptist worship. We shall look first at common characteristics in the decades 1521 to 1561, then at a few distinctive leaders and movements from this period, and finally at Anabaptist worship since that time.

Common Characteristics of Early Anabaptist Worship

The place to begin is not with liturgical texts or sacramental theologies but with people, probably more so here than in any other tradition. The Anabaptists were people who voluntarily put themselves at risk in order to achieve their desired worship reforms, and thousands were martyred for meeting for worship.

The first generation of leaders were varied. A few, such as Balthasar Hübmaier, George Blaurock (Cajacob), Michael Sattler (ca.1500–1527), and Menno Simons (1496–1561), were Roman Catholic priests. Friars and monks also joined the ranks of the Anabaptists. Yet status meant little to Anabaptist communities, and often reordination was considered necessary, as in the case of Menno Simons. It was character that mattered, not the individual's ecclesiastical status. Leaders were recognized by the local community they served, not apart from it.

Many of the early leaders were laity. Such men as Conrad Grebel (1498–1526), John Hut (ca.1485–1527), Pilgrim Marpeck (ca.1495–1556), Melchior Hoffman (1498–1543), Jacob Hutter (?–1536), and others were distinguished lay leaders. Some, such as Grebel, had been highly educated and were familiar with the new learning of the day; others such as Marpeck were self-taught theologians. New and important roles for the laity distinguished the Anabaptists from the clerical domination of the Lutheran, Reformed, and Anglican traditions. Calvin, even if he was never ordained, certainly acted as if he had been.

A further implication of lay leadership was the increased importance of women, who often shared roles of leadership and acted on terms of equality with men. The Anabaptist movement represented a leveling upward of lay ministry. When persecution came, it was indiscriminate; wives frequently were martyred along with husbands. The leaders were the first to be martyred, but others were ordained immediately to keep the flock together.

Above all, the Anabaptists must be seen as people trying to recover the pure church of apostolic times, a goal nearly impossible for a state-controlled church to which all were forced to belong. Baptism was an important issue because it came to be the means of distinguishing between a pure church of known believers, visible to all, and a mass of people indiscriminately baptized as infants, a church that included good and bad alike. Baptism could be used to keep distinctions clear, since only professing believers in good standing could receive the Lord's Supper. Despite the label "Anabaptist," these people did not consider themselves rebaptizers since they believed those baptized as infants had not received actual baptism.

The earliest accounts speak of baptisms with a milk pail or in a village fountain, and to this day most Anabaptists baptize by pouring or sprinkling. Demands for immersion are a separate and later concern.

Baptism of believers only was the basic issue for the Anabaptists. Both sides in the infant baptism controversy used the same arguments over and over again. There seem to be two main grounds for argument, the witness of scripture and the witness of reason. That the church had been baptizing the children of believers at birth for well over a millennium was not considered an important argument, even though the practice had gone on virtually without challenge for all those years. The Anabaptist irruption was a dramatic new turn in Christian thinking and the practice of this sacrament.

The biblical arguments from both sides tended to be based on literalistic bits of exegesis. The Anabaptists argued that there was no clear mention of the baptism of children in scripture, to which the pedobaptists (infant baptizers) responded that the four *oikos* (household) passages (Acts 16:15 and 33; Acts 18:8; and 1 Cor. 1:16) included families in which there most likely were children. The pedobaptists further asserted that the baptism of infants was simply the Christian form of circumcision, which had pertained to all Jewish male children long before they had the possibility of belief. Anabaptists did not find the parallel convincing.

Anabaptists were prone to cite such passages as Matthew 28:19, "Make all nations my disciples; baptize men everywhere." A strict interpretation places making disciples first and the same argument could be derived from Mark 16:16: "Believe it and receive baptism." Menno Simons argued that "Jesus Christ, the eternal Wisdom who cannot err, the eternal Truth who cannot lie, has commanded this, namely, that we shall first preach the Gospel, from the hearing of which comes faith (Rom. 10), and that we shall baptize those who believe."[3] Pedobaptists refused to be as literal about the importance of verbal sequence. They preferred, instead, to cite Mark 10:14: "Let the children come to me." Anabaptists saw no baptismal reference here and refused to consider it relevant.

Zwingli made some strong points in favor of infant baptism by considering it to be a New Testament "covenant sign."[4] As in the Old Testament, so in the New, those who were being saved were placed within a covenant community whose bounds are marked by signs or seals. Baptism was the seal of that covenant and a pledge that the child would inherit salvation as promised to Christ's followers. Zwingli chided the Anabaptists for placing too much value on the outward and visible sign of baptism.[5] His basic argument, that baptism of families is consonant with the biblical witness, was an important assertion for the defenders of existing practice.

The arguments on the basis of reason were also irreconcilable. Luther had struggled to defend infant baptism by claiming at first that God had imputed faith even to children and eventually arguing that the faith of others in the community was effective and that God commanded baptism of children.[6] Such arguments were far from convincing to Anabaptists, and Menno Simons argued that "young children are without understanding and unteachable; therefore baptism cannot be administered to them."[7] Both sides agreed that baptism without faith was simply magic and unworthy of Christians. Menno Simons argued that instruction in faith clearly had to precede baptism, for children must know to what they are committing themselves; that meant postponing baptism to an age of accountability. This was certainly the rational approach, but it tended to make baptism contingent on human preparation for it rather than a free gift offered by God indiscriminately to the children of believers. The Anabaptists reflect the humanistic learning of the Renaissance but not the desacralized universe of the Enlightenment. Baptism is a very important life event for them.

If the people who made up the church were careful about entrance into it, they were no less zealous about exits from the community. To keep the church pure, there must be ways of dismissing those who do not live up to the creedal and moral standards expected. The purity of the church was guarded through the use of the ban (Matt. 18:15–18) and shunning (1 Cor. 5:11). The Schleitheim Confession of 1527 defends the ban as a biblical practice of admonishing "twice in secret and the third time openly" for correction and expulsion of errant members.[8] Controversy raged over how extensive were to be the consequences of such banning. The ban was intended to exclude those who by sins had already cut themselves off from the church. When other stages of correction failed, the Mennonites (the largest Anabaptist group) developed a process of shunning. But to what extent should this reach, even within the family? Did 1 Corinthians 5:11 mean separation from bed and board of married couples or not? Various Mennonite groups disagreed.

This was the legacy, of course, of the medieval practice of penance with its extreme penalty of excommunication. But in Anabaptist hands it acquired a new personal and local quality. The excommunication—the ban—was not just from holy things but from all social contact and was intended to lead the sinner to repentance and readmission. A solemn reconciliation of the repentant sinner to the church was effected through the laying on of hands as the prodigal son or daughter was welcomed back into the community. "But as in the beginning one is received into the church by means of a sign [that is baptism], so also after he fell and was separated from the church he must likewise be received by a sign, that is through the laying on of hands, which must be done by a servant of the gospel."[9]

The force of this internal discipline was to keep the church pure. In contrast to the magisterial reformation, with its powers of coercion, the Anabaptists ruled by spiritual discipline. But more often than not, they were victims of persecution by the state church. Throughout most of the sixteenth century, the Anabaptists knew unremitting persecution from those who felt they were a threat to both church and state. Late in the century, the Mennonites found respite in the Netherlands, but by then persecution and martyrdom had been a way of life for half a century. This habit of living on the margin of society shaped their worship in many ways.

The attacks of a hostile world drove some Anabaptists to shun the world altogether. The most thoroughgoing worldly avoidance came among the followers of Jacob Hutter, who formed communities where property was held in common. The Hutterian Brethren found community in goods essential to a godly life, and their life-style became a form of connubial monasticism withdrawn from the world. Eventually, the Old Order Amish Church also achieved withdrawal from much contact with the world but without communal ownership.

Frequently, Anabaptist literature referred to the three witnesses or baptisms of 1 John 5:8: "the Spirit, the water, and the blood." In Hübmaier's theology, the Christian "like Jesus has a baptism yet to be accomplished, perhaps martyrdom itself in which he shall give his final witness of a good conscience."[10]

It is easy to see parallels between the Anabaptists of the sixteenth century and much of popular late-medieval piety. But it is difficult to trace direct connections except to say that the same kinds of humble piety manifested similar dissatisfactions with established religion. The areas of Europe in which Anabaptists flourished had also been fertile soil for many late-medieval groups of laity who sought more perfect lives. Some of them, too, had found that the outward and visible sacraments of the church could be dispensed with for inward communion with Christ. Anabaptism was part of a continuing ferment of unofficial religion, bubbling up often where least expected.

Much Anabaptist piety was shaped by response to intense persecution. Beginning in Zurich in 1525, Anabaptists were subjected to fierce attacks, and many of the early leaders perished in 1527. Persecution continued for men and women alike, and the number of martyrs ran into the tens of thousands. It is not surprising that in the wake of such continual violence a piety of the suffering church on earth evolved. The blood of which they spoke and sang was all too often their own, shed in martyrdom.

But they refused to take part in government or warfare or anything that shed the blood of others. For some of the Anabaptists, the vision of the imminent coming of Christ was the sustaining factor. Since the kingdom of God was at hand, severe persecution was only further proof of how soon this would be. One could endure persecution, even martyrdom, in this world when the promise of the next world was so close. Such chiliastic hopes fueled the fervor of their worship as they awaited a kingdom not made with human hands.

An important index to this piety of martyrdom was hymnology. Although some leaders, such as Conrad Grebel, deplored the use of hymns in worship as leading to pride, hymn singing soon came to be an important part of worship for many Anabaptists, in sharp

contrast to Zwingli's prohibition of it. A variety of leaders wrote
hymns for their people. The first Anabaptist hymnbook, the *Ausbund*
(selection), was published in 1560 and remains in use today among
Old Order Amish, the oldest Protestant hymnal still being used.

These hymns are no ordinary ones. They are filled with the language of suffering and martyrdom.[11] Not only do they keep alive the
memories of those who have already given their lives for their faith,
they anticipate that true Christians now singing will join their prede-
cessors in suffering. The identification of the present age with apostolic times comes readily in such a community of suffering. The most
recent *Mennonite Hymnal* (1969) reflects the mainstream of modern
American hymnody.[12] But hymn singing is still unaccompanied by
instruments in most Mennonite churches.

Another reflection of piety under persecution came in a book that
became an important shaper of piety among the Anabaptists, just as
did *Foxe's Book of Martyrs* (1554 and 1563) by John Foxe (1516–
1587) among English Protestants. This was *The Bloody Theater, or
Martyrs' Mirror* by Thieleman van Braght (1625–1664),[13] published
in final form in 1670. Its predecessor was *The Offering of the Lord*
of 1562, with accounts of the martyrs' deaths combined with a
songbook recounting their courage in the face of death. Martyrolo-
gies have had as much importance in Protestant worship as in
Roman Catholic, although this fact is largely overlooked.

The eucharistic piety of Anabaptists had much in common with
that which Zwingli had articulated. Although not all the doctrine
came from Zwingli, there was a common inheritance among many
early Anabaptist leaders of the humanistic learning that lay behind
Zwingli's critique of Roman Catholic eucharistic faith and practice.
The tendency to dissociate physical things from spiritual uses, so
characteristic of Zwingli, was readily accepted by many Anabaptists
in their eucharistic theology. Some went much further than Zwingli
in the direction of spiritualizing the sacrament so that physical elements were no longer considered necessary. Among some Dutch
Anabaptists it is possible there were survivals of late medieval sac-
ramentarianism surviving from such men as Wessel Gansfort
(ca.1420–1489). Gansfort had emphasized the importance of commemoration over physical eating. Such teachings had been reinforced by the teaching of Erasmus, who had stressed the symbolic
aspects of the eucharist.

Thus a common feature among most Anabaptists with regard to
the Lord's Supper was a tendency to see it largely as a commemorative event; indeed, it was often called the "Lord's Memorial." Above
all, it was a communal event of the visible church of saints gathered
in the Lord's name. Therefore it was necessary to make certain that
the body of Christ present as the congregation be pure and undefiled.

In recalling the Lord's death and suffering together, there was a strong sense of the community's identification with Christ's suffering. "Whoever drinks of this cup has first surrendered himself and testifies with it that he is prepared to pour out his blood for the sake of Christ and his church insofar as faith and the test of love demands it. Whoever gives his body and pours out his blood as indicated, he does not give his own life nor spill his own blood, but rather the body and blood of Christ. For we are members of his body."[14] For those who faced death together, the sense of unity with Christ and one another must have been unusually strong. A favorite theme was the reference in the *Didache* (an early church manual, "The Teaching") to the wheat scattered on the hills and brought together to make a single loaf.[15]

The fact that it was a community of love made the purity of the gathering even more crucial. And so the eucharist had a strong ethical character. The wicked were to be expelled, not only lest they eat and drink judgment upon themselves but "so that we may break and eat one bread, with one mind and in one love, and may drink of one cup."[16] Thus the eucharist tended to be a focus for the moral values of the community.

In general, the text of the Lord's Supper was not committed to writing. An exception to this is Balthasar Hübmaier's rite *A Form of the Supper of Christ,* compiled in 1527.[17] This rite makes clear the importance of worthy partaking and contains a period of personal self-examination to see if one is willing to suffer for Christ, an exhortation to brotherly love, and further exhortation to live uprightly.

The usual Anabaptist eucharist was much more informal. It was presided over by the locally chosen leader, whose role was largely that of teacher and shepherd. This leader led the Lord's Supper and did most of the preaching. The service usually included hymn singing, scripture reading, prayer, preaching, and the breaking of bread, without a set form except for reading the institution narrative.

The frequency of the eucharist could vary greatly. In general, Zwingli's quarterly eucharist would probably have seemed about right to many groups, especially given the emphasis on the purity of the church it presupposed. But there were instances of more frequent communion. Williams cites the "extraordinary frequency" of some Polish Brethren, who recorded that " 'The Lord's Supper we attend often and, indeed, where possible every day.' "[18] Certainly, that was the exception.

For most, the eucharist became an occasional event. The usual Sunday service consisted of reading and expounding the Bible, hymnody, and prayer. According to the Schleitheim Confession of 1527, the pastor presides in reading and expounding scriptures and "leads out in prayer." The pastor also disciplines the congregation, bans "in the church," and lifts "up the bread when it is to be broken." When the pastor is martyred, "another shall be ordained . . . in the same hour so that God's little flock and people may not be destroyed."[19]

Most of the observance of the traditional church year disappeared. It was charged against certain Anabaptists in Lithuania that they had not only destroyed the rest of the liturgical year but even eliminated Christmas and Easter. The only marks in time were occasional baptisms, ordinations, marriages, burials, and the more or less quarterly celebrations of the Lord's Supper.

Marriage, in particular, was an occasion of particular concern. Although they did not consider marriage a sacrament and repudiated monastic vows of celibacy, the Anabaptists found new significance in marriage as a covenantal relationship closely related to baptism. Far more was at stake than just a civil contract, since those in the Anabaptist community were already in covenantal relationship to one another. Not only were converts "rebaptized" or "reordained" in the eyes of the world but sometimes "retrothed," as married converts declared anew their relationship as new members of Christ's body. Remarriage of a banned spouse who had been reconciled to the community with his or her former partner was not unknown.[20] In certain groups, the absence of belief on the part of one partner could be used as a reason for divorce according to Paul (1 Cor.7:15).

In many situations, Anabaptist worship had to be in secret or inconspicuous for there was always the danger of mob violence as well as official persecution. Where toleration was possible, especially in Poland, meetings for worship were held on the estate of a friendly nobleman or in modest meetinghouses erected for that purpose. To this day, the Amish prefer to meet for worship in private homes, moving each week from one farmhouse to another. Movable benches are set up so the community can gather to worship in the main living room of the house and then are set aside until the next time. Less conservative Mennonites have built modest churches, usually centering in a pulpit with a small altar-table and perhaps a font. Pipe organs may or may not be present. The modest character of the buildings are a reflection of the reluctance of Anabaptists to want to dominate society. As true sectarians, they provide a marginal relationship as a humble community or holy remnant on the margin of society. Never to be confused with a state church or with society at large, their practice of baptism for believers only is a perfect expression of their relationship to the culture.

As might be imagined, prayer was stressed as a consequence of baptism. To be baptized, in effect, made one a person who could join in intercessory prayer with and for the community. Thus, although the pastor usually led the group in prayer, it was often picked up by members of the community. In some congregations, periods of silent meditation for prayer were also provided. Aside from those of Hübmaier, written orders of worship and forms for prayers seem to have been rare. Prayer was often expressed spontaneously as the Spirit prompted.

Preaching was a major portion of all worship. In most instances it was expository preaching from biblical passages, and a primary role of the pastor seems to have been that of being a scholar of God's word who both through preaching and teaching applied the meaning of scripture to daily life. Hübmaier provided for the practice of prophesying (as had Zwingli), when the congregation was free to question the preacher's handling of a biblical text. In the life of these often-persecuted communities, God's word was paramount, and the hungry sheep were carefully fed by preaching.

Distinctive Leaders and Movements

It is difficult to make general statements about the Anabaptists, since such a variety of leaders and movements is subsumed under their name. Comments on a few leaders and their special concerns will suggest the diversity of Anabaptist worship.

As indicated, Balthasar Hübmaier resembles in some ways the more magisterial Reformation, not only in seeing a positive role for the magistrates with regard to the church but in producing his own liturgies for baptism (and confirmation) and for the Lord's Supper. In some ways he is a bridge figure in Anabaptist worship, linking the old tradition and the new Anabaptist concerns.[21]

John Hut was one of the early Anabaptist leaders, a bookbinder and bookseller by trade. He became convinced that baptism should be postponed to the age of thirty, the age at which Jesus was baptized. This thoroughgoing biblicism was not generally endorsed by Anabaptists, but it does reflect the high view many of them placed on the biblical accounts of baptism by John the Baptist. For Hut, there were three stages to baptism: an outer in which one announced one's faith and enrolled in the discipline of the church, an inner redemptive one of suffering through the cross, and the final eschatological sign to prepare one for the last day. Baptism thus had a strong eschatological flavor as well as identification with the suffering of Christ through baptism.[22]

Pilgram Marpeck was by trade an engineer and forester. Self-taught as a theologian, he helped shape the concepts of baptism for many. His was one of the "most carefully developed of the Anabaptist baptismal theologies."[23] Marpeck was certain that regeneration began before and apart from baptism, but the outward act of baptism had an importance for him as a sign participating in the reality of what it signified. Baptism could be spoken of as a "waterbath in the Word," in which one pledged to lay aside the old life and follow Christ. The inner conversion preceded but the outward bath was used by the Spirit too. Marpeck considered children as born innocent. Baptism was not necessary for their salvation, but Marpeck advocated a rite of dedication of infants. The doctrine of predestination (predetermined salvation or damnation) was generally repudiated by Anabaptists.

For a small number of Anabaptists, the crucial figure was Jacob Hutter, who was able to give leadership to a group of sectarians who developed a communal life together. In these communities of Hutterian Brethren organized for common production and consumption there appeared a form of realized eschatology, a heaven on earth. But what was most radical for its time has tended to be among the most conservative in the continuity of worship forms. Hutterite worship was essentially Zwinglian when it came to the theology and practice of the Lord's Supper. It insisted that the elements have no power of their own but that the communal act of remembrance is all-important. Even the sermons became standardized, and various sixteenth-century forms are still used among the Hutterian Brethren.

The chief leader of what was to become the most widespread of the Anabaptist groups was Menno Simons. His followers are the Mennonites and the more conservative Amish. Simons had been a priest who was converted to Anabaptism and spent most of his later years shepherding communities in the Netherlands and northern Germany, shaping and nurturing an enduring tradition. Not only was his life spent in defending his people from outside interference but much time went into stilling controversy within the flock, especially over the severity of the practice of shunning when nuptial ties were involved. His legacy was the relative tranquillity and stability that he was able to bring out of the numerous sect members who came to claim his name. Most Mennonites celebrate the Lord's Supper twice a year, often with foot washing.

Strictly speaking, the Brethren Church and the Church of the Brethren are not Anabaptist churches. Although the Brethren originated in the early eighteenth century from Pietistic Lutheran and Reformed backgrounds, they do have some common features with Anabaptists. The insistence on believer's baptism is the most obvious common thread, but their practice (suggested by the nickname Dunkers) differed in that they baptized by triple immersion. They also had a common tradition with Anabaptists of nonresistance, placing them among the great exponents of pacifism along with the Quakers.

A distinctive aspect of Brethren worship is the practice of foot washing (John 13:3–12). Although known early in the West (Ambrose), Roman Catholics and Protestants have only made this a part of Holy Week services in recent years. The Brethren found it a deeply meaningful part of the Lord's Supper and have observed the ordinance on a regular basis for nearly three centuries. The ancient love feast is held at least annually in many Church of the Brethren congregations. They have also followed carefully the biblical injunction to anoint the sick (James 5:14), and this has been part of their pastoral care throughout their history. The importance of these two rites is deeply ingrained and greatly valued among Brethren.[24] More conservative communities insist that women be veiled during worship and practice closed communion (for members only).

The Anabaptist Tradition Today

How has the Anabaptist tradition fared in the modern world? Perhaps the question should be phrased "despite the modern world," for the fact that it has survived and thrived is partly owing to its ability to insulate itself from the world and other worship traditions. Whether this will continue, especially in the case of the more liberal groups, is open to question.

Groups who have suffered so much for the institution of their particular form of worship are not apt to take it lightly. The radicalness of Anabaptist worship in discarding set forms of worship, and in allowing each community to order its own worship according to its own wisdom and needs, was a feature not easily surrendered. While other traditions have become subject to cultural as well as extraneous liturgical influences, the Anabaptist element has managed to keep its tradition relatively intact. Change is inevitable in any worship tradition: if not change in the verbal elements of the worship, at least in architectural, musical, and cultural forms. But it is characteristic of the Anabaptist tradition that it has clung to many of its original forms with great tenacity and thus may be closer to its sixteenth-century origins than the less radical traditions of the time: Lutheran, Reformed, and Anglican.

While these more conservative traditions underwent major shifts during the Enlightenment or the romantic era of the nineteenth century, the Anabaptists managed to remain relatively untouched. In a sense, they had already undergone their own rationalism in the sixteenth century in the guise of Renaissance humanism. This had the effect of raising serious questions about the existing sacramental system. Yet the early Anabaptists found profundities in believer's baptism as life-and-death commitment that rarely had been known in traditional Christianity since the early church.

The context of Protestant America in the nineteenth century proved more of a challenge: namely, to conform to the prevailing

American frontier patterns in worship. This was less a temptation
than it might seem because of the relative isolation of American
Anabaptists. The fact that most worship long remained in German
or other non-English languages helped keep most Anabaptists dis-
tant from acculturation, although eventually that barrier fell except
among the Amish and Hutterian Brethren. A wider range of hymnody has been introduced, especially as hymnbooks moved from
German to partially English and then largely English. The newest
Mennonite hymnal has only fifteen texts in German. Still, there are
remnants of distinctive history, as in the hymn by Jörg Wagner
(?–1527) from the *Ausbund* of 1564:

> He who would follow Christ in life
> Must scorn the world's insult and strife
> And bear his cross each day,
> For this alone leads to the throne;
> Christ is the only way.
>
> Christ's servants follow Him to death
> And give their body, life, and breath
> On cross and rack and pyre.
> As gold is tried and purified,
> They stand the test of fire.
>
> Renouncing all, they choose the cross,
> And claiming it, count all as loss,
> E'en home and child and wife.
> Forsaking gain, forgetting pain,
> They enter into life.[25]

For all practical purposes, the Amish protected their worship by
simply opposing all forms of acculturation. Among the Hutterian
Brethren the solution was similar, since worship was confined to
their communities in Montana, Washington, Minnesota, North Dakota, South Dakota, Manitoba, Saskatchewan, and Alberta.[26]

More liberal Mennonites have faced increased pressure to accultu-
rate in recent years not from persecutors but from ecumenism, which
has accepted them and made them welcome among a wide spectrum
of worship traditions. The problem is that other traditions are often
well researched, have produced their own liturgical scholars, and
have carefully articulated reforms that they are consciously pursu-
ing. Mennonites have had relatively little need in recent centuries to
articulate and defend their own tradition. Today we sense a confrontation of "hard" traditions with highly articulate reasons for advocating certain liturgical reforms and "soft" traditions that have
hitherto operated without benefit of scholarship or liturgical com-
mittees.

The challenge is whether Mennonites will cherish their Anabaptist tradition enough to avoid compromising it by acculturation with other traditions.[27] Or has the time come when that tradition can safely assimilate practices that currently are changing other Protestant traditions: use of the lectionary, a fuller observance of the church year, more frequent eucharistic celebrations, set forms for prayer, and standard orders of worship? A sign of compromise is the increasing use of instrumental music in worship. Yet many Mennonite congregations also retain *a cappella* (unaccompanied) singing of hymns, often with great beauty.

One of the greatest successes of Anabaptist worship is that most communities are small enough that they can maintain a resolutely sectarian identity, whereas many Baptist churches in America have taken on a dominant role in the total community and inevitably adopted a church-type image. For a small gathered community, believer's baptism functions remarkably well. Somewhat more problematic is the practice of the ban and shunning. These still function among the Amish but, among more acculturated Mennonites, are increasingly difficult to maintain. Yet the image of a self-disciplining community has proved to have remarkable viability. Those who become disaffected easily find places in more lenient churches in American culture. But the close union of worship and ethics continues to function well in many Mennonite communities, as it has for over four and a half centuries.

6

Anglican Worship

Starting with the coronation of William and Mary in 1689, English monarchs have vowed to uphold, as head of the Church of England, "the Protestant Reformed Religion." A hundred years later, the title chosen for the American branch of Anglicanism was "the Protestant Episcopal Church." Yet nearly two hundred years later, the term "Protestant" had become so opprobrious to many Anglicans that by 1979 it had disappeared from the latest American prayer book except in the historical documents.

The changing attitude of some Anglicans to the word "Protestant" tells us something of the movement of this tradition from the desire to identify with the "best reformed churches" of Europe to the wish to shun such an honor. Today, Roman Catholic and Anglican worship often appear similar, yet major changes have come about in both traditions. Ironically, much of the current similarity has developed by denying many practices considered typically "Catholic" a century or so ago. Indeed, in recent years, the amount of change in what is considered Catholic worship has far exceeded that in traditions clearly labeled Protestant.

If the term "Protestant" is problematic for some Anglicans today, it was not always so. Using the political analogy to locate worship traditions in the context of relative conservatism with regard to late medieval worship, the Anglican tradition emerges as farther to the right than most Protestant traditions, but not as far to the right as some. If our criterion is the retention of much medieval ceremonial, vestments, images, Marian devotions, private confession, and Latin rites, many Lutheran churches were considerably more conservative than the sixteenth-century Church of England. If we concern ourselves with the theology of the sacraments in general and the eucharist in particular, Calvin stands closer to the medieval tradition than does Cranmer. Indeed, Bucer's plea to retain in the 1552 *Book of Common Prayer* the words "may worthily receive the most precious body and blood of thy son Jesus Christ . . . that he may dwell in them, and they in him" went unheeded and disappeared from the English rite. In terms of eucharistic doctrine, Cranmer's Church of England stands somewhat left of the Kirk of Scotland, which, we have seen, in 1560 had condemned the regarding of sacraments as only "naked and bare signs." Even before the advent of Puritanism, Anglican iconoclasm was far more thorough and consistent than that in Lutheran lands.

For most of its history, then, the Anglican tradition belongs somewhat right of center but not nearly as far to the right as it became in the nineteenth-century Catholic Revival. Other traditions also began to lean to the right in that century until suddenly, in the modern period, the recovery of medieval patterns has almost entirely lost its appeal for most Christians. Some intractable Anglicans now appear far to the right as the last custodians of late-medieval practices. In the process of the journey to the present, Anglicanism was also assailed in the eighteenth century by forces neither Protestant nor Catholic but deriving from the Enlightenment.

Today, the Anglican tradition of worship is usually the most readily identifiable even after nearly four and a half centuries. During that time, it spanned the globe and flourished in a wide variety of cultures. That a tradition could survive so many historical vicissitudes is a sign of great inner strength. What, then, is the key to the survival of Anglican worship in such a readily identifiable form? Many would say it is the persistence in Anglican worship of the *Book of Common Prayer* (hereafter *BCP*). And that would be hard to deny, although with each successive revision more variants appear. The Anglican tradition, more than any other, is a tradition of a book, a single book, the prayer book. No other liturgical tradition is so closely identified with a single document. Even the addition of a hymnal was relatively late in coming.

The history of the Anglican tradition as the "prayer book tradition" has been written by many authors, although by no one so successfully as the late Geoffrey J. Cuming in his masterful *A History of Anglican Liturgy.* [1] There is no need to repeat that history here except to outline the important dates of the various editions of the *BCP.* We shall, instead, relate those components of worship that shape and define a tradition other than printed service books to see how they function among Anglicans.

Archbishop Thomas Cranmer (1489–1556) was largely the architect of the first *BCP,* which became mandatory for all churches in England on Pentecost, June 9, 1549. On November 1, 1552, it was superseded, being "explained, and made fully perfect" by the second prayer book. This had a short life because of the return to Roman allegiance under Queen Mary, July 19, 1553. Another change in the reign brought the Elizabethan *BCP* of 1559, only slightly altered from 1552. The beginning of the Stuart reign saw a new version in 1604 and the Restoration produced a further revision in 1662. From 1645 to 1660, the *BCP* was abrogated by Parliament in favor of the *Directory for the Public Worship of God.*

An attempt to produce a Scottish *BCP* in 1637 met with failure. The independence of the United States saw production of the first American *BCP* in 1789; in use for over a century, it was revised in 1892, 1928, and 1979. Meanwhile, other countries and Wales, Ireland, and Scotland made their own revisions. There was a flurry of these around the world in the 1920s and a veritable storm of revisions in the 1970s and 1980s. While still retaining the 1662 *BCP,* the Church of England published *The Alternative Service Book 1980,* which is expected to remain in use until the end of this century. At present, the results of recent revisions are being consolidated in various Anglican provinces around the world.

We shall trace the origins of Anglican worship in the Tudor period (to 1603), subsequent developments under the Stuarts (1603–1714), the Georgian period (1714–1830), the period from 1833 to 1928, and the last sixty years. In the space available here, we can only mention the main outline of developments. More detail will be found in the standard studies cited in the notes and the bibliography.

The Origins of Anglican Worship

We must begin with the people of England, Wales, and the Channel Islands. Major social, political, and economic events were changing their perceptions of reality with unprecedented swiftness. The nationalization of the monasteries by King Henry VIII in 1536 and 1539 affected far more than just the religious communities themselves. By resale of monastic properties, constituting nearly one fourth of the national wealth, a major sector of society was tied much more closely to the crown, upon whom depended their title to lands. The end of the monasteries also removed from the scene one major form of worship, that of monks and nuns. Although cathedrals and collegiate churches survived to carry on daily choral services, most people had little contact with them. Closer to home was the suppression of chantry chapels (for memorial masses) in 1545 and 1547. This brought about a massive shift away from piety surrounding the dead, since there were now no more daily masses or offices said for them in parish churches or elsewhere. This subtraction from parochial life affected wealthy patrons and guilds of workers in towns.

A major result of the English Reformation was the reshaping of the very language people spoke and read. As the preface to the 1549 prayer book makes clear, the goal that "all the whole realm shall have but one use"[2] was part and parcel of a new nationalism in which uniformity rather than diversity was seen as a laudable goal whether in spoken language or liturgical practice. Cranmer deliberately chose the current language of the London streets as his vehicle for liturgical change,[3] although remnants of older speech remain: "hath holpen his seruaunt Israel," for example. Cranmer was contemporary but not avant garde; the new possessive "its" does not appear in his work.

The normal practice of the time was for people to read aloud even in private. Cranmer's prose is spoken prose, and its regular cadences, its parallelism and symmetry, are meant for the ear, not just the eye. He succeeded in shaping English piety by his literary genius more than by his theological acuity. Thus, while a Latin collect achieves its force by terseness, Cranmer arrives at expressiveness by expansion in English. Unfortunately, his genius did not extend to poetry, as he himself recognized and clearly demonstrated in his translation of *Veni, Creator Spiritus.* For lack of poets, English Christianity, unlike Lutheranism, had to wait nearly two centuries before metrical hymnody became common.

Another major shift in social life was the advent of widespread literacy. Simply to combine the words "book" and "common" indicates a major social change, and when one couples them with "prayer" we have a revolution in process. A century earlier, the first English printer, William Caxton (1422?–1491), had brought printing to England and made a liturgical revolution feasible. Mass-production printing brought the possibility of standardized texts; in 1541, a standard Sarum breviary was imposed on the whole Province of Canterbury. In 1538 a royal injunction ordered that the English Bible be placed in all churches, and in 1543 it was ordered to be read in churches. The new literacy had begun to set the stage for liturgical change as an increasing number of lay people began to read and all began to hear the scriptures in their own tongue. The *Prymer,* a popular devotional book, helped prepare the way. The first *BCP* was printed with a royal mandate that unbound copies not sell for more than two shillings, promoting wide distribution. Thus literacy and scriptural piety went hand in hand.

A most important shift in piety involved the meaning of participation in worship. As we have noticed, the late medieval period tended to equate participation with seeing. But the English Reformation gives clear preference to hearing; participation is identified with being able to hear. The rubrics are specific: "The priest . . . shall begin with a loud voice," "The minister that reads the lesson, standing and turning him so as he may best be heard of all such as be present." "And [to the end the people may the better hear]."[4] Such rubrics we may take for granted; in 1549, they were revolutionary.

A new vision of participation is operative not only in the prayer book but also in the reordering of church buildings that ensued. Visual participation is not negated; the most conspicuous change in churches during the Elizabethan era was the installation of painted tablets of the Decalogue, Lord's Prayer, and Apostles' Creed, replacing the visual judgment scene as the focal point with verbal iconography. But we must not think the level of active participation to have been high in the modern sense, which involves unison prayer and congregational song. The 1549 *BCP* is far from clear on who is to say the prayers and psalms in the daily offices and the eucharist. Probably the Lord's Prayer is said by all ("we are bold to say"), but the general confession is "made, in the name of all those that are minded to receive the holy Communion, either by one of them, or else by one of the ministers or by the priest himself."[5] By 1552, things have become more explicit. In morning prayer, there is a "general confession, to be said of the whole congregation after the minister, kneeling," and the creed is definitely congregational ("Minister and the people, standing") and the second Lord's Prayer ("Minister, clerks, and people . . . in English, with a loud voice.")[6] The penitential addition to the 1552 eucharist likewise involves a congregational response.

It is probably no accident that most of the clearly congregational parts in 1552 are also largely penitential. Although the 1552 additions to morning prayer and the eucharist are attributed to the influence of the Reformed tradition, particularly Bucer, they reflect a strong element of conservatism from late-medieval piety. Penitential attitudes were certainly major currents in popular piety. Probably the most influential, and certainly the most visual, of Cranmer's metaphors occurs in the "Prayer of Humble Access": "We be not worthy so much as to gather up the crumbs under thy table."[7] Despite its allusion to Matthew 15:27, the prayer is original with Cranmer. Even modern Anglican revisers have not dared remove this canine reference.

An important factor shaping the liturgical life of the average Englishman or Englishwoman was a drastic shift in the image of time. Time is an important instrument of communication, and it came to signify some quite different things in the sixteenth-century Church of England. Although late-medieval Christians attended mass weekly, if not daily, councils had to keep clamoring at them to receive communion at least once a year. Now, suddenly, they were being urged to receive communion not yearly but weekly, "upon the Sunday or holy day," and if people were negligent the prayer book provided an official exhortation to urge them "to dispose themselves to the receiving of the holy communion more diligently."[8] The 1549 prayer book presupposes "daily Communion" in "Cathedral churches or other places."

Such a radical change proved impossible, and 1552 concedes that every parishioner "shall communicate, at the least three times in the year: of which, Easter is to be one."[9] As often happens with minimums, this became the standard for several centuries. It was an advance over the former tendency "to communicate once in the year at the least" which 1549 recounts.[10] But Cranmer was also insistent, in addition to frequent communion, that the communion in holy things not be confined to the priest alone. The *BCP* of 1549 says that "the Priest on the week day shall forbear to celebrate the Communion, except he have some that will communicate with him."[11] This would not be a problem in cathedral and collegiate churches but clearly it was in parish churches, a fact explicitly recognized in 1552, which categorically mandated that there be "no celebration of the Lord's Supper, except there be a good number to communicate with the priest," the minimum apparently being "four, or three at the least."[12]

A 1552 rubric provided for such occasions; without sufficient communicants, the service was to go through the service of the word, the sermon or homily, the general intercession, and a concluding collect.[13] The service of morning prayer was also mandatory on Sunday morning, and 1552 indicated that the litany should be used "upon Sundays, Wednesdays, and Fridays." The result was usually an uninterrupted sequence of four items: morning prayer, litany, ante-communion (first part of the Lord's Supper), and sermon. For three centuries, this became the normal Sunday-morning pattern of worship for Anglicans, extended on a few occasions each year by the completion of the eucharist. In their rubrics, the state services, concocted to commemorate events in the seventeenth century, simply take the combined services for granted.[14] It is no wonder that the Puritans complained about the "longsomeness" of the service in 1603, and John Wesley in 1784 attempted some abbreviation of "the service of the Lord's Day, the length of which has been often complained of."[15] Improbable as this pattern may seem, it endured for most of Anglican history. The combined services provide a rich dose of scripture: a chapter from both testaments, an epistle and gospel, plus ample psalmody and canticles. Because 1552 and its successors provided no introits or psalms and an Old Testament lesson had long ago disappeared from the eucharist, the combination achieved some of the balance of Old Covenant and New that post-Vatican II services have attempted. But the service must have seemed long and tedious, and the sermon at the end must have had to contend with the onset of lethargy.

The good news was the unexpected success of morning and evening prayer as daily services. With the exception of Sunday matins and vespers, such daily services had centuries ago ceased to hold much interest for the laity. The 1552 *BCP* ordered that the clergy were "bound to say daily the morning and evening prayer" and the curate was to bring a church bell "that such as be disposed may come to hear God's word, and to pray with him."[16] Throughout the centuries, this was done and continues in England to this day. People came to daily prayer and praise probably more than even Cranmer had dared hope.

The yearly cycle saw changes too. There was great reduction in the number of holy days and fasting. The latter had economic consequences, especially for the fishing industry. Feast-day propers (prayers and lessons) were provided for the major christological feasts, holy week, New Testament saints and angels, and All Saint's Day but not for the galaxy of postbiblical saints that had filled the calendar. The liturgical focus was clearly on Sundays and on the events of the New Testament. A major factor in shaping English piety for several centuries was the martyrology of John Foxe known as *Foxe's Book of Martyrs* (first English edition, 1563). This supplied a new set of postbiblical saints and was often read in families along with the Bible.

Major changes also happened in the life-cycle celebrations. The medieval period in the West had seen a gradual breakup in the unity of initiation as baptism, confirmation, and first communion were slowly pulled apart.[17] Although Elizabeth I and Edward VI were both confirmed soon after birth according to patterns of the early church, the Church of England in 1549 simply completed the developing medieval split by requiring that children be able to say the Apostles' Creed, Lord's Prayer, and Ten Commandments and answer questions from the Catechism before confirmation. This requirement ratified what had long been customary, the complete dissolution of any connection between baptism and confirmation. Following the late-medieval pattern, confirmation remained the choice of a fortunate and pious few until the rule of James I (1603–1625), when confirmation became common for everyone. The Puritans were more medieval than they realized in calling confirmation "superfluous."

Confirmation had undergone a sea change in the process. A bit uncertain in nature in 1549, it became in 1552 largely a graduation exercise. Even Luther and Calvin might have approved, and Bucer had a hand in it. God is asked that the child may "continue thine for ever, and daily increase in thy Holy Spirit,"[18] but there is little sense of sacramental grace left in the 1552 rite. The emphasis is on education and its progress, on human achievement rather than on God's gift.

Baptism was to be a public service, although provision was also made for private baptism "in time of necessity." And baptism was

to be administered on Sundays or holy days, "when the most number
of people may come together," that they may receive the child into
the church and "every man present may be put in remembrance of
his own profession made to God in his baptism."[19] Not until 1662
was provision made for the baptism of adults, the presumption being
that all people had been baptized as infants. The child was to be
baptized by being dipped three times in the font (submersion) with
provision for pouring "if the child be weak." A form for blessing the
water in the font was provided in 1549 but disappeared in 1552. An
order was also provided for "the Purification of Women," renamed
in 1552 "The Thanks Giving of Women after Child Birth, Commonly Called the Churching of Women."

Most familiar of all the new rites was that for marriage, which
basically followed that common in southern England. The traditional purposes of marriage were cited (procreation, a remedy
against fornication, and for "mutual society, help, and comfort"), the
vows already long familiar in English were exchanged, and the ring
given with the promise, "With my body I thee worship." The Sarum
promise by the woman "to be bonere and boxsum in bedde and atte
bord" did not make it into the prayer book. A final rubric mandated
that the newly married couple receive communion on the same day
as their wedding.

Ministry for the sick and dying was provided in the form for
"Visitation of the Sick" and "The Communion of the Sick." The first
provided for prayer and confession, the latter for reserved sacrament
"the same day there be a celebration of the holy communion in the
church,"[20] otherwise a fresh celebration in the sickroom. The reserved sacrament option disappeared in 1552.

The tone of the funeral service was changed from fear to hope, the
dominant theme being set by chapter 15 of First Corinthians. A
proper psalm, collect, and lessons were provided in 1549 for a celebration of the eucharist, but these were omitted in 1552.

The rites of ordination were limited to three orders, no provision
being made for ordination to minor orders. The ordination rites first
appeared in 1550 and were revised in the 1552 book. Continuity with
the medieval rites is conspicuous, including use of the imperative
formula "Receive the Holy Ghost" and the giving of the Bible and
chalice in 1550, or the Bible alone in 1552, to the newly ordained
priest.

The changes in the familiar worship space must have seemed as
drastic as the adjustments in time. Few churches were built during
the first century of the English Reformation, although churches that
had become redundant were allowed to decay or were destroyed. But
the familiar parish church continued to function as before, as basically two buildings, the nave (congregational part) and the chancel

(clergy part). The big difference was that now the laity could enter the chancel, once the exclusive property of clergy and patron.[21] Thus the actions of people and clergy were brought together at the eucharist instead of being kept separate by the rood screen (partition with cross above it) that closed off the chancel. The medieval concept of two distinct spaces persisted, but the function of the chancel had come to be the eucharistic room, the rest of the church being used for the service of the word and daily offices. After the offertory (collection), "so many as shall be partakers of the holy communion, shall tary still in the choir, or in some convenient place near the choir, the men on the one side, and the women on the other side."[22]

By 1552, most of the altars had been replaced by wooden tables, which might be placed in the nave or in the center of the chancel, parallel to the long sides. For sake of uniformity, the priest was to be "standing at the north side of the table": that is, facing half the communicants. Thus the people participated by seeing all that is done, the priest no longer having his back to them, and they participated by greater proximity, sharing with him the same space, the chancel.

If the chancel had changed in both appearance and function, the nave had begun to feel different too. Long before the Puritans came into power, there had been massive destruction of images or anything else—such as inscriptions—that might lead the unwary to believe in purgatory, the intercession of the saints, or any form of idolatry. At Ely Cathedral, for example, the heads were systematically knocked off the saints' images carved in the fourteenth century, while foliage and innocuous forms were usually left untouched. Thus the purgation of buildings was largely accomplished in the sixteenth century. The chantry chapels were gone, turned into schools, private pews, or places for family monuments. The naves had been filling up since the fourteenth century with pews, and the congregation had already become immobilized as it began to sit for worship. Nor was the Reformation (or any movement since) able to pry them loose again. Great care was taken that "the minister shall so turn him, as the people may best hear"[23] and it is clear that audibility was a great concern in all the rubrics. No architectural alteration was needed for the new baptismal rites. It is quite explicit in 1549 that the participants "must be ready at the church door" or, in 1552, "at the font." Thus the fonts stayed where they had been, near the main entrance to the church. The ancient fonts usually remained in use, since baptism by dipping continued for about a century and a half. The Reformed and Lutheran practice of having the font in a visible place near the pulpit or altar-table seems to have had little appeal to Anglicans.[24]

One of the greatest successes of the English Reformation was in public prayer, especially daily morning and evening prayer. The model was the medieval development of the monks' prayer services as an ascetic daily discipline, yet Cranmer had a distinctly Reformation purpose, the systematic reading of all of scripture. Curiously, this marriage of monastic discipline and Reformation agenda worked well for clergy and laity alike. Even the latest revisions depart little from the style Cranmer developed, although an alternative today could have been an even earlier cathedral-type model based on repetitious praise and prayer.

Cranmer's intent, as he makes quite clear, was that he believed (wrongly) that the "Godly and decent order of the ancient fathers" was a scheme for daily reading through from "all the whole Bible."[25] He also provided that "the Psalter shall be read through once every Month."[26] By combining materials from the medieval daily prayer services of matins, lauds, and prime into morning prayer and from vespers and compline into evening prayer, Cranmer devised a scheme for systematic reading of the Bible and psalter. The "number and hardness" of the old rules had been modified to rules "few and easy" by simplifying things with elimination of "Anthems, responsories, invitatories, and such like things, as did break the continual course of the reading of the scripture."[27] Inspiration for some of this work of Cranmer came from Cardinal Francisco de Quinones (1480–1540) of Spain, whose "Breviary of the Holy Cross" of 1535 and 1536 anticipated a number of the reforms found in the *BCP.*

The daily office succeeded better than anticipated by becoming a popular service rather than the full eucharist. The biblicism of the daily office appealed to a wide spectrum of Protestants, its simplicity appealed to everyone (evening prayer is outlined in two pages in 1549), and the possibilities for large amounts of active participation possible through congregational recitation of psalms, canticles, and prayers had wide attraction. The amount of active verbal participation is high, although there is little visual action.

Although preaching a sermon or reading a printed homily was mandated at the eucharist, it was not easy to improve the quality of preaching in parish churches without massive retraining of the clergy. Luther had provided postils as collections of sermons for nonpreaching ministers, and in the same way Cranmer and associates issued the first *Book of Homilies* in 1547 and their successors published a second book in 1571. These thirty-three homilies served two functions: They provided a fall-back measure for nonpreaching clergy, and they functioned as a source of authoritative doctrine as is acknowledged in articles 11 and 35 of the official Thirty-nine Articles of doctrine.

No direct connection between preaching and morning or evening prayer was made, since it was expected that the service of the word of the eucharist would always take place on Sunday morning. Although many of the Edwardian and Elizabethan bishops themselves provided examples of great preaching, it was a favorite jibe of the Puritans that mere reading of homilies (as many clergy were content to do) was not preaching. The creation of a tradition of preaching clergy took several generations to accomplish.

Similar problems were faced in the area of church music.[28] Music and texts for vernacular singing could not be produced overnight. Indeed, it took three centuries for hymn singing to be domesticated in the Church of England. There was no theological objection to hymnody, as there was in much of the Reformed tradition, but neither was there the same impetus given toward it as characterized Lutheranism. Cranmer complained about the lack of poets, and hymn singing in England languished until it was eventually pioneered by Congregationalists and Methodists in the eighteenth century.

Psalm singing did not meet the same obstacles, and a strong tradition of singing the psalms began early in the English Reformation, especially to the metrical paraphrases of Thomas Sternhold (ca.1500–1549) and John Hopkins (?–1570). Congregational singing of these psalm versions became popular, providing an additional source of active participation.

Service music fared well and included an early setting of the 1549 eucharist, *Book of Common Prayer Noted* (1550), by the court organist John Merbecke (1523–1585). This work was advanced by a series of gifted composers, especially William Byrd (1543–1623), who composed settings for evensong, helped develop verse anthems that were to become part of evensong, and wrote much service music and offertory motets (polyphonic chants). This period of musical giants also provided Thomas Tallis (ca.1505–1585), who wrote settings for the Anglican liturgy, responses for evensong, and tunes that were adapted for hymns. A later generation produced Orlando Gibbons (1583–1625), composer of cathedral music, psalms, and anthems. Thus was launched a great musical tradition, although its cultivation was largely confined to cathedrals, chapels royal, and collegiate churches until the nineteenth century. After 1662, the prayer book provided for the possibility of an anthem at morning prayer and evening prayer, but robed choirs in the chancel did not become common in parish churches until the nineteenth century.

Pipe organs were common in some of the larger parish churches from the thirteenth century onward, yet there was massive opposition to their use in the Elizabethan period, the convocation of Canterbury failing by a single vote in 1562 to order their removal from all churches. Much destruction of organs occurred during the period of the Commonwealth. The chief musical acts of worship in parish churches during this period were congregational singing of metrical psalmody, congregational service music, and, sometimes, organ music.

Developments Under the Stuarts

The Stuart period (1603–1714) is notable for the failure, despite much effort, to achieve forms of worship acceptable to all English Protestants. The next chapter discusses the beginning of a new tradition of worship by the Separatists and Puritans, including some of the highlights of the struggle for further reform within the Church of England as well as outside of it. Suffice it to say here that, for almost exactly a century, Puritanism remained one of the strongest spiritual forces within the Church of England but that finally the Puritan intolerance of others was reciprocated and the movement was forced out of the established church rather than comprehended within it.

The whole period of the Stuart reign is marked by a series of changes in the centers of gravity in both popular piety and political power. When these were at odds, the country became polarized. Archbishop William Laud (1573–1645) tried to return things too far and too fast to the old order. His fall was rapid and he died proclaiming himself a good Protestant, just as his predecessor, Cranmer, had died protesting his fidelity to Catholicism. Yet during this period of turmoil a form of normative Anglicanism asserted itself in such men as the saintly rector of Bemerton, George Herbert (1593–1633). His poetry expresses the emerging Anglican via media, especially in a poem with a sustained metaphor of two women (churches), one too gaudy and painted (Roman Catholics), the other naked and unkept (Puritans).[29] Great leaders adorned the church, including Bishops Lancelot Andrewes (1555–1626), John Cosin (1594–1672), and Jeremy Taylor (1613–1667), all of whom contributed to developing a national tradition in worship.

Some changes of lasting significance occurred during the Stuart period. The Canons of 1604 ratified the minimum of three eucharists a year and presumed a minimum of ceremonial.[30] During the seventeenth century, state services were appended to *BCP*s to commemorate the Gunpowder Plot (1605), the death of Charles I (1649), the return of Charles II (1660), and the accession of the reigning monarch.

Archbishop Laud brought about a major reordering in the chancels of churches by urging the replacement of altar-tables in their ancient position against the east wall, although not without opposition from Bishop John Williams of Lincoln (1582–1650).[31] In the 1640s, the Puritans completed the work of iconoclasm begun under

Edward VI. But an event of great moment occurred as the aftermath of the great London fire of 1666, which destroyed sixty-seven parish churches as well as St. Paul's Cathedral. Sir Christopher Wren (1632–1723) rebuilt fifty-two churches and the cathedral. Applying a careful analysis of the spatial requirements of Anglican worship as practiced in the Restoration period, he determined that such worship demanded an auditory church. "Ours," he said, "are to be fitted for Auditories," and he calculated exactly how far a preacher's voice could effectively be heard in each direction.[32]

It is easy to be dazzled by the aesthetic brilliance with which Wren adapted continental baroque forms for his task. More important is the fact that, almost single-handedly, Wren created a distinctive spatial form for Anglican worship. It was a brilliant matching of space to worship, a tradition that centered on the reading of scripture, prayer, psalmody, and preaching with occasional (but important) sacramental celebrations. The result is a one-volume building with no chancel, an altar table against the east wall enclosed on three sides by a communion rail, a font near the door, and combined reading desk, clerk's desk, and pulpit. Religious images were few except for the mandatory tablets (Decalogue, Creed, and Lord's Prayer). It was a form that was to be standard for two centuries. In the eighteenth century, James Gibbs (1683–1754) embellished the exterior by marrying a staged tower and spire to a classical portico.

A series of brilliant cathedral preachers such as John Donne (ca.1573–1631) helped develop an Anglican tradition of pulpit rhetoric. Various collections of private prayers were produced such as the *Preces Privatae* (private prayers) of Lancelot Andrews and the devotional books of Jeremy Taylor, *Holy Living, Holy Dying,* and *The Golden Grove.* A notable experiment in prayer was the married religious community at Little Gidding from 1625 to 1646, which flourished under the guidance of Nicholas Ferrar (1592–1637). Distinguished composers continued to serve the church, notably Henry Purcell (1659–1695). As staunch a Puritan as John Milton (1608–1674) was moved by "A Solemn Music," and many Puritans cultivated musical skills in private life.

The Georgian Period

The period from the death of Queen Anne (1714) until the accession of Queen Victoria (1837) represents a period in Anglican worship that few would care to reproduce today. Yet, it presents a time of some developments that were to bend the future, the origins of a new liturgical tradition in Methodism, and the emergence of a series of sister churches to the Church of England. Nonconformity had been evicted from the national church and proceeded to develop along the lines of the Reformed, Puritan, and Quaker traditions, with very little influence any more on the worship of the Church of England.

In 1688, an internal schism had forced some of the most capable bishops and clergy out of the national church when they refused to renege on their vows of allegiance to James II. The Nonjurors, as they were called, became a minority church, but this gave them freedom to experiment with liturgy at a time when any reforms were unlikely in the established church. No convocation met from 1717 to 1852, so *BCP* revision was impossible. The Nonjurors made good use of their liberty, publishing various rites that tended to resemble the 1549 *BCP* and the newly identified rites of the early church. Contacts with the Episcopal Church in Scotland brought Nonjuror rites into greater currency.

Various other private attempts were made to revise the prayer book on the basis of liturgical antiquarianism compiled from primitive sources or on the basis of new theological currents that tended to find Trinitarianism and the Athanasian Creed repugnant.[33] There continued to be a minority party of those who placed a high value on the sacraments and episcopacy.[34]

The eighteenth century was not their time. Many Anglicans, from Archbishop John Tillotson (1630–1694) on, advocated a latitudinarianism that sought to minimize theological and liturgical distinctions among Christians. In Tillotson's case, it meant a strictly memorialistic approach to the eucharist and distaste for the Athanasian Creed (creed of the late fourth or early fifth century, of unknown origin). But such a position was moderate as Christian rationalism moved further and further in the direction of deism. Anything supernatural, based on special revelation, or founded in personal providence became repugnant, and divine intervention in history seemed unthinkable. It is no wonder that the observance of the eucharist fell to a low ebb in this period. Bishop Benjamin Hoadly (1676–1761) could go considerably further than Zwingli, referring to Christ as "He, who was once present with his Disciples and is now absent." The eucharist was purely in memory of Christ.[35]

If the sacraments fell to a low importance at this time, they did not vanish altogether for two reasons. Most people were biblical literalists and continued to defer to the commands of Jesus. And it was believed that sacraments could remind people of the necessity of the ethical life, enabling them to resolve to abide by moral precepts for the common good. Worship in general, and the sacraments in particular, were subverted to the cause of morality and social order. For deism, the end of worship was not communion with God but social harmony. Ceremonial was dismissed as useless and became minimal. The impetus of deism was not from Protestantism but from

forces of the Enlightenment extraneous to Christianity. These took
even more extreme forms in Catholic France.

Resistance to such approaches came from a variety of individuals
and groups: theologian Bishop Joseph Butler (1692–1752), the Methodist movement with its strong emphasis on sacramental life, and the
Evangelicals with a Calvinistic theology and commitment to personal religion. But they were largely countercultural movements and
did not reverse the pervasive blandness of Anglican worship, which
dreaded "enthusiasm" throughout much of this period. The evangelical influence continued within the Church of England and helped
raise the level of preaching above mere moralistic harangues.

The visual and musical components of worship in this period of
rationalism were minimal. No seventeenth-century Puritan would
have been offended by churches in which visual symbols, even the
cross, were lacking altogether, and ceremonial minimal. Vestments
were unknown, the use of incense in church unheard of, candles rare,
and holy communion three times a year considered sufficient in most
parishes.

A major positive step in this time was the emergence of Anglicanism as a worldwide community. Anglican worship had been conducted in North America as early as 1579 (Drake's Bay, California),
and Anglicanism became the established church in many of the
American colonies. The fate of the church in the United States was
uncertain after the American Revolution, since ties to England had
made it suspect, but a clear sign of recovery and independence was
the process of preparing the first American *BCP*, which was approved in 1789.[36] It performed some liturgical fine-tuning on the
1662 book, borrowed its eucharistic prayer from the Episcopal
Church in Scotland, and, unlike previous *BCP*s, included a small
collection of hymns.

The Catholic Revival

The near-century from 1833 to 1928 saw changes in Anglican
worship only slightly less striking than those of the Reformation era.
A revolution occurred in the nineteenth century, a complete change
of direction. Yet, it was brought off without changing a single word
of the *BCP*. This revolution meant reversal of three hundred years
of moving ever farther away from medieval practices in worship. It
was also a rejection of a century and a half of rationalism that had
shown little patience with either Protestant or Roman Catholic
supernaturalism.

We shall refer to this movement as the Catholic Revival, preferring that to Anglican Revival used by Yngve Brilioth.[37] Various

components of it are described by other labels, often applied by opponents: the Oxford Movement, Puseyism, Tractarianism, and Ritualism. It was not a move toward current Roman Catholic worship of the post-Tridentine era but to the worship of the late Middle Ages as practiced in England. (The small Society of Sts. Peter and Paul was a glaring exception to this generalization.)[38] The Catholic Revival in Anglicanism was an attempt to return liturgically to the period before the dissolution of the monasteries (1536 and 1539) although some held the early fourteenth century as the ideal. Indeed, a late manifestation was often labeled "British Museum religion," since so much was based on research of the past. The attraction was certainly not contemporary Roman Catholicism; Edward B. Pusey (1800–1882), one of the chief leaders, found many current Roman Catholic devotions particularly repugnant. The return was to be to a point before the parting of the ways. Certainly there were strong elements of romanticism and a large dose of nationalism involved. The Catholic Revival also had strong appeal in England and America despite the era of Jacksonian democracy. We shall not trace the history of the movement but only its effects on parish worship.[39]

First and foremost, people had changed. The industrial revolution, new wealth from a global empire, rising educational standards—all had shaped people in new ways. Sir Walter Scott (1771–1832) had touched a sensitive nerve of romanticism in his novels and poetry and made the past seem marvelously appealing. As G. K. Chesterton remarked, the nineteenth century saw the Middle Ages by "moonlight." The limitations of rationalism were increasingly apparent, especially in light of the excesses of the French Revolution. The industrial age was bringing new problems. The Victorian era was marked not only by piety but also by wealth and leisure. When else has the study of church architecture been a popular hobby? Church music came to attract vast interest. The standards of taste that helped reshape Anglican worship in England were imitated in countries around the world as replicas of English village churches sprouted up, even in India and Tasmania. Without such changes in popular thinking and taste, changes in worship would have been stillborn.

In America, Anglicans were confronted by the rapidly expanding frontier churches and the new freedoms of Jacksonian democracy. Yet, rather than accommodate to such expressions of Americanization, Anglican worship preferred to stay staunchly loyal to the prayer book. Hymn singing was encouraged, however. The Catholic Revival was both strongly supported and vigorously resisted in America, increasing the styles of worship possible using the same prayer book. These ranged from those characterized by a minimum of ceremonial to the very elaborate. Whatever the style, the worship of the Protestant Episcopal Church, unlike that of other traditions in America, stood out as distinct in refusing to adapt to prevailing frontier patterns.

In a time of widespread social change, piety made its adjustments too. Despite the conservatism of reaching to the past, it was a time of optimism. Worship was involved in social change, as articulated by Frederick Denison Maurice (1805–1872), and the linkage of worship to justice sensed by Maurice was elaborated by such leaders in the next century as Percy Dearmer (1867–1936), William Temple (1881–1944), and A. G. Hebert (1886–1963). Piety found its way into a variety of types of social reform. The most immediate effects in worship were abolition of pew rents and that grossest symbol of inequality, the private pew, owned by individuals. Many of the ritualists were involved in inner city missions, especially in London. The new patterns in worship went hand in hand with the restoration of religious orders for nursing and education of the poor. Victorian piety tended to be practical piety, perhaps a survival of the moralistic piety of the previous century, and the various worship reform crusades came from people who were concerned enough about their common worship to be willing to fight over it.

The observance of time shows major changes in some segments of Anglicanism, less in others, and almost none in a few. Whereas, as we have seen, the normal pattern for the Sunday service had been a combination of morning prayer, litany, ante-communion, and sermon, the new pattern came to be to separate these and to celebrate the eucharist each Sunday and holy day. The "Shortened Services Act" of 1872 facilitated this in England. In America, the pattern often came to be an early eucharist on Sunday morning and a later morning prayer and sermon. Gradually, the chief service might become the eucharist on the first Sunday of the month and eventually on every Sunday. In short, the most significant change was to move from a pattern where there were far fewer celebrations of the eucharist than there were baptisms, weddings, or funerals in most parishes to one in which the eucharist became the normal weekly service.

Such a shift had been anticipated (but lost) by Methodists in the eighteenth century and accomplished (and kept) by the early 1830s by Disciples of Christ, Mormons, Plymouth Brethren, and the Catholic Apostolic Church. Anglicanism changed from a minimally sacramental church to one that made the sacraments central in its worship in thousands of parishes.

Sacramental theology changed as well with new emphasis on Christ's real presence in the eucharist, on baptism as accomplishing regeneration, and on the value of sacramental confession. Confession to a priest became a highly controversial issue, especially after Pusey's sermon on that subject in 1846.

This was also seen in the keeping of the yearly calendar, with much more emphasis placed on the seasons and feasts and with substantial visual and musical support. Vestments and other textile arts brought color to what had been (literally) black and white fabrics (except occasionally a maroon carpet and cushion on the altar-table). Keeping time with the liturgical year was also marked by the introduction of hymnody, much of it based on seasonal hymns from the Middle Ages or written by such poets as John Keble (1792–1866), whose chief work, significantly, was called *The Christian Year* (1827). Anthems and propers multiplied to give occasions distinct focus in the cycle of salvation history. A revision of the table of lessons in 1871 in England led to more emphasis on the liturgical year.

If the keeping of time was changed significantly, a more conspicuous change was in the worship space itself.[40] Following the work of the Roman Catholic architect A. W. N. Pugin (1812–1852), the Cambridge Camden Society (1839–1868) took the lead for three decades in developing and enforcing a new Anglican orthodoxy in church architecture. Their ideal was a village Gothic church of the early fourteenth century in England. They advocated separate and distinct chancels, which removed the laity from clergy and holy places. The whole was to be carved, painted, and glazed with a large variety of medieval images, especially those with symbolic references.

This was a large order. It involved undoing the results of the gradual evolution of church buildings designed on a commonsense basis for worship according to the *BCP,* an evolution that had been in process for three centuries. To assert that everything done to churches for three hundred years was not only wrong but very wrong took nerve and determination, but ultimately the Victorians triumphed. Chancels were made useful by filling them with lay choirs robed as pseudo-monks and minor clerics. A "dim religious light" gave buildings an aura of mystery where the new vestments and "instrumenta ecclesiastica" sparkled in the pious gloom.

Under the Victorians, the minor arts thrived—colored tiles, stained glass, iron and brass work, bookbinding, woodcarving—all designed to make worship visually glorious. In America, a cathedral building movement was launched with the building of Albany Cathedral in the 1880s. Symbolism flourished as buildings were designed to make symbolic references apart from obvious function. The image of church buildings changed to that of numinous holy places of refuge and retirement from the blandness of daily life.

An important part of Victorian life among Anglicans was daily family worship, led by the father for the family and household servants. It is best documented by Victorian novelists, who describe daily routines of morning and evening prayer and scripture reading.

Morning prayer in church on Sunday continued to thrive, and the invention of gas lighting gave a new boost to Sunday evening prayer, which often became an important musical event.

For more advanced Anglo-Catholics, especially those living in the newly established Anglican religious communities, it became necessary to supplement the *BCP* with various unauthorized breviaries or missals with richer calendars and wider assortments of prayers. Prayer collections such as those of Dean Eric Milner-White and *The Kingdom, the Power, and the Glory* also saw wide use. While endorsing the model of public worship from fixed forms, these unofficial collections enormously broadened the options open for both private and public prayer.

The nineteenth century saw a series of great preachers. John Henry Newman (1801–1890) won many to the Oxford Movement through preaching. F. W. Robertson (1816–1853) of Brighton, England, and Phillips Brooks of Boston, Massachusetts (1835–1893), were other outstanding preachers in an era known for princes of the pulpit. The evangelicals had long stressed the importance of preaching for conversion. In the shift to more sacramentally centered worship, preaching came to function in a new way in the context of the eucharist. While still concerned with conversion and morality, it took on new dimensions in stressing the corporate memories of the church as found in the cycles of the church year. Twentieth-century preaching produced even greater diversity.[41]

Music also flowered. American Episcopalians had a collection of hymns in the 1789 *BCP,* and the number of them increased gradually throughout the nineteenth century until a separate hymnal was published in 1871. In England, hymn singing developed more slowly, partly because it was considered "a snuffling Methodistical trick."[42] Not until midcentury did hymn singing become popular in the Church of England with the publication of such books as *The Hymnal Noted* (1851) and *Hymns Ancient and Modern* (1861). The leading figure was John Mason Neale (1818–1866), whose ability as translator restored a wealth of ancient and medieval hymns to the Victorians.

The period also saw a flowering of choral music in parish churches. The new and refurbished chancels became an ideal location for lay choristers after the model of cathedral and collegiate choirs. In essence, the local band of musicians and singers was brought down from the rear balcony, dressed up, and placed in the chancel. A variety of musicians composed new hymn tunes and anthems: Arthur Sullivan (1842–1900), John Dykes (1823–1876), and John Stainer (1840–1901), to name a few. It was also a time of rediscovery of the possibilities of organ music, especially after Samuel Sebastian Wesley (1810–1876) publicized the riches of Bach. The quality of church music continued to improve, especially with such music editors of hymnals as Ralph Vaughan Williams (1872–1958) and Canon Winfred Douglas (1867–1944). A great advance was made in active participation through the introduction at long last of congregational hymn singing. Choral music invited a more passive form of participation yet added another element to total involvement in worship.

The Past Sixty Years

The 1920s saw a spate of liturgical revision, mainly to accommodate the broader needs that the Catholic Revival had brought to public awareness. The most signal failure in England was the refusal of Parliament to authorize new revisions of the *BCP* in 1927 and 1928. In America, a new *BCP* was approved in 1928 and, a dozen years later, the much-beloved *The Hymnal 1940*. Other English-speaking countries published new prayer books or liturgies: Canada, 1918; Scotland, 1929; South Africa, 1929. Most had previously used the 1662 *BCP*. In a sense, all these books represent the end of an era more than the beginning of a new one. They represent the harvest of nineteenth-century practice and scholarship.

The new era, although it built on many nineteenth-century developments, especially new prominence for the sacraments, has also frequently involved the repudiation of many Victorian tendencies, especially those aimed at reproducing medieval worship. Thus the modern liturgical movement rejected much of the clericalism, the architectural revivalism, the sentimental music, the individualism, and the general preference for things medieval that had characterized the previous era. Anglican worship also broke out of the tight confines of English nationalism and the Anglican tradition to embrace elements from all periods of Christian worship and all traditions, both eastern and western.

The 1930s saw the origins of a new Anglican liturgical movement, in contact with but not dependent upon the current Roman Catholic liturgical movement. The most visible evidence was the Parish Communion movement in England, promoted by the Parish and People movement (1949–1968)[43] and the parallel Associated Parishes movement (1947–present) in the United States. Among a variety of adherents, the best-known proponent was A. G. Herbert, whose *Liturgy and Society*[44] (1935) was a landmark. Other liturgical scholars, notably Gregory Dix (1901–1952) and E. C. Ratcliff (1896–1967), focused attention on the period of the early church. Gradually, the early church, rather than the medieval, came to commend itself as a model for modern worshipers.

The ecumenical movement brought wider contacts with global

Christianity, especially after the first Faith and Order Conference in Lausanne in 1927. During the period before World War II, the liturgical movements of the various churches moved on more or less parallel tracks; after the war, convergences began to appear. In the years after Vatican II, the new Roman Catholic agenda (plurality of forms, simplification of rites, three-year lectionary, contemporary language, and recovery of primitive forms in preference to medieval and Tridentine formulations) came to appeal to Anglicans and others. The result has been very similar changes in worship among both Anglicans and Roman Catholics. Some Anglican traditionalists have preferred to remain in the Victorian period, whether of the Anglo-Catholic style or the evangelical style.

The triumph of the liturgical movement was signaled in the United States by the 1979 *BCP,* which reflects the movement's chief concerns, and *The Hymnal 1982.* In England, *The Alternative Service Book 1980* is in force until the end of this century. It has largely replaced the 1662 BCP, which still remains legally in use. Other countries have produced similar books, such as *An Australian Prayer Book* (1978), *The New Zealand Liturgies* (1984), and the Canadian *Book of Alternative Services* (1985). Most of these give evidence of significant changes in parish life.

A greater recognition of the variety of people has led to a greater concern for adaptability of styles. It is noteworthy that the Episcopal Church published *Lift Every Voice and Sing* (1981) with songs from black churches and *El Himnario Provisional* (1980) for Hispanics, and these cultural traditions were recognized in *The Hymnal 1982.* More active roles for the laity have been encouraged, and lay leadership of prayer and readings, spontaneous intercessory prayer, and actions such as passing the peace are now common.

The cycles of time have changed as more and more parishes have made the eucharist the chief Sunday service, with almost everyone present communing—the reformers' chief goal, at last, realized. A much more varied yearly calendar has introduced new and previously unfamiliar feasts in America or Canada (Baptism of the Lord, Reign of Christ), moved some propers (for Transfiguration to the Sunday before Ash Wednesday), and eliminated others (pre-Lent). The calendar and lectionary in England is that of the Joint Liturgical Group;[45] that in North America, an Anglican version of the Roman Catholic Sunday lectionary and weekday lectionary. New calendars of saints, with many noted Anglicans, have been developed in several countries.

The process of initiation has been the subject of considerable debate, because of attempts to establish a more unified initiation rite by combining baptism, laying on of hands, and first communion. Nevertheless, a distinct rite of confirmation is still provided. Reaffirmation of baptism vows is a new possibility. Services similar to the Roman Catholic Rite of Christian Initiation for Adults appear in *The Book of Occasional Services* (1979).[46] The same book provides materials for a public healing service and the provisions for "Ministration to the Sick" and "At the Time of Death" are greatly developed in the 1979 American *BCP.* The new marriage rites stress equality of both partners. In most nations, the new Anglican ordination rites discard the medieval features to take as their model the third-century rite of Hippolytus.

Much effort in recent years has gone into renovating worship space to carry out the ideals of the liturgical movement. This has meant prying altar tables away from the wall in order to allow the celebrant to face the people (as Cranmer advocated). Chancels have again become problematic as they were before the Victorians, and there has been a general effort to declericalize worship space, removing the distinctions the Victorians made between space for clergy and choir and that for the people. There has also been an effort to make baptism a congregational service, which has sometimes meant relocation of the font in front of the congregation, Baptism of infants by dipping (as Cranmer expected) is again made possible by new and larger fonts. Anglicans have recovered new interest in liturgical arts, especially in contemporary textiles and stained glass in England and America.

In one sense, the forms of daily prayer have probably changed least, the durability of Cranmer's daily offices being a surprising liturgical phenomenon. New services for midday and night offices have been added in the American *BCP.* The biggest change has been to contemporary language after four centuries of the language of Cranmer. After initial opposition and resistance, contemporary language has become more and more accepted for public prayer.

Preaching has been reinvigorated by new concern for the lectionary. This has meant, for many preachers, new efforts for careful exegesis and expository preaching. A key theme of evangelicals has become common property, the importance of God's word in shaping the lives of hearers.

Church music, too, has undergone several changes in this period. In the 1960s and 1970s much folk and pop music was sung in churches. Some of this has persisted, and new ethnic strains have made their contributions. In the new hymnals, more "quality" music from both past and present appears, but the newer varieties of congregational song are represented too. Thus the newer hymnals are distinguished by being far more comprehensive than any previous ones. There has been a broadening in the range of musical instruments, especially guitar music to accompany solo or choral singing, but the versatility of the organ has more than commended itself.

Thus Anglican worship has continued to evolve. On some points Cranmer has been vindicated, but on others the trend has been to move to items of which he had no knowledge concerning the worship of the early church. The texts of the new *BCP*s derive both from Hippolytus and Cranmer. The musical, homiletic, and architectural styles embrace possibilities of which neither dreamed. Yet there survives a distinct Anglican ethos of worship, with loyalty to the prayer book paramount even though now in differing national versions. Despite these regional variations, Anglican worship is still the most readily identifiable of all the Protestant traditions of worship.

7

Separatist and Puritan Worship

We have already discussed in chapter 5 one tradition of Free Church worship, the Anabaptist. We now turn to another tradition, which can with equal accuracy be called "Free Church" but whose historical origins and developments are quite different, the Separatist and Puritan tradition.

Although we shall use this name based on historic origins, the modern descendants of the Separatist and Puritan tradition are known today as Congregationalists, some varieties of Baptists, and Unitarian-Universalists. Many Congregationalists have joined with other traditions in new churches such as the United Church of Canada (1925), the United Church of Christ (1957), and the United Reformed Church (1972).

The sixteenth-century places of origin of Free Church worship were widely scattered. Whereas the Anabaptists originated on the continent of Europe, the Separatists and Puritans came into being in England (although some development occurred in the low countries), and full flowering first came in America. Relations between the two Free Church traditions in the closing years of the sixteenth and early seventeenth century are intriguing but tenuous. In general, they seem to have evolved largely independently of each other. Yet Anabaptists and Puritans have enough in common that we can call them both expressions of Free Church worship, even though they are historically and geographically distinct.

The original inspiration for the Separatist and Puritan tradition came from within the Reformed tradition, but the context is that of Anglicanism. Thus, unlike the original four traditions—Lutheran, Reformed, Anabaptist, and Anglican—we have now reached a tradition that is one step removed from the heritage of late-medieval worship. In its very origins, it represents a move farther to the liturgical left than most of those traditions that made the break directly from the medieval church. Unlike the Anabaptists, it is a

secondary movement from the medieval sources, just as the later
Quaker movement is tertiary. However, in several ways, especially
the effort to retain a national church, English Puritans as a whole do
not represent as radical a leap to the liturgical left as the Anabaptists.
The Separatists being excepted, Puritanism belongs in a place just left
of center.

If the Separatist and Puritan tradition is derivative from the Reformed tradition within the Anglican matrix, it is still distinctive
enough to be defined separately from either. In a sense, the Separatist
and Puritan tradition is a type of hyper-Calvinism. Whereas Calvin
certainly used a biblical criterion in making liturgical decisions, he
could do so with considerable flexibility. It is noteworthy that the
subtitle of his service book is "According to the Use of the Ancient
Church," not the New Testament Church alone. Calvin had no
inhibitions about using matters not provided for in scripture, and he
was willing to discard some practices, unquestionably scriptural,
which had been contaminated by subsequent use. Calvin used a
criterion of all things being done decently and in order for the
purpose of edification. Nonbiblical practices could be tolerated or
even encouraged if they met this criterion, and biblical practices
ignored when they failed to meet it.

By and large, the Puritans did not heed Calvin's belief that

> God did not will in outward discipline and ceremonies to prescribe in
> detail what we ought to do (because he foresaw that this depended
> upon the state of the times, and he did not deem one form suitable for
> all ages), here we must take refuge in those general rules which he has
> given, that whatever the necessity of the church will require for order
> and decorum should be tested against these. Lastly, because he has
> taught nothing specifically, and because these things are not necessary
> to salvation, and for the upbuilding of the church ought to be variously
> accommodated to the customs of each nation and age.[1]

In opting for "whatever the necessity of the church will require"
there is considerable leeway for innovation. Calvin's final word is, "If
we let love be our guide, all will be safe."

Such vague "general rules" were not enough for the Separatists
and Puritans. Their most distinctive mark was a rigorous biblicism.
Horton Davies has demonstrated convincingly their desire to use
"The word of God as the supreme liturgical criterion."[2] If the worship of God is so important, then God does not leave to human
discretion how God is to be worshiped. God wills how humans will
worship their Creator and God has made the forms of such worship
clear in scripture. Although they could not agree always on details,
the Separatists and Puritans were rigorous biblicists in worship and
church polity. The first distinction between the Reformed tradition

and the Separatist and Puritan tradition, then, is the extent of the use of the Bible.

The issue is largely that of authority. The Puritans wanted absolute authority for anything in worship, and that authority could come only from God's word itself. Human inventions could not be tolerated in worship because they were creaturely self-assertions against God's will. It was impudent for humans to think they could improve on how God wished to be worshiped. "The acceptable way of worshiping God," the *Westminster Confession of Faith* proclaimed, "is instituted by himself . . . he may not be worshipped according to . . . any other way not prescribed in the Holy Scripture."[3]

There were certain systemic problems to this approach to worship. First, it was difficult to use the Bible as a legalistic book of liturgical prescriptions. Most of the Bible's mentions of Christian worship are quite incidental. Thus even the Puritans could not agree on just what the Bible prescribed. Was the Lord's Prayer to be followed literally or treated only as a pattern, as more radical Puritans argued? Speaking in tongues is certainly scriptural (1 Corinthians 14), but the Puritans shied away from such a practice. Agreement on just what the Bible prescribed was far from simple and frequently impossible. Nevertheless, there was general confidence that such a consensus could eventually be reached and enforced, creating worship pleasing to God and completely obedient to God's will.

The second distinction between the Separatists and Puritans and their Reformed mentors was in the preference for liturgical subsidiarity: liturgical decisions being made at the lowest possible level, whereas the Reformed tended to make these on the national level. This became increasingly apparent as the Independents (Congregationalists) came to power among the Puritans and was a fact of life among Separatists from their very beginnings. In practice, this meant that worship was to be ordered on the level of the individual congregation, although certain guidelines might be provided from higher authority. The principle was to order worship by the local body of worshipers, not by the regional or national church. It was argued that this liturgical autonomy had the benefit of making worship more immediately relevant than worship using fixed forms, although such forms could be used when desired. Prayers, especially, could be composed extempore, and sermons were prepared for specific people and occasions rather than read from published homilies. The needs of the local people were always the primary concern. This means that relevance really has a priority almost equal to biblical authority, so that relevance and authenticity are united. One does not pray a fixed prayer "For Fair Weather" when wanting to end a drought but, rather, voices the actual concerns of real people. Such relevance comes about because congregational autonomy allows one to order worship within biblical norms to fit real situations.

Congregational autonomy would make it seem difficult to generalize about worship in this tradition until we recognize that the degree of predictability in most Free Church worship is usually high. Orders of worship tend to be similar, the concerns voiced in prayer soon become familiar, and even the sermons have much in common. Far from being wildly erratic, the services are usually highly predictable, sometimes almost approaching the uniformity of traditions based on a service book.

We shall look briefly at the origins of the Separatists, move on to the Puritan agenda under adversity (1558–1644), then treat the Puritans in power from 1629 on in America and from 1644–1660 in England. We shall then discuss developments as established churches in America (to 1833), as Nonconformity in England after 1689, and finally look at twentieth-century developments in England and America. For the sake of convenience, we shall hereafter refer to this tradition simply as the Puritan tradition, without intending to negate the Separatist contribution.

The Origins of the Separatists

The English Separatists are difficult to lump together, because their liturgical directions are so idiosyncratic and their membership was usually confined to single congregations. Yet their size is no indication of the degree of influence they had on Free Church worship in both England and America, where they have helped to shape the worship of many millions. In general, they were impatient reformers. Robert Browne's book *A Treatise of Reformation Without Tarrying for Any* (1582) could well serve as their motto. As the title implies, they were not optimistic or even desirous of reforming a national church with its great "mingle-mangle" of the pious and the wicked. Rather, their concern was with pure congregations gathered to worship according to God's will.

These small groups were exclusive and sectarian, but they found what they sought: pure congregations in which the Lord's Supper could be properly celebrated. Their boldness brought danger, and they were subject to frequent persecution from the crown. John Greenwood (b. ?), John Penry (b. 1559), and Henry Barrow (b. ca.1550) were all hanged in 1593. They opposed the Puritan agenda, with its goal of reform of the national church and worship for a "promiscuous multitude," just as much as they resisted the established church. As a result of persecution, various Separatist groups found it safer to flee to the Netherlands, where they found more sympathetic tendencies among the Reformed. This also brought contact with the Mennonites, which may have been significant. The "strangers' " churches in London, established for foreigners resident in the country, had also influenced their course.

One is struck by the centrality of concern among these groups about the Lord's Supper and the importance of worthy communicants. Even Calvin had been too lenient and was not above criticism, since, it was said, new light had dazzled his eyes after the long Roman darkness. Discipline was all-important, and special requirements applied to clergy. Indeed, important as the Lord's Supper was, without proper clergy it could not be celebrated, and the Pilgrims in Massachusetts went without the eucharist in the absence of an ordained pastor until one came in 1629.

Several of the better-known Separatist congregations and pastors deserve mention. Robert Browne (ca.1550–1633) became convinced that only gathered churches could offer worship pleasing to God by separating themselves from the wicked. In common with other Separatists, he felt that only with ministers who preached could the Lord's Supper be administered; otherwise it was like placing a seal on a blank document.[4] Set forms were disregarded; the ingredients of the normal service were half an hour of prayer, an hour of sermon, and commentary on or dissection of the sermon by a lay person. Apparently the eucharist was led without notes or text by the minister. In 1582, Browne's congregation from Norwich found it safer to flee to Middleburg in the Netherlands. His later life turned in a different direction, and Browne spent the last half of it as rector of an Anglican parish.

The Pilgrims, later examples of Separatists, became famous for their role in American history. Their minister John Robinson (1575–1625) was an Anglican clergyman who moved to the liturgical and ecclesiological left. His secret congregation at Scrooby Manor, Nottingham, settled in Leyden in 1609; some of the congregation, without their pastor, moved to Plymouth, Massachusetts, in 1620. Robinson made a strong case for free prayer: "If our prayers be not conceived first in our hearts before they be brought forth in our lips, they are an unnatural, bastardly, and profane birth."[5] Accordingly, prayer from books was eschewed in favor of prayer from the heart. The influence of the separatist Plymouth Colony Pilgrims on the worship of the Massachusetts Bay Puritans is hard to determine, but the resemblances between their worship and that narrated in 1645 by the Boston pastor John Cotton (1584–1652) are strong.

Another in this assortment of Separatists was John Smyth (1554–1612), whose career and opinions moved increasingly to the left after he was ordained as an Anglican. He moved through a Puritan phase and then led a Separatist congregation in Gainsborough, which fled with him to Amsterdam in 1608. There he baptized himself and began to reject infant baptism. His congregation repudiated him and he founded a new congregation that held to believer's baptism. At the end of his life, he came under Mennonite influence but died before he joined them. His friend and successor as pastor, Thomas Helwys (ca.1550–ca.1616), returned to London in 1612 and established the first Baptist congregation in England. Only believers were admitted to baptism; pouring was the usual method of administration. (Immersion became general only from the 1630s.) Another Anglican clergyman, Roger Williams (ca.1604–1683), helped found the first Baptist church in America in 1639.

Even among Separatists, the early Baptists were a small remnant. But the advent of Helwys's General (Arminian) Baptists in London in 1612 and the Particular (Calvinist) Baptists in Southwark in 1633 marks the beginnings of a major segment of the Free Church worship. How much influence the Anabaptists, in the form of the Dutch Waterlander Mennonites, had on them is debated. Certainly, many of the tendencies of the Baptists seem to have been formulated in common with other Separatists. During the Commonwealth era the number of Baptist congregations grew considerably, and they have been a permanent part of English and American Christianity ever since. Only the issue of who were fit candidates for baptism divided them from independent Puritans, with whose views on worship they generally agreed.

The Puritan Agenda

The much larger group known as Puritans developed and elaborated a consistent agenda for the completion of liturgical reform in the Church of England. Many of the same concerns that were expressed early in the reign (1558–1603) of Elizabeth I in the "Admonition to Parliament" (1572) were reiterated in the Millenary Petition of 1603, in the *Westminster Directory* enacted by Parliament in 1645, and again as the "Exceptions" of the Puritan ministers in 1661 at the Savoy Conference held with Anglicans in the Restoration period. After 1689, the Puritans were allowed to go their own way with no hope of ever persuading the Church of England to follow their agenda.

The origins of Puritanism can be traced to the more radical Protestants of Cranmer's time, especially Bishop John Hooper (ca.1495–1555). During the reign of Queen Mary (1553–1558), 788 reformers, both moderate and advanced, were forced to flee to about eight locations in Europe. Unintentionally, by martyring 288 reformers in her five short years as monarch, Mary did more to establish Protestantism than any other person in English history. Many of the exiles made their way to Geneva or other centers of the Reformed tradition and returned home after Mary's death, determined to shape the worship of the Church of England after the model of "the best reformed churches," especially Geneva.[6] One opponent warned that the wolves were coming home and had already sent their books ahead of them.

For the next eighty-five years, there was to be guerrilla warfare to capture the soul of the national church. The real issue was not polity, for there were Episcopal Puritans such as Archbishop Edmund Grindal (1519?–1583) and Bishop Miles Coverdale (1488–1568), Presbyterian Puritans such as Thomas Cartwright (1535–1603) and Edmund Calamy (1600–1666), and Independent Puritans such as John Cotton (1584–1652) and Philip Nye (1596–1672). Nor was theology the basic issue, since most Anglicans moved within a Calvinistic framework although without Calvin's high sacramental doctrine. Strong Calvinism was maintained by Archbishop John Whitgift (ca.1530–1604), that harrier of the Puritans, in his Lambeth Articles of 1595 and evidenced by Anglican participation in the Synod of Dort (1618–1619).

No, the essential controversy was liturgical: How complete should the reformation of worship be? The first eruption was over vestments, which had been in contention even at the consecration under Edward VI of Bishop John Hooper in 1550 and was exacerbated by the Ornaments Rubric in the 1559 *Book of Common Prayer* that the ministers should "use such ornaments of the church as were in use by authority of Parliament in the second year of the reign of King Edward the Sixth."[7] This and similar legislation in the 1559 Act for the Uniformity of Common Prayer apparently turned the clock back to 1549. Convocation in 1563 protested the restoration of vestments, and Archbishop Matthew Parker (1504–1575) in his *Advertisements* of 1566 did not satisfy the Puritans, although he ordered "a comely surplice with sleeves" at the eucharist rather than traditional mass vestments.[8] Parker apparently believed that such things were unneeded, but he was not dealing with Lutherans. The Puritans felt they could not be constrained to go against conscience, as indicated by a representative tract, *A Brief Discourse Against the Outside Apparel and Ministring Garments of the Popish Church.*[9]

The battle escalated in 1572 with the first "Admonition to Parliament," which, besides urging reform in church government (most of the bishops having proven themselves obdurate to desired reforms), attacked various objectionable practices such as the use of wafer bread, kneeling for communion, admission of papists to communion, and vestments. It was directed "not only in abandoning all popish remnants both in ceremonies and regiment, but also in bringing in and placing in God's Church those things only, which the Lord himself in his word commands."[10] Elizabeth outmaneuvered the document's proponents, and it came to nothing. (Ironically, during much of her reign, the Channel Islands maintained an Anglican Church run on Presbyterian Puritan principles, and not until the end of the reign [1603–1625] of James I were they made to conform to Anglican practice.)

Given these advances and setbacks, it is not surprising that the Puritans developed a consistent identity and a consensus on what they desired in worship. Their chief complaints vary little for over more than a century: The *BCP* had halted short of complete reformation, there was still too much popish ceremonial in Anglican worship, no scriptural warrant could be found for much that endured, and existing worship was far from edifying. All this must be seen in the context of an Anglican parish worship that was far more devoid of ceremonial than it has been for a hundred years. The complaints were not about such clergy vestments as chasubles and copes but about surplices; the churches were not full of images but had been cleansed of them; the prevailing theology was anything but Roman Catholic. Yet the Reformation, in the minds of Puritans, was still far from complete despite the good intentions of Cranmer and his generation.

Who were these people so avid for further change? By and large, the Puritans were the educated middle class of the time. They were literate people who were on their way up socially and economically and had learned that politics could serve their personal advancement. In modern terms, they were pious yuppies. Sir Walter Mildmay founded Emmanuel College in 1584 as a seedbed, among others at Cambridge, for Puritan preachers. Literacy had made these people much less dependent on visual images for information than their ancestors and at the same time made words, printed and spoken, far more important for the communication of truth. The linear mentality, of things happening one after another as in reading or preaching, had a stronger grip on their imagination than the all-at-once simultaneity of the visual.

Their piety had been deeply affected by the new possibility of reading the Bible. Here was true authority, God's own word, now in print for all to see and heed. It is not strange that an important part of the Puritan concept of ordained ministry based it upon knowledge of scripture, especially via the original languages. The ordained minister was primarily a trained scholar of God's word.

Since the Bible was so important, Puritans developed additional forms of public biblical study. Chief among these were prophesyings, vaguely reminiscent of those practiced by Zwingli in Zurich. These provided an occasion for Puritan clergy to meet to compare their biblical exegesis and to comment on the interpretation of texts by their peers. Such sessions were considered subversive by the state church, and participants were vigorously persecuted. But the prophesyings suggested a practice that became common in seventeenth-century Puritan worship: congregational response to the preacher's handling of scripture.

A continuing strain of medieval piety that remained most congenial to Puritans was the penitential emphasis. This was reinforced by the Calvinist stress on humanity's rebellion against God and the total depravity of the race. But a consequence of this was a kindred distrust of human authority that finally proved stronger than the divine right of kings. If kings went against God's will, they too could be destroyed in the name of God's law. Above all, Puritans feared anything that smacked of idolatry, that confused the contingent with the Creator.

Among these confusions were human ceremonies, of which the three most offensive, most frequently condemned in Puritan literature, were the sign of the cross in baptism, the giving of the ring in marriage, and kneeling for the eucharist. None was biblical—that is, willed by God—and the first and last suggested dangerous doctrines; baptism was not effectual for those not elect, and communion elements per se were not to be adored. Vestments and other ceremonies likewise lacked God's sanction and therefore were mere human inventions and relics of popery.

The changes already under way in church architecture appealed to the Puritans. The royal injunctions of Edward VI and Elizabeth I had provided for pulpits in all churches and slow and distinct reading of services. Archbishop Laud's attempt to put the altar-table back against the east wall was opposed by Anglicans of various parties, including Puritans.

There were important Puritan concerns about the keeping of time. Holy days were condemned as "having no warrant in the word of God," in favor of emphasis on the Lord's Day. Sabbath keeping[11] increasingly became a Puritan hallmark despite (or because of) the royal publication of the *Book of Sports* in 1618 and 1633, which advocated Sunday archery and dancing. Indeed, in England and Scotland, sabbatarianism far exceeded that in any Calvinist community on the Continent. Not only was work proscribed but keeping the day holy meant avoiding recreation, even taking a walk. The traditional calendar was criticized, especially the season of Lent, which the Puritans disparaged because the whole year was to be kept holy.

In the life cycle they desired that "confirmation, as superfluous, may be taken away." There was a general tendency to secularize weddings. Yet it was the Puritans who reversed the traditional list of the purposes of marriage, exalting mutual help and society as the chief end. Funerals were often discouraged, because many eulogies presumed too much about the virtues and destination of the deceased.

Real Puritan strengths came in preaching, which was expected to be both biblical and relevant. Texts were dissected "painfully" (in detail) and then applied to life, often in vivid terms.[12] Anglican preachers, who were content to read the published homilies rather than write their own sermons, were called "dumb dogs" unfit for ministry. Real sermons were demanded, of preachers who knew both scripture and the life concerns of their people. The length of sermons, often an hour or more, made them a major part of any gathering for worship. Active participation was enhanced by inviting the congregation to comment on the preacher's interpretation of scripture.

Some of the most strenuous critiques raised against the *BCP* were about prayer. Collects were condemned as being too short and saying too little. Litanies were criticized as being like a tennis ball bouncing back and forth.[13] The model of prayer encouraged could be printed or free, as long as it was edifying. There were several Puritan prayer books, especially the Waldegrave Book of 1584, republished in Middleburg in 1586.[14] The Reformed tradition provided the model. Increasingly, objections arose that printed forms were inadequate since they often failed to be relevant. The Separatist objections to forms began to appeal to Puritans and defenses of prayer extempore (prepared for the time) became frequent. Relevance came to be stressed in prayers as in preaching. Demands for the flexibility to pray for a concrete local circumstance became part of the Puritan rhetoric. Debate on this issue continued until recent times, with little new being said by either side.[15] (The modern consensus seems to be that both set forms and spontaneous prayer are important in public worship.)

The Elizabethan injunctions had encouraged the singing of plainchant and allowed hymns before and after services. The Puritans adamantly opposed using hymns of human composure in favor of the psalms sung in worship. Metrical paraphrases of psalms by various poets were popular and sung with relish. Although many Puritans cherished music in private life, they condemned instrumental and choral music in worship as neither biblical nor edifying.

Puritanism in Power

The Puritan liturgical agenda, then, was intact long before there was an opportunity to practice such worship legally. Opportunity came first in Salem and Boston, Massachusetts, in 1629 and 1630 under the Massachusetts Bay Colony venture. As Francis Higginson (1586–1630), first teacher of the Salem Church, voiced it as England disappeared over the stern of his ship, "We do not go to New-England as separatists from the Church of England; though we cannot but separate from the corruptions in it; but we go to practice the positive part of Church reformation, and propagate the gospel in America."[16] Unlike the Separatists in Plymouth, the Boston Puritans considered themselves Anglicans, worshiping as Anglicans should but were legally prevented from doing in the homeland. They were still an established church, and Congregationalism remained such until 1818 in Connecticut, 1819 in New Hampshire, and 1833 in Massachusetts. Boston was a city set on a hill to show the world what truly reformed religion, especially worship, was like.

They were not alone. Anglicans in Virginia, with less self-consciousness, could boast by 1614 that the surplice was not found there either.[17] John Cotton, pastor in Boston, described *The Way of The Churches of Christ in New England,*[18] giving insight into their worship. But by then, the Puritans had come into power in England and probably had little patience for being lectured by a colonist when they were now free to reform "Mother Church" as they saw fit.

The Westminster Assembly (1643–1649), convened by the Long Parliament in 1643, undertook reformation root and branch. In worship, this took the form of *A Directory for the Public Worship of God,* ratified by Parliament on January 3, 1645, and put into effect on August 26, 1645. This replaced the *BCP* for fifteen years as the official worship document of the Church of England. While it was more than just a book of rubrics, it was less than a book of prayers. Rather, it was an attempt to attain unity without uniformity, representing "a synthesis between previous Independent Puritan and Separatist practices."[19] Prayers were not included, but the subjects to be covered in prayers were carefully listed, the book providing "some help and furniture" to aid ministers in praying. The order for the Sunday service was provided in detail, with provision for the eucharist. Practices were also prescribed for baptism, marriage, visitation of the sick, and burial of the dead. Public solemn fasting and days of public thanksgiving were commended, while all holy days except "the Christian Sabbath" were proscribed. The parallels with the *BCP* are obvious; the omissions—confirmation, churching of women, and Ash Wednesday—are equally significant.

The omission of the holy days is particularly significant. Sunday was to be observed with diligence; civil laws enforced that. But in addition, a pragmatic approach was developed of responding to God's works in present history rather than events of the past. This took the form of days of thanksgiving for blessings presently experienced and days of fasting and humiliation at signs of God's displeasure. Time was organized with a sense of God's saving acts close at hand. In 1649, we are told, "the Lord was pleased to command the wind and seas to give us a jog on the elbow, by sinking the very chief of our shipping in the deep."[20] Another consequence of abolishing the church calendar and lectionary (list of scriptural passages) was that preachers were now free to preach their way through the entire Bible in course. The principle that all of scripture was written for human benefit could be observed by reading and preaching on every verse over a number of years.

The shape of the week also changed, with the addition of a pattern of midweek services or lectures designed to be edifying. One New England preacher used these series over decades to do a complete system of theology.[21] Sunday afternoon services were common. John Cotton tells us that in Boston the Lord's Supper was celebrated "once a month at least,"[22] more often than in most English parishes.

In New England, initiation through baptism at birth led in early youth to public profession of faith and admission to the Lord's Supper. Public profession was not confirmation but an individual's own profession of religious experience and an opportunity to "own" the covenant of the local congregation, the foundation document for each local church. With declining piety, succeeding generations could not always profess religious conversion. The Half-Way Covenant of 1662 allowed such persons to be voting members of the parish and to receive the Lord's Supper. Their children could be baptized but that generation could not have church membership and receive the Lord's Supper unless they could claim conversion themselves.[23] For the Baptist minority, these problems were solved by believer's baptism.

Architecturally there was not that much for Puritans to change in England. In the eastern counties of England, Parliamentary visitors (the Puritan counterpart of Episcopal visitors) purged churches of the few remaining images and inscriptions.[24] Biblical texts were inscribed on the interiors of naves and the Laudian arrangements of the altar-table discarded. While Independents favored pew communion, the Presbyterians set benches around the Lord's Table for communicants.

America, on the other hand, provided a vast laboratory for experiments in building meetinghouses.[25] The earliest of these were the "pyramids" (square buildings with pyramidal roofs), of which only the one in Hingham, Massachusetts (1681), survives. In the early eighteenth century, a more elegant form developed with the pulpit in the middle of one long side, an ornate pulpit window behind it, and the main door opposite. The congregation was arranged on three sides of the pulpit and the hinged shelf table that stood below it for the Lord's Supper. Most meetinghouses had balconies on three sides to bring people close to the pulpit.

We have already noted the Puritan concern that prayer be edifying and relevant. This led to the long or pastoral prayer before the sermon. After the sermon, the *Directory* tells the pastor to "turn the chief and most useful heads of the sermon into some few Petitions."[26] By giving outlines only, the *Directory* encouraged that prayer come from the heart through the prompting of the Spirit, not from a book. Richard Baxter (1615–1691), Matthew Henry (1662–1714), and others wrote manuals for family prayers. Family devotions came to be a very important daily routine and usually consisted of metrical psalms, a chapter of scripture, and prayer.

Preaching was the major portion of any service and was largely expository. Congregational participation was encouraged by inviting the congregation to question the minister's handling of a text.[27] This provided an abundance of active participation, which could be rather vociferous at times in attempts to discern God's word for the congregation.

As might be expected, music was limited to the psalter; it is noteworthy that the first book published in America was *The Bay Psalm Book* (Cambridge, 1640). The Puritans did not favor the use of biblical canticles in worship even though they were scriptural. Considerable efforts went into improving the quality of psalter singing.[28]

After the Restoration, Puritans in America were not forced to conform, only to tolerate other forms of English Protestantism. In England, the failure of efforts at compromise in 1661 led to the expulsion of over two thousand Puritan clergy when they refused to use the new *BCP* after St. Bartholomew's Day, August 24, 1662. The Puritan movement had been forced outside of the national church. Hopes of completing the reform of the national church according to the Puritan agenda were dead after 1689. Puritanism found its expression though the churches of nonconformity: Congregationalists, Presbyterians, and Baptists. The vitality of the movement is shown in the fact that these groups built more than a thousand church buildings in England in the twelve years after they were first legally allowed to do so in 1689.

Later Developments

The period after 1689 in England saw Congregationalists, Presbyterians, and Baptists settle into their own forms of respectability. Among Congregationalists, an important new development was the advent of hymnody, pioneered by Isaac Watts (1674–1748). Watts began with materials modeled on the psalms, trying to make David "speak like a Christian" by such hymns as "O God, Our Help in Ages Past" (Psalm 90). But his hymnody moved to things David never contemplated: "Jesus Shall Reign" or "When I Survey the

Wondrous Cross." Watts's hymnody was not accepted without controversy, but Methodism soon did much to popularize his work in another tradition.

The eighteenth century was a problematic time for English Congregationalists and Presbyterians as the liberal tendencies of the time affected these groups, moving many of them in a Unitarian direction. The Enlightenment era brought lack of concern for the sacraments in worship, although in the early eighteenth century Judge Samuel Sewall pled for a weekly eucharist in Boston.[29] The Lord's Supper moved to the periphery of Puritan worship and its message was largely interpreted in moralistic terms: namely, "Be good." Neither the theology of Calvin nor that of Cranmer survived to make the Lord's Supper seem an encounter with the living God. The final step was taken by a young Unitarian clergyman, Ralph Waldo Emerson (1803–1882), who in 1832 refused to celebrate the Lord's Supper altogether.

Yet a counterculture factor was operative, also shaping the Puritan tradition, especially in America. From 1725 to 1760, The Great Awakening introduced such novelties as itinerant preachers, lay preachers, preaching for the experience of conversion, and controversy about the admission of the unconverted to the Lord's Supper. In general, the Awakening gave an opportunity for minority groups such as Baptists to compete with the various established churches and to find new prominence. Revivals were considered "Surprising Works of God" at this time, and Jonathan Edwards (1703–1758) carefully analyzed the permanence of the "religious affections."[30] Emotion became a more pronounced part of worship, vigorously promoted by some preachers. Some conclude that the Awakening brought new dominance to the preacher and an end to congregational response to the sermon.[31]

In the nineteenth century, Unitarians, who had taken over many Congregational churches in America and England, often proved the most liturgically creative of Free Church people, especially James Martineau (1805–1900) in England.[32] In America, Unitarianism tended to reflect East Coast sophistication and emphasis on the cerebral in worship. Refinement appeared in the introduction of organs and eventually choirs among Unitarians and Congregationalists. The visible evidence of this was the reorientation of the meetinghouse to a church form with the pulpit opposite the main entrance on a short end. These buildings with their refined and ornate detail reflected the full sophistication of the Federal style, merging eventually into Greek revival in the 1830s. The development of Sunday schools profoundly affected worship and architecture. Sunday schools often began with quasi-worship assemblies before dividing into individual graded classes. New spatial requirements for these activities often led to raising the church building so as to put Sunday school space in the basement or additions to the church building for educational purposes.

East Coast propriety met a vigorous challenge in the 1830s and later as evangelists from the West, reflecting a new tradition of Free Church worship, began bringing new revival techniques east. The remainder of the century showed tension between these newer and more boisterous forms of Free Church worship and the propriety of the older Puritan tradition. Each, in turn, accepted bits of the other. Horace Bushnell (1802–1876) gave a significant theological argument against the western revival system in worship by insisting in *Christian Nurture* (1847) that infant baptism was appropriate and "the child is to grow up a Christian, and never know himself as being otherwise."[33]

An interesting development in England was the group often called by outsiders "Plymouth Brethren," but which prefers simply to be called "Brethren." A variety of leaders, including an Anglican priest, John Nelson Darby (1800–1882), led it from 1831 on and helped develop an informal style of worship in which any group of laity could celebrate weekly the breaking of bread. Ordained clergy were considered superfluous. Worship was conducted with great simplicity in which any man present could preach and celebrate the sacraments. Thus they gave an opposite answer to the question "Can we have the eucharist?" to that given by the early Separatists who had made celebrations contingent upon clerical leadership. These communities had at last achieved that elusive goal, a weekly eucharist. From the early 1830s on, they (and in America the Mormons and Disciples of Christ) have kept the celebration each Sunday.

Twentieth-century Developments

In the twentieth century, the Separatist and Puritan tradition in worship has become increasingly difficult to define and to characterize. This is because it has been subject to a variety of external pressures: the success of the nineteenth-century Frontier tradition, the appeal of the re-catholicized Anglican tradition, and the attractions of the post-Vatican II Roman Catholic agenda. At the same time, various mergers have combined Congregationalists with other worship traditions. In general, the modern adherents of the Puritan tradition tend to be found in theologically rather liberal denominations such as the United Church of Christ, the American Baptist Churches in the United States, and the Unitarian Universalist Association.

After more than a century and a half of disestablishment, Congregational churches (United Church of Christ) or Unitarian Universalist churches often remain the historic downtown churches in much of New England and the Midwest. Members of these churches tend to be well educated and sophisticated. Frequently they are the social and political liberals of their regions. Thus it is not strange that the worship of such congregations tends to appeal more to the mind than to the emotions and the worship focuses more on highly cerebral preaching than on emotional appeal or on sacraments. The rationalism of the Enlightenment still prevails with regard to the sacraments. In general, these are not the churches that are attracting large numbers of new Christians.

There are historical reasons for this. We have mentioned the resistance in the nineteenth century to revivalism in worship with its heavy emotional content. The Puritan tradition, having outgrown its biblicism, overcame many of its inhibitions about innovation in worship. The revival techniques were not especially appealing. But in the late nineteenth century, this tradition found new possibilities in aesthetic approaches to worship. Twenty years after the Anglicans, Congregationalists on both sides of the Atlantic began building Gothic churches, instituting robed choirs, and installing many of the art items the Parliamentary visitors has smashed two centuries earlier. In addition, there was even a tendency to adopt fixed forms of prayer, which could be printed each week in the Sunday bulletin, made possible by the invention of stencil duplicating by a Chicago businessman, Albert Blake Dick (1856–1934).

Aestheticism had great appeal in many of these churches in the first half of this century. It is no accident that one of the most influential books about worship was *Art & Religion* by Von Ogden Vogt (1879–1964), published first in 1921.[34] Although ordained as a Congregationalist, Vogt was pastor of an Unitarian congregation in Chicago with a magnificent Gothic building and sophisticated art. In Vogt's writing, the experience of the beautiful and worship are similar.

In the period after World War II such an approach to worship had less appeal, and congregations shifted to recovery of some of the sixteenth-century characteristics, especially emphasis on penitential acts and a new openness to the historic creeds. Although Congregationalists, Baptists, and Unitarians were not likely to adopt Reformation liturgies, they were more willing to acknowledge the horror at human sin and estrangement that those historic rites reflect and to emphasize the importance of recovering the corporate memories of salvation history. Preaching moved from preoccupation with dealing with "real-life situations" to the confrontation of the biblical witness.

Early in the century, several individuals made important contributions to worship. Walter Rauschenbusch (1861–1918) raised Christian awareness of the social powers of evil and published a volume,

For God and the People: Prayers for the Social Awakening (1910).[35] Others, such as Congregationalists Washington Gladden (1836–1918) and John Oxenham (1852–1941), Methodist Frank Mason North (1850–1935), and Presbyterian William Pierson Merrill (1867–1954), helped develop a new hymnody of the social gospel. Such hymns as "Where Cross the Crowded Ways of Life" or "In Christ There Is No East or West" express new concerns for social problems. Important shifts were occurring in both prayers and hymns toward articulating the unity of worship and justice.

Sometimes this went so far that worship seemed to be a means of energizing crusades for justice. Teachers of religious education were prone to see worship as a manipulative tool that should use psychological techniques to educate and motivate. The point became irrevocable that one could not ignore in worship the struggles for justice, and when the civil rights and women's rights movements erupted, they had important consequences for worship, especially in this tradition.

A different path was pioneered by P. T. Forsyth (1848–1921), English Congregationalist pastor and theologian. In many ways, he anticipated the theological interests of the period after World War I in resurrecting a high doctrine of the church, the sacraments, and preaching. Such books as *The Church and the Sacraments*[36] and *Positive Preaching and the Modern Mind*[37] gave guidance and depth that mere aestheticism alone could not provide, and they were recognized as classics by the 1950s.

Because the Free Church tradition practiced subsidiarity in worship, individual pastors could often lead in quite contrary directions. Certainly one of the most distinctive was William E. Orchard (1877–1955), pastor of the King's Weigh House Chapel in London. Orchard led the way in producing *The Order of Divine Service*[38] for English Congregationalists and published a collection of prayers, *The Temple.*[39] Eventually, he became a Roman Catholic priest. Few pastors in this tradition went as far as Orchard in valuing set forms, yet familiar patterns became common. The so-called "hymn sandwich" service usually consists of three hymns, scripture reading(s), choral music, unison prayers, a pastoral prayer, a sermon, an offering, and a benediction, all in varying combinations, to be sure, but with few if any significant differences. Even the pastoral prayer is usually predictable in what concerns it will voice and in the kind of language it uses. And the number of hymns known by most congregations is far from immense.

There have been periodic attempts to give guidance to such worship. In 1948, *A Book of Worship for Free Churches*[40] was published by the Congregational-Christian Churches, although it was not widely used. The most recent publication is *Book of Worship: The*

United Church of Christ.[41] Intended primarily for the pastor's use, it shows the influence of recent liturgical scholarship combined with a zeal for inclusive language. More a congregational service book is *A Book of Services*[42] of the United Reformed Church in England and Wales.

Both books are strong indications of the appeal of the post-Vatican II Roman Catholic agenda for liturgical reform. The most important influences have been the use of the ecumenical (now common) lectionary in America and that of the Joint Liturgical Group in England, with concomitant rediscovery of the values of the traditional liturgical year, especially Holy Week. The possibility of a variety of forms, especially for the eucharistic prayer, has also been accepted. And there is evidence that more frequent eucharistic celebrations are occurring, perhaps not as frequent as the early Separatists or the Plymouth Brethren achieved, but certainly moving in that direction.

8

Quaker Worship

The most radical discontinuity with the medieval tradition occurs in a worship tradition originating in the seventeenth century, that of the Religious Society of Friends, commonly known as Quakers. Its radical character places this tradition farthest left in our political analogy. Yet in another sense, much of Quaker worship has been the most conservative in its internal history by remaining closer to its own early practices and ideals than any other western tradition, Protestant or Roman Catholic.

Just why the most radical disjuncture should occur in the seventeenth century rather than as a consequence of the Enlightenment or the present era of future shock is difficult to explain. The Quakers were by-products of Anglicanism's mature age, the Stuart period, and, of course, the advent of Quaker worship cannot be dissociated from the ferment of English Puritanism, whose triumph had finally come. Quaker worship is a tertiary development from medieval worship just as Puritan had been secondary after the Anglican and Reformed traditions. Unlike the earliest Puritans, some of whom had been ordained as Roman Catholic priests, the Quaker leadership had no direct connection with Catholicism. Nor were they clergy; the chief leaders were all lay people. Thus, both in person and in circumstances, Quakers were twice removed from the western matrix of medieval worship.

The whole medieval apparatus and most Protestant adaptations of it disappear in Quaker worship. In classical Quakerism, there are not only no clergy but also no service books, no outward and visible sacraments, no preaching, no choirs and organs, and virtually no ceremonial. Quaker worship is the most ascetic of all traditions, for it is disciplined to rely not on external promptings but on inward resources alone. Thus it constitutes a radical break not only from medieval worship but also from its Protestant matrix as well, since sermons, psalmody, prepared prayers, and most else that character-ized Puritan worship are negated.

There is one point of contact with medieval life that should not be overlooked, and this is the long tradition of mysticism with its insistence on the primacy of direct and immediate encounter of the individual with God. The great Quaker theologian Robert Barclay (1648–1690) quotes approvingly the twelfth-century mystic Bernard of Clairvaux (1090–1153). Although there are differences between them, the medieval mystics give words to help express Quaker expe-riences. There is an invisible connection between the corporate mys-ticism of Quakerism and the medieval tradition.

For such a radical tradition, stability has been a remarkable fea-ture. Cranmer might be puzzled by Anglican worship today, but the Quaker founder, George Fox (1624–1691), would probably feel quite at home were he to return to many of today's Friends' meetings. Although modified in the American West almost two centuries after the original impulse, the stability of the Quaker tradition is remark-able.

It is difficult to know in what context to discuss the worship of the Shakers. The early background of this movement evolved as an offshoot from English Friends, and this is the closest historical con-nection. Again, the influence of the American frontier had an impact on Shakers: the popularity of hymn singing, for example. In many ways, Shaker worship is most closely related to Quaker worship: the break with the past, stress on corporate mysticism, freedom of ex-pression, equality, mysticism, absence of clericalism and visible sac-raments. On the other hand, Shaker worship is certainly unique in many ways. But as a movement that exists today only in two tiny communities, I do not choose to call it a separate tradition and shall treat it here.

We shall discuss the formative period of the Quaker tradition from its beginnings to its encounter with the American frontier (1646–1837), pause to look at Shaker developments (1774–1989), and then trace Quaker developments to the present (1837–1989).

Origins of the Society of Friends

Quaker worship began in 1646 with the experience of the Inner Light by George Fox. An uneducated shoemaker's apprentice, Fox underwent several years of personal turmoil and search, which led to a sense of peace with self and God and strong dissatisfaction with the worship of the established church, then under Puritan leadership. His personal conflicts resolved, Fox embarked upon a lifelong career as reformer and missionary. His preaching in the streets and public places often led to imprisonment (six years altogether), but he persisted undaunted. Fox's skill as an organizer is reflected in his 1668 "Rule for the Management of Meetings," which became, in effect, the charter for the Society of Friends. He traveled in Europe and North America, spreading his ideas, and left a *Journal* that was published posthumously in 1694.

The last decades of the seventeenth century saw the establishment of a number of Quaker communities in Great Britain and North America. Robert Barclay became the Quaker theologian par excellence; his *An Apology for the True Christian Divinity as the Same Is Held Forth and Preached by the People, in Scorn, Called Quakers* was originally published in Latin in Amsterdam (1676) and in English (1678). Three of the fifteen "propositions" he proposes for debate deal with worship and provide a careful defense of Quaker practice. His contemporary, William Penn (1644–1718), founded Pennsylvania in 1682 as an experiment in religious liberty, with freedom of worship for all monotheists. Penn's *No Cross, No Crown* (1669) is a classic of Quaker devotion. Another important leader, James Nayler (ca.1618–1660), came under the influence of a radical group, the Ranters, who treated him as Christ, but he was eventually reconciled to the Quakers.

As time went on, Friends found it increasingly necessary to develop terms to describe what they experienced in worship. Some of this vocabulary has been adopted by other groups and may constitute the Quakers' most important contribution to Christian worship simply by articulating so well various experiences of worship: "centering down," "finding one's inward center," voicing a "concern," "putting oneself forward," "waiting on God," a "gathered meeting," and "sense of the meeting." Strangely enough, there has often been a mutual attraction between these people of the far left and Anglicans of the far right, who sometimes find that "Quaker worship is a powerful corrective."[1] Although far apart liturgically, there has been a common interest in mystical forms of religion.

At the heart of Quaker worship is the belief that the inner light is accessible to all and that the purpose of worship is common waiting upon God in stillness and quietness. It is a very simple idea but one not accomplished simply, as non-Friends soon discover when they attempt to imitate Quaker worship.

Considerable self-discipline is necessary for the process of "centering down" or "finding one's inward center." It demands self-restraint and self-abnegation to avoid "rushing into words" once the community is assembled. There is considerable need for repressing personal identity for the good of the group's corporate mysticism. One cannot come with a prepared agenda. Only under the compulsion of the Spirit can one speak without fear of forwardness. And then such speech is a message for the group, spoken in the Spirit for the building up of the body. The gifts of the Spirit are all for communal edification (1 Cor. 12:11).

There are few forms of leadership in worship. Elders function simply to bring people back when they have gone beyond the acceptable bounds (such as making a political speech) by gentle reproval. The elders indicate the termination of a meeting for worship by standing and turning to greet those next to them. In some monthly meetings (congregations), "recorded ministers," those who have frequently been vehicles of the Spirit's communication, are seated on benches facing the community so they can be better heard when they speak. "Deacons" eventually evolved to look after charity and weddings and burials. Special honors usually were paid to visiting Friends as a matter of courtesy, and those who traveled much (such as Fox) played important leadership roles as "traveling Quakers."

When the presence of the Spirit is experienced, it is common to speak of the occasion as a "gathered" meeting. For this, it is not necessary that there be speaking at all. A completely silent meeting may be a gathered meeting, whereas one in which people have been loquacious does not necessarily indicate that the presence of the Spirit was experienced. Hidden behind the term "gathered" is the concept of quality. It suggests an experience of the presence of the living Christ that comes not by human activity but solely from the working of the Holy Spirit.

The practice of Quaker worship cannot be separated from the Friends themselves; they are the true texts that must be studied to comprehend this worship tradition. The people who worship as Quakers are certainly distinctive. From their heroic age in the seventeenth century down to the present, Friends have practiced a kind of worldly asceticism. But unlike most ascetics, they have lived married lives within the world. Their style of life has often distinguished them from other Christians. In the early years, their clothing and speech set them off from others; today it is more often their social and political causes.

Until 1689, Quaker worship was proscribed by Puritans and Anglicans, depending on who was in power. Four Quakers were hanged on Boston Common in 1659–1660 for not exercising what one Puritan told other sects was their "free liberty to keep away from us." Yet, while the English Puritans went underground after 1660, Quakers met openly in defiance of civil law. Thousands were imprisoned rather than forsake the type of worship they felt God willed.

It is not strange, then, that Friends formed close communities, although always within normal civil life. They never tried to hide from society, and their distinctive dress, speech, and manners always gave them away. Their children were gently persuaded to marry within the Society, and the next generation was carefully nurtured by the community as "birthright" Friends. Many Quakers were in business, and names such as Cadbury, Rowntree, Fry, and Barclay attest to their commercial acuity and reputation for honesty that brought prosperity. The Friends also produced more than their share of social reformers, such as Elizabeth Fry (1780–1845), the prison reformer. Significantly, many women were involved as missionaries, some witnessing to the sultan of Turkey, who offered them a place in his harem, and others to the pope, who was less hospitable.

If the Spirit can speak to all in worship, the logical implication is that all humans are equal. Without practicing outward forms of baptism, the Quakers were the first to insist that in worship there is neither slave nor free, male nor female, laity nor clergy. Robert Barclay states the Quaker concept of ministry as not being

> *Monopolized* to a certain kind of Men, as the *Clergy* (who are to that purpose Educated and brought up, as other carnal *Artists*) and the rest to be despised as *Laicks;* but it is left to the *free Gift of God* to choose any, whom he seeth meet thereunto, whether Rich or Poor, Servant or Master, Young or Old, yea, Male or Female.[2]

In such egalitarian worship no clergy were necessary, for all were practicing their ministry to one another.

Women had the right to speak (despite 1 Cor. 14:34), but it was recognized that women's concerns were often different from those of men. Until well into the nineteenth century, therefore, men and women often met separately for worship, although in the same building. There were provisions for joint meetings for worship and for business. Friends were the first to encourage women to act as equals in worship.

At the center of Quaker worship is the most inclusive degree of "full, conscious, and active participation" because there are no qualifications as to sex or social status. The modern concern for linking worship and justice had its beginnings among Quakers, although not articulated as such. Everyone can speak in meeting because all are equal before God, if not before human beings. Since all distinctions are broken down in worship, this carries over into the rest of life. It was because of what they experienced in worship, not for abstract reasons, that Friends were the first to oppose slavery and first to treat women as social equals. Barclay observes that "God hath *Effectually* in this day *Converted many Souls* by the *Ministry of Women;* . . . Which manifest Experience puts the thing beyond all Controversie."[3]

Since worship dictated the life and mission of the movement, Quakers anticipated much that would be discovered in other traditions. Centuries later, F. D. Maurice, Percy Dearmer, and Virgil Michel would express it in terms of liturgy and justice. Quaker ethics also proscribed kneeling before humans, use of honorific titles, fancy clothes, war, sports, and the swearing of oaths. Such avoidance of social distinctions and competition was simply the logical consequence of worship, where the Spirit chooses its own instruments regardless of human distinctions.

The same sense of social equality applied in meetings for business. All participated in discussions but no votes were taken, since they might push the minority into a losing situation. Instead, the clerk sought the "sense of the meeting"; if none could be discerned, decisions were postponed. It was a radical form of democracy because everyone counted. Fox urged congregations to hold monthly meetings for business; regional meetings were held quarterly, and larger areas (such as New England) had yearly meetings.

Quaker worship is not for everyone because it excludes all instincts for personal aggrandizement and places a premium on things not congenial to the natural man or natural woman: humility, self-restraint, reticence, and meekness. People with such qualities are requisite for Quaker worship; otherwise it becomes something of a hollow parody. Nor do such qualities come easily even to birthright Friends but are acquired in lifelong communal discipline. Those who transgress too much may be "disowned" (expelled) by the monthly meetings.

One of the finest examples of a Friend is the American John Woolman (1720–1772). His *Journal,*[4] published in 1774, reveals his sensitive and pious nature, especially in reflections after First-day (Sunday) meetings in which he wondered whether he had put himself forward in speaking. His worship life overflowed into crusades against slavery, military service, and the abuse of Indians. Woolman's sensitive self-restraint and concern for others in speaking at worship illustrates the type of person who helps to make Quaker worship a genuinely communal experience.

At the heart of Quaker piety is a strong corporate mysticism based on the sense that God speaks to the community through the voices of individuals. As Robert Barclay puts it, "Many candles lighted, and put in one place, do greatly augment the light." This is not an individualistic form of mysticism but one in which the public worship of the community is all-important. Indeed, the term for public worship is "meeting." Barclay speaks of the "necessity to the entertaining of a Joint and Visible Fellowship . . . and seeing the Faces of one another, that we concur with our Persons, as well as Spirits."[5]

Friends believe their worship to be utterly dependent on divine activity and not on human preparation, which was often lampooned as "will worship" and "self-pleasing." George Fox ridiculed a "hireling ministry" paid to preach sermons. If worship is enabled by God, it is presumptuous of humans to prepare sermons and prayers instead of leaving to God what is said. Such efforts, it was asserted, are only attempts to earn the praise of other humans and therefore are inherently sinful as based on "Man's Wisdom, Acts, or Industry."[6]

At the same time, biblical piety runs deep for it is clear that the same Spirit immediately present to worshipers is also the Spirit that dictated scripture. The Spirit cannot contradict itself; anything said contrary to scripture must be of human origin. First-day schools are an important part of Quaker life and focus on biblical studies. Family worship and personal devotions focus greatly on scripture reading; a high degree of biblical literacy is one of the presuppositions of Quaker worship. Yet the scriptures only declare the "Fountain"; they are subordinate to their author, the Spirit.

In many ways, the Quakers refuted the dominant Calvinism of Anglicans and Puritans alike. If, they argued, there was immediate access to God in the Spirit, this gave the Spirit higher authority than scripture, which, though true, was "secondary." Furthermore, Friends have a higher doctrine of humanity than the total depravity which was such an important part of Calvinism after the Synod of Dort, 1618–19. Nor was the atonement limited, since the Spirit is accessible to all (although most "wound it to death"). Thus predestination was emphatically challenged. The Spirit could speak to anyone, and he or she could recognize it just as if one were outdoors at noon and acknowledged that the sun was shining.

Furthermore, Friends rejected Calvin's understanding of humanity's need for visible signs in the form of visible sacraments. This is an extremely important shift in theological anthropology. For Calvin, signs are essential to humans; for the Friends, they are unimportant. The Calvinistic union of the spiritual and the physical is repudiated among Quakers because of the immediacy of the Spirit. Visible sacraments are simply not necessary when one can experience the Spirit directly in community.

Quakers argued that Christ did not intend the sacraments to be continued after his death. They could cite the disappearance of foot washing or the anointing of the sick as both "commanded with no less Authority and Solemnity."[7] The baptism of John was merely a figure, and the Lord's Supper was ordained for a limited time for the weak only and not meant to survive beyond the earliest Christians.

Barclay argues that "the Baptism of Christ, under the Gospel, is the Baptism of the Spirit and of Fire,"[8] which he contrasts to outward water baptism. The only baptism that counts is the inward one of the Spirit. In the same fashion, Quakers could claim communion with the risen Lord, not through eating and drinking perishable items but through spiritual communion with him. "The *Body* then of Christ, which believers partake of, is *Spiritual,* and not *Carnal;* and his *Blood,* which they drink of, is *Pure* and *Heavenly.* "[9]

Such disjuncture of the physical and spiritual is not for everyone, yet in Quaker piety it has worked well. Far from producing an otherworldliness, Friends have been in the forefront of engagement in works of reform and mercy. Whereas others would feel drawn to these same works by the God made visible in physical sacraments, Friends have excelled in the same works on the basis of spiritual sacraments. It is not an anthropology for most people; for Quakers it is supremely successful.

An excellent index to Quaker worship is the kind of meeting place that Friends erected. Fox had made a career of decrying the magnificent "steeple houses" of the establishment and had not infrequently invaded them during services to challenge paid preachers. But even Quakers found shelter necessary, and early in the movement they began to build meetinghouses. These were always modest buildings, often domestic in character, hidden inconspicuously down side streets and alleys.

In time, a distinct form emerged. It lacked a steeple or tower on the outside and contained no liturgical centers (pulpit, font, altar-table) on the inside. The whole interior was gathering, movement, and congregational space. The focus was entirely on people. The space was filled with benches, with often a row or two slightly elevated and facing the rest as a place for elders or recorded ministers. There is no art or other visual focal point to distract attention from the gathered community itself.

The acoustics make speech easily audible in small intimate spaces. By the eighteenth century, it had become common to have movable partitions in the middle to screen off space so women and men could meet separately on most occasions. Windlasses survive in some older buildings for raising and lowering the partitions, and various forms of folding partitions were also tried. The exterior often expresses the interior dualism by two sets of doors. In the nineteenth century the division of the sexes disappeared, and single spaces now predominate. As radical an innovation as it was when it began, the Quaker concept of worship space has changed little, and seventeenth-century meetinghouses in England, Rhode Island, and Maryland still function as originally designed.

If simplicity was a feature of Quaker space, it was even more so of time. Friends repudiated naming days or months after pagan gods, so days of the week and the months were simply numbered, which was deemed the biblical method. This means one speaks of First-day worship or Tenth-month meeting. Special days were considered human inventions: "We cannot, therefore, consistently unite with any in the observation of public fasts, feasts, and what they term holy days; or such injunctions and forms as are devised in man's will for divine worship."[10] The sole emphasis remained First-day meetings for worship.

The life cycle was equally simple. Being a "birthright" Friend was valued, but others went through "convincement" to "conversion." Converts could give testimony to having received baptism by the Spirit, and then the monthly meeting would appoint Friends to confer with them and "inquire into their lives and conversations" and, "if satisfactory to the meeting, a minute be then made thereon, signifying its acceptance of such persons as members of our society."[11] Marriages were celebrated by the couple making their vows to each other publicly, without benefit of clergy. Likewise, at funerals, members of the community might express a concern.

As could be expected, preaching was not part of classical Quaker worship. Yet the movement spread by preaching in the streets of cities by what were called "threshing" meetings. Fox cried "Woe to the bloody city of Lichfield!" and people flocked to hear what he had to say a century before the Wesleys took to the streets. Women preachers and exhorters were common two centuries before they were seen in other churches. But preaching was not to be prepared for worship. None were to speak except as the Spirit prompted.

Music was not categorically excluded, but it had to be spontaneous. People might sing their concern or a portion of a psalm or some lines especially significant to their witness. But *"Artifical Musick, either by Organs or other Instruments, or Voice, we have neither Example nor Precept for it in the New Testament."*[12]

In a sense, all Quaker worship is prayer, but it need not be verbalized. The silent waiting on God is often an inarticulate offering of one's self. And when one speaks, it is as if the voice of God were speaking to the community. At the same time, one must not pray formally without the "Motion of the Spirit." Speaking to God and listening to God shape all that happens in Quaker worship. It also must be kept in mind that most Quaker families practiced "calling together of their children and household, wait upon the Lord in their families."[13] This family worship flows into the larger community gathered on First-day for worship. Above all else, such worship comes from the Spirit: "Ever since we were a people we have had a testimony against formal worship, being convinced by the precepts of our Lord Jesus Christ, the testimonies of his apostles, and our own experience, that the worship and prayers which God accepts are such only as are produced by the influence and assistance of his Holy Spirit."[14]

The Shakers

The worship of the Shakers, or the United Society of Believers in Christ's Second Appearing, to give them their correct name, is unique especially in the sustained use of dance in worship. This practice and their hymns have influenced others.

The Shakers began in England as an offshoot of a small Quaker sect known as "Shaking Quakers." An uneducated housewife, Mother Ann Lee (ca.1736–1784), assumed leadership in 1766 and brought seven followers to settle in Watervliet near Albany, New York, in 1774. For the next decade, her life consisted of travel about that area and New England, preaching repentance and shepherding her followers.[15] She made several cryptic statements applying words of Christ to herself, which her followers interpreted after her death to mean that she had been the female incarnation of the Godhead or Christ's second appearance, this time in female form. Foremost of her religious priorities were celibacy (sex being the source of sin), confession, the sharing of worldly goods, millennialism, and ecstatic utterances in worship.

After her death, the development of the tradition was shaped by a variety of leaders. Father Joseph Meacham (1742–1796) presided over the "gathering into order" of the movement as the organization of celibate communities proceeded, beginning with New Lebanon, New York, in 1787. Shaker missionaries went west and often gathered converts from frontier revivals. Eventually, nineteen communities were established as far west as Indiana, south to Kentucky, and north and east to Maine. At the height of the movement, there were about six thousand people living celibate lives in various communities. Each community was divided into "families" of thirty to ninety men, women, and children. The community organization included elders and eldresses who were in charge of spiritual matters and heard confessions, deacons who managed temporal matters, and trustees who dealt with the outside world. The New Lebanon community leadership coordinated all others.

A series of distinguished leaders presided over the far-flung colonies. James Whittaker, Lucy Wright, Henry Blinn, Frederick Evans, and Anna White were influential leaders at various times and saw the Shakers through successive periods of development.

From early on, the Shakers were given to ecstatic outbursts of exclamations as the Spirit moved them in worship.[16] Heavily millenarian in belief, their worship celebrated the new reign of Christ on earth, beginning with the foundation of the United Society. Their worship came to have recognized physical exercises and gestures such as shaking off the devil. Other physical manifestations of ecstasy—barking, shaking, and laughing—attracted and amazed worldly visitors, who flocked to witness such spectacles when they were permitted to be present.

In time, dances for the whole community were worked out that included both slow shuffles and vigorous whirling movements in which the men and women moved in separate ranks according to established patterns. The most distinctive part of Shaker worship came to be the importance placed on dance. One Shaker document argued, "God has created nothing in vain. The faculty of dancing, as well as that of singing, was undoubtedly created for the honor and glory of the Creator; and therefore it must be devoted to his service, in order to answer that purpose."[17]

Shaker worship involved the highest degree of active participation of body and mind in worship that Christianity has ever developed. Dance was accompanied by singing hymns or the exclamation of meaningless syllables. Why were such worship forms lost? As converts decreased after the Civil War and the average age of community members advanced, older members became too feeble for such vigorous activity and dance was given up, "as it was considered necessary to maintain a perfect union among the members, a service in which all may participate as One."[18] The solidarity of the community took precedence over their most distinctive worship form.

An important era in their worship development was the period known as Mother Ann's work, 1837–1847. During this period, mystical outbursts pervaded the communities and various visitations were experienced from the Spirit world, especially Mother Ann, Indians, and various other celebrities such as Mother Lucy (Wright) and George Washington. These visitations found expression in "spirit drawings," which imparted visual images and messages from the spirits.[19] The same period saw an edict from the leadership at New Lebanon for each community to build outdoor shrines for worship on nearby mountaintops. These consisted of a carved stone surrounded by a fence. Later, an order went out to destroy all such spots.

There are important characteristics of the people who worshiped as Shakers. Most were farm folk who preferred a simple life and relished the view that it was a "gift to be simple." They valued education, but for most it did not include higher education. A number of Shakers published theological documents defending their faith and elaborated a belief structure proclaiming the need for "The Manifestation of Christ in the Female," asserting that "Ann Lee was the distinguished female who was chosen for that purpose."[20] The codification of rules for behavior went on especially in *The Millennial Laws* of 1821 and 1845.[21] These decrees guarded every detail of daily life, such as that only initials should be put on tools or clothing and that meetinghouses should have a white exterior and a white and blue interior.

Like the Quakers, the Shakers emphasized the equality of the sexes in worship and in leadership roles in the community. Men might work in the fields and women indoors, but both sexes were considered equal.[22] This found expression in the language of hymnody, which frequently used female imagery for God and balanced masculine images with feminine ones.[23]

The combination of a highly regulated form of daily life with a strong mystical piety helped give Shaker worship its ecstatic quality. Worship provided an outlet for emotional expression, yet always within a communal experience. Although individuals produced the spirit drawings, wrote new hymns, and composed tunes, such piety always found expression in the context of a community that both encouraged and regulated personal expressions of piety. Confession to the elders or eldresses, separation from the world, and common ownership of property all served to strengthen the corporate nature of Shaker piety.

Shaker worship demanded special spaces. The meetinghouse stood at the center of each colony. Ten of these were built in the late eighteenth century by Moses Johnson,[24] and examples of his work still survive at Sabbathday Lake, Maine (1794), Canterbury, New Hampshire (1792–93), and Hancock (from Shirley), Massachusetts (1792–1795). The liturgical space in these and all other Shaker meetinghouses is entirely movement space, although seating was sometimes provided for the elderly or for spectators from the world. Like Quaker meetinghouses, there are two doors, one for men and one for women; the elders and eldresses usually lived above the worship space.

These buildings provided an important experience of empty and nondirectional space in which the whole focus was on simplicity. No one place was more prominent than any other. The community itself supplied the only ornament and it was free, unhampered by pews or liturgical centers, to express its faith through movement. The ascetic beauty and flexibility of surviving Shaker buildings make them worthy of attention today.

Worship was offered daily by the total Shaker community in the meetinghouse, and the "families" might meet for prayer. The ministry could call for special events, but basically the calendar was marked only by Sunday observances. As with the Quakers, there were no visible sacraments, since they were only "figures or symbols of spiritual substances, which were to take place in a future day."[25] There might be private ceremonies of signing away of private property when new members joined the community or to signal acceptance of orphans. And there were sad occasions when some individuals returned to the ways of the world, either voluntarily or through expulsion, and their property was returned.

Although the movement spread at first by field preaching, this was not an important part of worship. Explanations and interpretations of Shaker life were occasionally delivered at worship services for the benefit of spectators from the world who might be present.

Spontaneous outbursts might be delivered on occasion at the prompting of the Spirit. This often took the form of prayer, which could address the Deity in extravagant terms or in nonsense syllables.

The relationship of dance to music is close. Unlike the Quakers, the Shakers developed a large repertoire of hymnody,[26] some of which, such as "Simple Gifts" of 1848, consists in part of sung rubrics for dance movements: " 'Tis the gift to come down / Where we ought to be." Hymns were sung both as a part of dance and while standing still. Most hymn singing was unaccompanied; however, the Canterbury, New Hampshire, community eventually installed a pipe organ. In the educational process, music education was taken seriously. The Shakers produced a number of tunes for their own singing and adapted others. Their most distinctive contribution to hymnody was the expression of their own theological views with female imagery for God and passages about the end of the present world. Shaker theology found its best expression in hymns that all could sing. Various Shaker hymnals were produced, and both words and tunes provide unique contributions to hymnody.

Today, Shaker worship is confined to two small communities at Sabbathday Lake, Maine, and Canterbury, New Hampshire. But the Shakers inspired others to sense the possibilities for worshiping with the whole body, provided hymns, advanced the concepts of feminine imagery in Christian worship, and showed how ascetic space can be eloquent as a setting for Christian worship. As a variant of the Quaker tradition, the Shakers had an influence all out of proportion to their small numbers.

Developments in Quaker Worship

Quaker worship has continued to evolve beyond its seventeenth-century origins and eighteenth-century maturity. In the early decades of the nineteenth century, controversy erupted over the teaching of Elias Hicks (1748–1830), who tended to stress the Christ within over against the authority of the Bible and the historical person of Jesus Christ. From 1827–28 on, the Hicksites developed as a branch that stressed inner experience as of supreme importance. In opposition, orthodox Friends emphasized the authority of scripture and written doctrine. The Hicksites became intensely involved in social action, especially in the antislavery movement. Unitarianism and other liberal currents of the day found their expression in Quakerism among the Hicksites.

A far more important development occurred in the West. As we have seen several times already, the frontier acted as a liturgical "black hole," swallowing up the established traditions of the more staid and sober East Coast and casting them out transformed. The traditions that went through such drastic transformations thrived and grew dramatically on the frontier; those that refused to change remained minority elements unless replenished by fresh immigration.

Certain Friends, especially in Ohio and Indiana, saw the transformations that were occurring in other traditions and the resultant growth on the frontier and decided to adopt similar techniques for the promotion of Quakerism, which had always had a strong missionary thrust. On the frontier, this meant adopting many revivalist measures, even though they had little in common with classical Quakerism, including full-time Quaker ministers, who could conduct revivals and preach for conversion. Eventually it meant a move to structured or programmed worship, much like that of other frontier churches. Traditional Quaker silent meetings were not designed to attract prospective converts; they were for the already converted. But meetings with preaching, hymn singing, and altar calls could and did produce new Quakers, although it altered many of the most distinctive characteristics of Quaker worship.[27]

In the years 1837–1840 an English Quaker, Joseph John Gurney (1788–1847), toured America urging the adoption of the revivalist techniques. He persuaded many in the Midwest, and the success of the new techniques began to be reflected in numerous converts. His followers, known as Gurneyites, spread across the Midwest, conforming largely to existing frontier patterns, even to attempts to introduce visible sacraments.[28] Opposition to these innovations in worship came from East Coast Friends, particularly from the followers of a Rhode Island Quaker, John Wilbur (1774–1856), who became known as Wilburites. In Indiana and Ohio and points west, Gurneyites prevailed; ironically, there now exists a Friends seminary in Richmond, Indiana, producing candidates for a paid clergy.

The result is a division in the Quaker tradition. The classical Friends, largely on the American East Coast and in England, practice unstructured worship in which there are no clergy and worship revolves around silent waiting on God. On the other hand, probably the larger number of American Friends today have clergy and services that are programmed with preaching, music, and prepared prayers. Sometimes these services are semistructured, giving time to individual witness in the context of other prepared items. Both patterns have their advantages; unstructured worship is clearly that of the classical period of Quaker worship while structured worship represents an adaptation to a cultural period, the American frontier, where such change was considered necessary. Thus Quaker worship survives today both by adapting and by refusing to change.

9

Methodist Worship

The Methodist tradition of worship began in the eighteenth century, much later than those we have already considered. Not only had the controversies of the Reformation era long disappeared but the battle over control of the Church of England that had marked most of the previous century had finally been put to rest. Indeed, too much peace was probably the greatest problem in English religion at the time, manifesting itself in general indifference. But such peace also brought about the possibility of a less partisan and more universal approach to worship.

By Methodist worship, we mean that of the disciples and descendants of John Wesley (1703–1791), his brother, Charles (1707–1788), and numerous other co-workers, most of them, in the initial stages, Anglican clergymen. This tradition of worship is located most obviously in those churches called "Methodist" or "Wesleyan" in the United Kingdom and the United States. It also continues, in varying degrees, in more than fifty other churches that have separated from Methodists at one time or another: the Salvation Army, the Church of the Nazarene, and various Holiness churches of the non-Pentecostal variety. Some, such as the Salvation Army, have modified the Methodist worship tradition drastically; others have been less innovative. At the same time, Methodists have been prone to merge with churches of other traditions, as in the United Church of Canada (1925), Church of South India (1947), and Uniting Church of Australia (1985), usually conflating worship practices along with denominational polity. At the same time, Methodists have assimilated others, such as the Evangelical United Brethren Church in 1968. Thus the Methodist tradition has often become anonymous as the result of divisions and mergers. It is easier to define the tradition's central core than its outer boundaries.

The place of the Methodist tradition in the scheme of Protestant worship is not immediately apparent. Because of the time distance

from Reformation controversies, John Wesley was able to rein-
troduce some features of late-medieval piety and practice: the eucharist as it implies a sacrifice, frequent celebrations of the eucharist,
vigils, and fasting. These practices alone could place Methodism to
the far right of Protestant worship traditions. On the other hand,
Methodism is a secondary or even tertiary tradition, reflecting later
developments within both Anglican and Puritan traditions. Pietism
is certainly present too, especially from the Moravian phase of the
Lutheran tradition. Significantly, Wesley made a pilgrimage in 1738
to the Moravian center at Herrnhut just after the heartwarming
experience at Aldersgate that began his most significant work.

The Puritan tradition is strongly represented; both of Wesley's
grandfathers were nonconformist ministers, and his mother's family
included influential Puritans from Dorchester, the Whites. Wesley's
alterations to the *BCP* reflect much of the Puritan agenda for worship as expressed in the 1603 "Millenary Petition" and the 1661
"Exceptions of the Ministers." Yet Wesley repudiated the emphasis
that Puritans (and many Anglicans) placed on predestination. At the
same time, Wesley's eucharistic doctrine is probably closest to that
of John Calvin.

But the matrix of Wesley's work was always his beloved Anglican
tradition. Whenever possible, he extolled the virtues "of a solid,
scriptural, rational Piety" and departed from Anglican practice only
when souls were at stake. Thus Wesley would break canon law by
invading others' parishes if it were necessary to save souls.

Methodist worship was also greatly transformed by the nineteenth-century experience of the American frontier and both shaped
and assimilated the Frontier tradition of worship. In turn, Methodist
worship provided the background for yet another worship tradition,
the Pentecostal.

Where do we locate Methodist worship on the scheme? It seems
most appropriate to consider it a central tradition, not unlike the
Reformed tradition. In the general context of American Protestant
worship, Methodist worship is probably as central as any.

We shall deal first with Methodism's eighteenth-century origins in
Great Britain, then look at worship on the American frontier with
its subsequent nineteenth-century developments, and finally turn to
the characteristics of twentieth-century Methodist worship.

Eighteenth-century Origins

The original reasons for the formation of the Methodist tradition
in worship were missional. John Wesley faced the problem of reaching unchurched masses in the new industrial and mining centers of
England. We shall call his method "pragmatic traditionalism": that

is, use the methods of current practice where they work; otherwise, search the universal tradition for practices that have worked in similar situations. Thus Wesley could accept field preaching (although reluctantly, at first) because it was both apostolic and effective; the love feast he defended because it was the ancient agape; and the watch night was simply a new form of vigils. Hymn singing could be justified on the grounds of biblical precedent, the ancient fathers, and Lutheran practice. In his pragmatic traditionalism, Wesley is not so much an innovator as a restorer. He is a good Anglican in his love of tradition, but it is a tradition that can liberate, that can reform the present. Wesley was a patristics scholar, and no one ever has shown better how relevant the early church can be to practice.

Methodist worship was a countercultural movement in the midst of the English Enlightenment. As we have seen, sacramental worship had been pushed to the margin of church life among both Anglicans and Nonconformists. Sacraments were reduced to social propriety (in the case of baptism) or ethical motivation (in the case of eucharist), with little thought that either sacrament might be divine intrusion into this well-ordered universe. It was not intellectually respectable to make the sacraments central in an atmosphere that so completely dissociated the physical and visible from the inward and spiritual.

If anything was unfashionable in Georgian England, it was enthusiasm. The Wesleyan movement was constantly denounced for producing Spirit-filled Christians or "enthusiasts" rather than staid pewholders. Enthusiasm was especially distrusted because it made religion primarily a matter of the heart rather than the head. Rationalism simply could not tolerate such enthusiasm. Yet Wesley did reflect some of the liberal currents of the time, especially his dislike for the stern denunciations of the Athanasian Creed.

Another reason Methodism was considered not socially respectable was that it reached out primarily to the poor.[1] In an era that placed so much emphasis on power and prestige, a few Anglican priests had no concern with advancement but identified with "the meaner sort," who were powerless politically and economically. To reach the poor urban masses, one had to go beyond the parish system and develop a whole new form of mission. This outreach shaped Methodist worship in definite ways.

Methodism, then, began as a countercultural movement in the midst of an era of rational religion. The members of the Holy Club of students and dons at Oxford were ridiculed for the methodical emphasis on sacraments and daily prayer, hence they were called "Methodists" or "sacramentarians." John Wesley's mission to America in 1735–1738 was far less successful than he had hoped, but it brought important contacts with the Moravians and in 1737 Wesley published in Charleston the first Anglican hymnal, *Collection of Psalms and Hymns.* Wesley's return to England led to his Aldersgate experience of inward assurance of salvation in 1738 and the radical step of preaching in the fields. From then on, Wesley's life for over half a century was incessant riding across the British Isles to preach, organize, and guide the people called Methodists.

Charles Wesley poured forth the greatest treasury of hymns in the English language, over six thousand of them. In 1784, John Wesley put his hand to revising the *BCP* for America. His *Sunday Service for the Methodists in North America*[2] was the rather conservative work of one who loved the 1662 *BCP* but saw the need to adapt it to the times. He accepted most of the 1661 Puritan "Exceptions" to the *BCP* and made a number of changes of his own. In particular, he tried to encourage a weekly eucharist by making the combined Sunday services less burdensome. This book provided the background for Methodist rites for over two hundred years. Contrary to his wishes, Methodists in England separated from the Church of England shortly after Wesley's death, while American Methodists had been organized as an independent church since 1784. Nevertheless, English Methodists kept a strong affinity for the worship forms of the established church.

One cannot describe the origins of Methodist worship without attention to the early Methodist people. Wesley faced the problem of ministering to the new urban poor in such places as London, Bristol, and Newcastle. The parliamentary system for creating new parishes had failed to provide a satisfactory means for reaching the vast population jamming the cities. The mines and "dark satanic mills" employed many of the countryfolk who had been forced off the land as "the deserted village" became a widespread phenomenon. Here was a new social system that the established church, largely staffed by younger sons of squires, was poorly equipped to serve.

New forms of mission had to be found in worship as well as new systems for health, education, and public welfare to minister to a largely unchurched population. The inhibitions that restrained educated and affluent people could be ignored. People could sing and shout with uninhibited joy. The level of active participation could be raised by encouraging people to sing with fervor, give personal testimonies, and pray spontaneously in class meetings. Although Wesley was careful not to confuse genuine religious affections with mere boisterous behavior, Methodist worship invited vigorous and loud participation. Scant wonder, then, that it was labeled "enthusiasm," for there was an abundance of outward signs of the Spirit's inward working.

With the fields ripe for harvest, the number of Anglican clergy willing to help was far from sufficient and Wesley early began to use lay preachers, eventually even some women. A constant problem was the lack of clergy willing to celebrate the eucharist frequently. Wesley took the conservative position, that ordained clergy were necessary for the celebration of the eucharist. Late in life, he felt forced to ordain elders (presbyters) for "those poor sheep in the wilderness" in America and finally for the British Isles. He did not take the liberal position of allowing lay leadership of the eucharist but found new roles for laity in preaching and pastoral functions in the societies and classes. Thus although there was a great increase in lay leadership of worship, it did not include the sacraments. Laity were enlisted "to feed and guide, to teach and govern the flock" of societies, penitents, and classes.[3]

Shifts in piety shaped the new Methodist tradition, especially in Wesley's insistence on the instituted means of grace. In his sermon on "The Means of Grace,"[4] Wesley makes it clear that these consist of searching the scriptures, receiving the Lord's Supper, and prayer. Elsewhere he adds to these, as "ordinances of God," "fasting, or abstinence."[5] Christians were to be immersed in scripture through frequent attendance at preaching services and in personal and group Bible study.

The Lord's Supper was of great importance. At a time when frequent celebration of the eucharist was rare in most parish churches, Wesley preached on "The Duty of Constant Communion," insisting that "do this" meant it should be done as frequently as possible.[6] Wesley himself received communion on "an average of once every four or five days" throughout his lifetime.[7] Such frequency had been rare in Protestantism since the sixteenth century, and it required great ingenuity for Wesley to try to provide sufficient Anglican clergy to meet the needs of Methodist people for the sacrament. Wesley observed that for many lukewarm Christians the eucharist could be both a confirming and converting ordinance.

Prayer was the third means of grace and was encouraged in the parish church services (Methodist services being scheduled at other than "church" hours), in the Methodist societies and classes, and in the family.

The "General Rules," which gave Methodism much of the character of a religious third order, encouraged fasting at regular intervals as an important religious discipline. This was about as countercultural as one could be in a self-indulgent century!

Another factor shaping Methodist piety was "Christian conference." Part of Wesley's genius as organizer was to provide support groups for converts, whom he organized in societies, bands, and classes. The Methodist society in a community would meet regularly for lay preaching services and for the eucharist whenever a clergyman was available. But small class meetings provided the place for examination of conscience, spiritual direction, testimony to one's religious growth, and prayer together. Thus worship and discipline were intimately related. Indeed, a ticket from class meeting was necessary for receiving the eucharist with the society. The small class meeting never existed in isolation but was always feeding people back into the larger society or the church. The early Methodist people prayed with their peers in class meeting, with the society in the local community, and frequently in the parish church. At its best, it brought a combination of public prayer, preaching, and the eucharist. Such a balance has been hard to achieve at any time in Christian history, but Methodists accomplished it during the eighteenth century in England despite formidable obstacles.

The structuring of time showed important changes for the Methodist people. Wesley hoped everyone would receive the eucharist weekly when possible. Lay preachers could provide weekly preaching services, and the class meetings met on a weekly basis under a lay leader.[8] The preaching services were regarded as supplemental to worship in the parish church: the Anglican Sunday morning prayer, litany, and ante-communion with sermon.

On a monthly basis, there were special services, such as watch night, Wesley's version of vigils.[9] Usually held on a moonlit night (for reasons of safety), these were times for preaching, prayer, testimony, and hymn singing. Occasionally, the love feast[10] would be held when eucharists were not possible. Administered with bread and water, this derived from the ancient church via the Moravians and was an occasion for sharing of prayer, testimony, and hymn singing. Testimony was a spontaneous sharing by any individual present with a story of God's grace in that person's life. In effect, it gave everyone a chance to proclaim God's work.

Unlike many of their contemporaries, the Wesleys regarded the Christian year with enormous seriousness. John Wesley's *Journals* show careful observance of prayer-book feasts such as All Saints' Day.[11] Many of the hymns of Charles Wesley were written to celebrate these events, "Hark! the Herald Angels Sing" and "Christ the Lord Is Risen Today" being the best known. In his *Sunday Service,* John Wesley could not refrain from tidying up the calendar, with Sundays numbered after Christmas until "the Sunday next before Easter" and after Trinity. Nevertheless, he could excise much: "Most of the holy-days (so called) are omitted, as at present answering no valuable end," a thoroughly pragmatic decision. Propers remain only for Christmas, Good Friday, and Ascension in addition to the Sundays.

Wesley added one annual event, the Covenant Renewal service, held New Year's Day.[12] Ultimately deriving from biblical precedents such as Joshua 24, the immediate source was a service developed by

Presbyterians Richard (1611–1681) and Joseph Alleine (1634–1688) in the previous century. In recent times, it has been somewhat duplicated by the annual reaffirmation of baptismal vows at the Baptism of the Lord as introduced since 1976 in many Methodist churches.

The lifetime cycle brought other changes. Wesley kept and defended infant baptism. But, like the Puritans, he saw no purpose in confirmation and omitted the rite from his prayer book. The conscious experience of conversion was the crucial event, but it had no liturgical reflection. This experience of new birth had far more practical consequences than infant baptism, for it brought full assurance that one's sin was forgiven and that one was justified with God. Conversion was an exhilarating experience of justifying grace. Recollection of this event could fill a lifetime with rejoicing. Converts were shepherded in classes and societies where the white flame of conversion could be kept burning brightly.

Wesley made some significant changes in the rites of passage.[13] With no apparent precedent he eliminated the giving away of the bride in the wedding service. He also removed the giving of rings (as the Puritans had advocated). The burial rite was changed to make the ultimate destination of the deceased seem less certain, Wesley finding the *BCP* service too presumptuous. Changes were made in the ordination rites, with forms for ordaining deacons, elders, and "superintendents."[14] All mention of the power to forgive sin was eliminated from the rite for elders. In general, Wesley had problems with any forms that presumed to know the spiritual state of the recipient, whether alive or dead.

There were significant developments in the place for worship. In 1739, Wesley persuaded himself "to be more vile" and began preaching in the fields and anywhere he could reach a crowd. He leap-frogged over five centuries of indoor worship to the days of the early mendicant friars and their preaching at market crosses. When possible, "preaching houses" were built to enable indoor preaching services. Wesley resisted the legal definition of these as dissenting chapels.[15] For many years, his model was the Octagon Chapel in Norwich (1756). Wesley's premise was that such octagonal buildings (with balconies) brought the largest number of people close to the preacher at minimum expense. Late in life, he built City Road Chapel in London (1778). A font appeared, and City Road Chapel functioned almost as a parish church. Eventually, Methodist chapels were built all over England and Wales, unpretentious brick buildings on back lanes without steeple or portico but usually with balconies, an elevated pulpit, and a communion table ringed with rails.

If the times and places of worship changed, so did the style of preaching.[16] Although emotions were not sought for their own sake, they were not avoided either. Methodist preaching was directed to the heart as well as to the head. It was a constant offering of a crucified Savior calling for conversion of life, a far cry from the tepid moral rationalism heard from most Anglican and Nonconformist pulpits of the time. More often than not, the preacher might be a neighbor or local man or woman who had received a call to preach and had been examined and licensed under careful supervision. The link between preaching and pastoral care was always clear. Wesley felt that simply making converts without careful spiritual direction afterward was breeding souls for damnation.

Wesley balanced both sides of the controversy over free and fixed forms of prayer by advocating both at every level of worship. His eucharistic rite concludes (after all the fixed forms) with the rubric, "Then the Elder, if he see it expedient, may put up an Extempore Prayer."[17] Such prayer was to be prepared for the time, not left to chance. Wesley always defended the *BCP* with its fixed prayers and used it faithfully each day. But he was equally firm on the need to supplement the official forms with prayer conceived for the occasion.

Furthermore, he expanded the numbers of those who were to pray in public so that class meetings involved spontaneous prayer offered by anyone present. And what was done in the public session of the class was replicated daily at home in family prayers. Being able to address the Almighty publicly and extemporaneously in prayer was an ability expected of any Methodist, even though read prayers were also encouraged. Wesley advised ministers in America to use the full liturgy "on the Lord's Day, in all their congregations, reading the litany only on Wednesday and Fridays, and praying extempore on all other days."[18]

Methodism's greatest contribution to ecumenical Christianity has been in the form of hymnody. The result of introducing hymnody to wide use in England was to allow a far greater degree of active participation so that all could express their worship with the best of their musical talent. Many of the over six thousand hymns by Charles Wesley consist of doctrine written as poetry, in some instances literally theological treatises versified.[19] But Charles Wesley was able to use the poetic forms of the time to achieve this without being tedious or didactic. "Come, O Thou Traveler Unknown," sometimes called the best of his hymns, is a poetic version of Genesis 32, Jacob at Penuel. What people sang became the theology they learned, and what they learned shaped their lives.

Frequently, the hymns are the best source of Wesleyan theology. The 166 *Hymns on the Lord's Supper,* published in 1745, are one of the greatest treasures in English of eucharistic piety.[20] They also are the chief document for Wesleyan eucharistic theology. With their emphasis on the eucharist as sacrifice, the work of the Holy Spirit,

and strong eschatological flavor, they seem to belong much more to
the early church or the present than to the eighteenth century.

The hymns gave the people much active participation in worship
and punctuated every service. Familiar tunes were used to make
them as singable as possible. On the other hand, Wesley's prayer
book makes no provision for service music, and organs were too
expensive. Nor did he approve of choir anthems, "because they
cannot be properly called joint worship." Music was a form for active
participation by everyone rather than passive listening.

Nineteenth-century Developments

The journey across the Atlantic brought a real sea change in
Methodist worship. Although many of the themes of Wesley's movement endured, they were transmuted by personalities and circumstances he could not have envisioned. The real founder of American
Methodism was Bishop Francis Asbury (1745–1816), whose role it
was to preside over the expansion of Methodism from the strip of
states along the seacoast to the vast heartland beyond the Appalachian mountains. Asbury, although English born, was attuned to the
new American situation. Wesley's pragmatism had great appeal to
him, Wesley's traditionalism very little. The result was a mostly
pragmatic reformation of worship for American circumstances.

Wesley's love for the *BCP,* his emphasis on frequent eucharists,
his affection for the church year—none of these survived passage
across the Atlantic. William Wade has shown that, unlike Wesley,
Asbury scarcely noted Christmas Day in his journals, let alone the
lesser feasts of the Christian year.[21] Although Asbury successfully
stopped an attempt to allow unordained men to administer the eucharist, it seems to have been more a matter of church discipline than
to defend a traditional approach to the sacrament. Asbury's piety
focused on preaching and disciplined life, not on sacraments and
fixed forms for prayer.

The key event came in 1792, a year after Wesley's death. The 314
pages of his prayer book were quietly laid aside in favor of 37 pages
of "Sacramental Services, &c." in the *Discipline* of that year. Jesse
Lee (1758–1816) tells us that the ministers were convinced that "they
could pray better, and with more devotion while their eyes were shut,
than they could with their eyes open."[22] All that survived this discarding were services for the baptism of infants and adults, the
second half of the Lord's Supper, weddings, burials, and the three
ordination rites. These became standard items in the *Discipline;* the
rest of the *Sunday Service* seems to have been little missed. After
1808, the *Discipline* was revised every four years, and minor changes

frequently appear. The rites in the *Discipline* were named the "Ritual" in 1848 and 1870.

The *Discipline* continued to carry a brief notice as to what should be included in the normal Sunday morning and evening services, especially insisting on the reading of scripture "chapters" or, later, "lessons." The 1828 *Discipline* was concerned to promote "establishment of uniformity in public worship," and frequent appeals were made that the "Ritual invariably be used," probably good evidence that it was not. New services were added in 1864 for the laying of a cornerstone and the dedication of a church building and for the reception into church membership of probationary members. The year 1876 brought the first recommendation of the use of "pure unfermented juice of the grape" for the Lord's Supper. This eventually became mandatory until 1988. Such a move resulted from the work of a pious dentist, Dr. Thomas B. Welch (1825–1903), who discovered in 1869 a means of pasteurizing grape juice that prevented fermentation. As a former Methodist preacher, Welch sought a non-alcoholic sacramental wine. He adapted technology recently developed by Louis Pasteur to make grape juice a possibility.[23]

As the century continued, others became concerned for the recovery of set forms, especially Thomas O. Summers (1812–1882), Dean of Vanderbilt Divinity School and general book editor for the Methodist Episcopal Church, South. He oversaw a reprint of Wesley's *Sunday Service,* edited a collection of prayers, *The Golden Censer,* [24] and developed a standard order of worship.

Summers's background was English and he reflects different developments in England, where Wesley's prayer book or even the *BCP* were used by some Methodists through much of the nineteenth century. The Catholic Revival in the Church of England brought a negative reaction from many British Methodists, who moved further from the forms of prayer-book worship and, as a result, from Wesley. In time, however, Methodists began to accept the Gothic revival[25] and some of the practices of the Catholic Revival.

These are the bare bones of nineteenth-century developments. The reality needs flesh and blood, and we must begin with the actual people involved. There seems to have been a split in worship between the settled East Coast and the frontier west of the Appalachians. Ralph Waldo Emerson remarked that England stopped at the Appalachians, America began beyond them. Churches on the seaboard tended to be in settled towns where conventional forms of ministry could function. Worship there tended to be relatively sober and sedate. By contrast, the frontier had few settlements but a widely scattered population of largely unchurched people who ventured up rivers and creeks wherever fertile land could be found to farm.[26]

People so isolated could not come to church, so Methodist circuit riders went to them. Incessantly on the move, these itinerant preachers were the friars of the time, mostly celibate, always poor, and obedient to the presiding elder (district superintendent). They visited families, preached to whatever groups they could assemble, and soon adopted the practice of bringing large crowds together for annual camp meetings (see chapter 10).

In the process, Methodism learned to adapt worship to the unchurched people on the frontier, who, first of all, had to be brought to Christian faith itself. Certainly no prayer book could appeal to largely illiterate people, but simple songs could. Sedate and fixed forms did not recommend themselves in such situations, but spontaneity and excitement did. For frontier people, freedom was important and structures not. So the frontier developed forms of worship that were demonstrative and uninhibited, abounding with shouts and exclamations and fervent singing. People who had sought freedom on the frontier were not about to sacrifice it in worship. They responded to worship that allowed them to shout their feelings about what the preacher was saying or engage in physical movements such as the altar call, at which converts were summoned to come forward to be welcomed at the communion rail.

A good representative of this period was Peter Cartwright (1785–1872), who preached all over Kentucky, Ohio, and Illinois as circuit rider and presiding elder.[27] As rough-and-ready as the people to whom he ministered, Cartwright was the epitome of pragmatism in introducing whatever new forms seemed effective in worship. He had little regard for tradition, much concern for whatever methods would win souls. His preaching and pastoral care brought many of the unchurched to Christian conversion. Their worship reflected the unpolished life-styles of these new Christians.

An important development in this period was the emergence of Christian worship among blacks, especially in the South and West.[28] Worship had a particular function for these oppressed people, playing a bonding role for the community in both suffering and hope. In many ways, blacks adapted the worship forms of whites, but it also was a reciprocal development as both cultures affected each other.[29] For example, white spirituals were fused with African culture to produce black spirituals that became a common treasure of church music.

Richard Allen (1760–1831) became the first black American bishop in 1816 and led in the formation of the African Methodist Episcopal Church. Like the church's name, the worship was of the Methodist tradition but in a different cultural style. Freedom was observed in the usual Sunday service, but a "Ritual" closely similar to that of the predominantly white Methodist churches appears in the Disciplines of most of the major black Methodist churches.

As might be expected, the piety of people on the frontier developed along different lines from that in England or even on the East Coast. The culture was highly individualistic and this tended to be the case with piety, best expressed in the camp-meeting songs that focused on first person singular. Charles Wesley's "Jesus, Lover of My Soul" would more likely have been, on the frontier, "My Soul, Lover of Jesus." The personal relation of the individual to God was paramount, and songs expressed contrition for sin, joy in salvation, and hope of sanctification. Simple lyrics could easily be memorized: "Come to Jesus just now / Just now come to Jesus." Much of the piety was otherworldly, as in hymns such as "This World Is All a Fleeting Show" or "There Is a Land of Pleasure."[30]

In all this, the institutional church played a relatively minor role. Those converted were put to work in helping to continue revivals or advance some good cause: distribution of tracts, Bible circulation, Sunday schools, missions, abolition, women's rights, and temperance. By the end of the century, the temperance cause had helped women discover political power in America and led to elimination of fermented wine at the Lord's Supper. All these movements were celebrated in songs used in worship. A very activist hymnody developed in addition to the personal "Jesus-and-me" type. Usually the demonic character of a particular evil (such as rum) was excoriated and then the triumph of virtue hailed.

Because Methodism expanded so rapidly, the discipline of the class meeting tended to disappear, although the worship function of these sessions was transferred to the midweek prayer service. Often led by laity, individuals continued to share their joys and sorrows as they prayed with and for one another. Such prayer was almost entirely spontaneous and interspersed with hymns.

The Wesleys' sacramental piety did not transplant in American soil. The only available alternative was the prevalent enlightenment attitude to the sacraments, which saw them as divine commands but not as essential means of grace. The Disciplines often mandated that people have access to the sacrament quarterly and made provisions for securing an ordained elder for such occasions. For a number of churches, this remained the norm although the Methodist Episcopal Church, South (1844–1939), always more conservative and Wesleyan, mandated monthly communion in some Disciplines and this survives in parts of the South. Wesley's eucharistic hymns disappeared entirely from the hymnal in 1905 and 1935, only to begin a slow return in the late twentieth century. Defense of infant baptism was the subject of many tracts and the chief point of conflict with

Baptists. Fasting was an early casualty, although temperance became an important crusade after the Civil War.

On the frontier, time took on a new sense of meaning. Much depended on the circuit rider's making his way around a vast area. The year was also punctuated by camp meetings. Peter Cartwright went to camp meeting in May 1801 and was converted. Gradually, local preachers were appointed and began to hold weekly preaching services, leaving it to the circuit rider to administer the sacraments on his next visit.

The weekly pattern included both Sunday and midweek services. Sunday morning services were somewhat more formal than the evening service, which was likely to place emphasis on altar prayers in which worshipers knelt at the communion rail (usually called the "altar"). The Disciplines suggest more scripture reading in the morning, probably to allow more time for altar prayers and singing in the evening. The midweek prayer services attracted the inner circle of church members. These included prayer, a lesson, testimony, singing, and a benediction.[31] As the century wore on, Sunday school also came to be an important part in church life, beginning with "opening exercises" of informal worship consisting of prayers and songs, before dividing into classes by age groups for study.

The traditional church year meant little but a new pragmatic calendar developed around local festivals. The quarterly visits of an ordained elder for the sacraments were red-letter days. In addition, periodic revivals were held, frequently lasting the better part of a week. There might be pilgrimages to nearby campgrounds for camp meetings; this gave way after 1874 to the much more refined Chautauqua meetings, a significant transition.[32] As the exodus of youth from farming communities accelerated, homecoming services became an annual feature, with dinner on the grounds. Methodists usually kept an annual watch night at New Year's Eve when others were less piously occupied. It was not the church year Wesley envisioned but one that functioned well in a period of Christianizing a continent.

In the life cycle, the chief change came about mid-century with the realization that Methodism was not just a religious society that could be attached to other churches but a church in its own right. The chief sign of this was the new "Form for Receiving Persons into the Church after Probation" of 1864. Probationary members were adults who had been baptized but for whom a six-month period of scrutiny was required after their baptism rather than before it. Eventually, as discipline slackened, the term was changed to "preparatory members" and finally applied only to those baptized as infants. The attempt to keep a disciplined church had finally been turned over to the Sunday school. In 1964, the term for the service introduced in

1864 was changed to "The Order for Confirmation and Reception into the Church," unleashing even greater theological confusion. But, with the stubbornness of a recent tradition, the term "Confirmation" proved impossible to dislodge even when attempts to remove it were made in the post-Vatican II reforms.

A significant change in the wedding rite was dropping the term "obey" from the betrothal vows as early as 1864 in the Methodist Episcopal Church and in 1910 in the Methodist Episcopal Church, South. This progressive act was balanced by restoring the giving away of the bride in 1916, recovering the ring ceremony in the 1860s, and making the service more like that of the 1662 *BCP*. Burial and ordination rites underwent minor revisions during this century.

If the times of worship changed throughout the century, places did likewise. The period began with much worship being held outdoors, in temporary brush arbors in wooded regions. Eventually, more-or-less permanent camp-meeting grounds were established, with tents for people to camp on the grounds for a week or so, and these finally gave way to cottages.[33] Eventually, Methodists built churches in virtually every town and village in America, some 39,000 of them. A reminder of the primitive brush arbors remains in many country churches in the form of outdoor tables for gathering "on the grounds" at homecomings.

As civilization intruded on the frontier, church buildings evolved through all the fashionable styles of the nineteenth century. Methodist churches were identifiable on the interior by always having a communion rail, which frequently encircled the altar-table and pulpit platform. The pulpit evolved from a wineglass form or tub pulpit to a desk on a platform behind which invariably stood three chairs: one each for minister, visiting preacher, and song leader. A pedestal font or portable basin completed the liturgical centers.

A major change in church architecture in the nineteenth century was brought about by the advent of the Sunday school movement. Many wooden churches were jacked up and a lower floor built beneath or else they were floored over at the balcony level. The climax was the advent of the Akron plan, invented by industrialist Lewis Miller (1829–1899) in Akron, Ohio, in 1868. Organ pipes, choir, pulpit platform, altar-table, and communion rail were tucked in descending order in a corner, surrounded by semicircular pews on a sloping floor. Adjacent Sunday school space could be opened by sliding doors on festive occasions, revealing the school's central space for opening exercises and classrooms on floor and balcony levels. It was a highly functional arrangement of space that occurred at a time of eclecticism in architectural style. Because of the eclectic styles, most leave much to be desired aesthetically but they do document the worship form.

These churches were especially designed for preaching, which was to be the principal focus and climax of the usual service. The type of evangelistic preaching for conversion that thrived on the unchurched frontier gradually became institutionalized, even for East Coast churches. The function of preaching seemed to be largely to call people to conversion or to rekindle the white heat of that moment of one's personal experience. Special seasons of the year might feature revival preaching, with emphasis on repentance and conversion.

A distinctive feature of nineteenth-century Methodist worship was that people knelt for prayer, usually facing the pew. Indeed, some editions of the 1905 *Hymnal* carried a rubric advising worshipers to face the preacher when they knelt. Prayer was important in worship but it became almost exclusively clericalized in the Sunday morning service in what came to be known as the "pastoral" or "long" prayer. In this, the preacher covered the whole gamut of prayer from confession to oblation, from praise to intercession, using Elizabethan rhetoric. In Sunday evening services, those who wished to were invited to kneel in prayer at the communion rail. In the midweek prayer service, all could express their concerns aloud in prayer. Some felt the need for more guidance, and collections such as Thomas O. Summer's *The Golden Censer* must have been used in some churches. But protests over increasing "formalism" occurred over such moderate innovations as a full order of worship for the first time in a Methodist hymnal in the 1880 *New Hymnbook*. An order had appeared in the 1870 southern church's *Discipline* and another followed in the northern *Discipline* of 1888. Family prayers flourished, and there was no lack of small books designed to guide families in praying together.

Music thrived in Methodist worship. The frontier had known black and white spirituals. A specific type of revival music developed, simplistic in wording, theology, and music but capable of expressing the heartfelt yearnings of new converts.

A peculiarly Methodist contribution was the work of Fanny Crosby (1820–1915), who, though blind, wrote over two thousand hymns. They represent the individualism of the day with concern for the state of one's own soul, such as "Safe in the Arms of Jesus," "Pass Me Not, O Gentle Savior," and "Blessed Assurance, Jesus Is Mine!" Few if any other women have had such an impact on Protestant worship in America as this devout poet. Hers was a hymnody of personal experience, and that was just what the times wanted.[34]

The more flamboyant music of Ira D. Sankey (1840–1908) accompanied the preaching of Dwight L. Moody (1837–1899) and was supported by Rodeheaver Publishers of Sacred Music, which flooded the market with books of gospel music. Charles A. Tindley (1856–1933), black pastor of a Philadelphia church, helped develop the black gospel hymn, and Thomas A. Dorsey (1899–1965) continued the tradition.[35]

Choral music was an innovation for nineteenth-century Methodists. It was found in revival services that music could melt the hardened hearts of sinners. Soloists, duets, quartets, and octets became increasingly frequent, first at revivals and then at normal services. Eventually, full-fledged choirs made their advent. Much of their original function was to manipulate emotions, creating an atmosphere for preaching for conversion. Gradually, choirs came to have other functions in worship. At the same time, instrumental music made its appearance, especially in the form of parlor organs and pipe organs. Wesley's belief that organs were better "not seen or heard" in Methodist chapels was long forgotten. Service music was late in arriving, not very apparent until the 1935 hymnal, although chants and some service music had appeared in the 1905 hymnal.

Twentieth-century Methodism

If the nineteenth century brought major developments to Methodist worship, the twentieth century saw equally as much change. We can only sort out the essentials here, but they reflect similar experiences among several other traditions in twentieth-century Great Britain and North America.

Nineteenth-century revivalism had filled the churches, but as the days of the frontier ended the price became apparent. Worship tended to be treated as a means to an end—making converts—rather than an end in itself. Making converts certainly worked, especially on the frontier and in unchurched areas, but with the closing of the frontier and with a Methodist church in every village, worship with this orientation had drawbacks. As Methodist people became more affluent and educated, they became more middle class and more self-conscious. Emotional displays were discouraged and spontaneity was relegated to the prayer meeting. Typical was a Vermont congregation which built a new Gothic church in the 1920s and resolved to discourage shouts of "amen" during the sermon.

The substitutes for emotionalism and spontaneity came to be aestheticism and new types of social activism. The combination did much to move Methodist worship toward greater social respectability. Aestheticism was manifested in efforts at "enriching worship," a phrase that did not seem redundant at the time. Such enrichment took the form of sophisticated architect-designed buildings in whatever style was fashionable. Methodists made the most of the second Gothic revival, popular at such places as Yale, Duke, Princeton, and West Point in the first four decades of this century. Indeed, Duke University Chapel remains the greatest Methodist monument of this

period. Such buildings on a much reduced scale were the goal of
Elbert Conover (1885–1952), who directed the Methodist architectural bureau and for decades advocated Gothic or Georgian revival
churches with divided chancels (i.e., altar-table at far end between
choir stalls) and a cross on the steeple.[36]

Aestheticism revealed itself musically in improving the "quality"
of music sung with more and more professionally trained musicians
employed in the larger churches. Choral responses replaced the people's parts as choirs became standard in all but the smallest congregations. The 1935 *Hymnal* reflected growing musical sophistication.
Lowell Mason (1792–1872) and John B. Dykes (1823–1876) were
still the favorite composers, but the number of their hymns had
dropped since the 1905 hymnal. Choral anthems were becoming
important parts of worship despite Wesley's reservations. An abundance of service music was provided in the 1935 hymnal for "the
Holy Communion" plus a collection of "Ancient Hymns and Canticles."

Methodists were in the forefront of uniting worship and social
action. The social gospel was captured in such hymns as "Where
Cross the Crowded Ways of Life" by Philadelphia pastor Frank
Mason North (1850–1935). A Methodist minister from Springfield,
Massachusetts, Fred Winslow Adams, led the effort to set up a new
Christian calendar through the Federal Council of Churches. In
1937, the Council published *The Christian Year*[37] with a new season,
Kingdomtide, reflecting the social gospel optimism of the time.
Other denominations were reluctant to accept this innovation, al-
though Congregationalists did so briefly. Only Methodists have re-
tained this reminder of the social gospel era.

A tendency to use worship as a means of promoting peace and
social justice flourished during this period. The prophets of the Old
Testament provided favorite lections and many sermon texts. There
was concerted effort to make worship relevant to daily life and the
topical sermon flourished. Typical was William L. Stidger's admonition to preach "to real-life situations." Solving problems in daily life
or resolving moral dilemmas tended to characterize Methodist
preaching during much of this period. Advocacy of social reforms
often replaced calls for conversion in the preaching of this period of
liberal theology.

Aestheticism and worship as social crusade may have held people's interest in the first half of the century, but in the quarter century
after World War II it became increasingly obvious that this was
insufficient. Twentieth-century Methodist liturgical scholarship had
been born with Nolan B. Harmon's *The Rites and Ritual of Episcopal
Methodism,* published in 1926.[38] After fifteen hundred copies had
been run off, the publisher broke up the plates, foreseeing neither

further sales for such an esoteric subject nor a future bishopric for the young author! But there were people who were interested. Bishop Wilbur P. Thirkield and Oliver Huckel published a *Book of Common Worship* in 1932,[39] compiling a large collection of prayers. Books such as Johnston Ross's *Christian Worship and Its Future*[40] and Fitzgerald Parker's *The Practice and Experience of Christian Worship*[41] began to appear. And pastors such as Oscar T. Olson of Epworth-Euclid Church, Cleveland, Ohio; Fred Winslow Adams, Wesley Church, Springfield, Massachusetts; J.N.R. Score, St. Paul's, Houston, Texas; and George Hedley, chaplain of Mills College, Oakland, California, were pointing Methodism to a new era.

In general, these men were neo-Wesleyan in their worship concepts. Their preference was for the fixed forms that Wesley had provided in his *Sunday Service,* now for a century and a half left in oblivion. Scholarly support came from the English Methodists, especially John Bowmer, *The Sacrament of the Lord's Supper in Early Methodism* (1957), John Bishop, *Methodist Worship* (1950), and J. Ernest Rattenbury, *The Eucharistic Hymns of John and Charles Wesley* (1948), to cite a few. Their work gave an important foundation for Methodist restorationism. Another impetus was given by the founding of the Order of St. Luke in 1946 under the guidance of Romey Marshall and William Slocum.[42] In its early years, this organization of Methodist clergy worked to restore the Wesleyan side of Methodist worship but moved to a new agenda in the 1970s.

The result of many efforts was the publication in 1945 of the first *Book of Worship,* approved by the General Conference in 1944. If we remember that a single order of worship had caused protests of "formalism" in 1870, the publication of an entire volume of services and prayers seventy-five years later was a significant event indeed. Two decades later, a second *Book of Worship* was authorized and published in 1965. By this time, the agenda had become much clearer. Methodists and others had found the liberal sentiments of the early twentieth century too glib after a decade and more of depression and war. Neo-orthodoxy now had a profound appeal reflected throughout the 1965 book. Many of the affirmations of the Reformation era now rang true, especially the dependence on God's grace in the face of human rebellion and sin. For Methodists, the liturgies of Wesley (which were largely those of the *BCP*s of 1662 and 1552) said it all very well. The only part provided in full in the normal Sunday order of worship was the confessional portion introduced into morning prayer by Cranmer in 1552. Penitential piety was back in fashion; Methodists had discovered sin again after fleeing from generations of hellfire preaching. In effect, a selective image of Wesleyan worship was being recovered: the emphases on confession and the creeds.

The 1965 *Book of Worship* and 1966 *Hymnal* signaled the fusion of the eucharistic rites of the northern and southern churches, printed next to each other in the 1935 hymnal. Now it was the same service but printed in versions for a full service of word and table and a shorter version for the table service, to be appended to the usual Sunday service. It is still quite clear that the eucharist was regarded as an occasional service, although by 1966 it was being celebrated weekly in some of the Methodist seminaries. Restoration of the sacramental half of Wesleyan worship still had a long way to go.

Scarcely were the new *Book of Worship* and *Hymnal* published before the post-Vatican II era of liturgy erupted. Much of the euphoria among Roman Catholic clergy reached Methodists too. Those were the 1960s when defiance of authority was almost mandatory, when the best-publicized Roman Catholic services were so-called "underground masses," which frequently ended up in print.[43] In 1965, Methodists had just published the last service book in Elizabethan English. But instead of being able to sit back and absorb the products of a process of liturgical revision that had lasted a decade, suddenly they had to begin the same work all over again.

The revolution of the 1960s was a time when all worship conventions and traditions were questioned. Even matters as seemingly sacrosanct as the 11 A.M. Sunday hour for worship were found to be entirely arbitrary. Some regarded this period as a temporary storm they could ride out by never venturing from harbor. More venturesome congregations entered with gusto into what was called "experimentation." For the timid, an early service could try balloons and banners and leave the eleven o'clock service undisturbed. The balloons are gone, now, and the banners fading, but one thing that has lasted is the realization that a large part of worship is visual experience. The visual participation that the medieval Christian knew is slowly becoming available to modern Christians. For Methodists, the change is seen most graphically by comparing the colors and objects offered in the Cokesbury church-supply catalogs of the 1980s with those of the 1950s.

In 1970, the Commission on Worship started the process of Methodist liturgical revision once again. By that time, the reformed Roman Catholic rites were becoming available and other churches were retooling to produce their own revisions (except the Presbyterians, who had just finished, it turned out, too soon). Four goals motivated the development of the new United Methodist rites: use of contemporary English, a classical and ecumenical shape to the rites, expressing contemporary theology, and the maximum of pastoral flexibility. The first new rite, *The Sacrament of the Lord's Supper*, published in 1972, was received with enthusiasm and inaugurated the *Supplemental Worship Resources* series, which eventually reached seventeen volumes.[44] Second-generation revisions of the five basic services (word, table, baptism, marriage, funeral) appeared in *We Gather Together* (1980); third-generation revisions in *The Book of Services* (1985), and final versions in *The United Methodist Hymnal* (1989).[45]

In the process of liturgical revision, it became apparent that when choices had to be made they were generally between late-medieval practices mediated through Cranmer or early Christian services documented by Hippolytus. In almost every case, the preference was for early Christian over late medieval. A good instance is in *An Ordinal* (1980)[46] where the laying on of hands is accompanied by a prayer of invocation rather than by the medieval imperative formula.

The most conspicuous change in American Methodist worship in recent decades has resulted from widespread use of a lectionary. The *Common Lectionary*[47] version of the Roman Catholic Sunday lectionary of 1969 has been adopted in slightly more than half of United Methodist congregations. It has brought a major shift to more exegetical preaching, aided by the availability of a variety of lectionary-based commentaries. An unexpected concomitant result has been the use of a much fuller calendar, with new feasts (Baptism of the Lord, Transfiguration, Christ the King) previously not observed by Methodists.

In most of the new rites there are clear parallels between the new rites of Roman Catholic and other Protestant churches. In two areas, the United Methodist rites are distinctive. The first is in the large number of eucharistic prayers, twenty-two in *At the Lord's Table* (1981) and twenty-four in *Holy Communion* (1987). Many are seasonal (Lent I) or for pastoral occasions (Christian Marriage), but in each case the entire prayer changes as in the Gallican liturgies of early medieval Western Europe. The other major change is in the process of Christian initiation, where an effort has been made to make the process complete at whatever age performed (with baptism, laying on of hands, and first communion), yet with possibilities for subsequent renewals through reaffirmation of baptism by individuals when they reach maturity (confirmation) or upon return to faith or by the entire congregation on an annual basis.

A major feature of recent years has been the concern to make worship fully inclusive. This has led many congregations to eliminate exclusively masculine language when referring to human beings ("man," "mankind") and to move in some quarters to change God language by eliminating pronouns and using more feminine images of God. "Father," "Son," "Lord," "King," and "kingdom" still remain in place generally despite protests. Compromises on God language mark the 1989 *Hymnal.*

The United Methodist Hymnal also recognized a high level of awareness of the need for ethnic and cultural pluralism. Songbooks for blacks, Asian Americans, and Hispanics were published in the early 1980s. A conscious effort was made to make the *Hymnal* as inclusive as possible for a denomination that includes more different constituencies than most American Protestant churches. The compilation of a hymnal is a highly political task, and the 1989 *Hymnal* certainly reflects that. It will be anathema to elitists of any kind, yet it will be the most representative hymnal ever compiled in America. Of course, pluralism leaves many wondering just what consensus is still possible today. Whether the revised services, the recovery of the psalter (noted and with antiphons), higher standards of visual design, and the wide variety of hymn texts and music will lead to a new consensus or promote further fragmentation remains to be seen. English Methodists have been through a similar process in recent years, resulting in *The Methodist Service Book*[48] (1975) and *Hymns and Psalms* (1983).[49] The next few years would seem to require time to assimilate so much recent change.

10

Frontier Worship

The most prevalent worship tradition in American Protestantism (and maybe in American Christianity) lacks any recognized name. I shall call it the Frontier tradition, in accord with the practice of naming traditions after their origins. (Frontier-revival tradition might be more accurate but is a bit too cumbersome to bear much repetition.) The importance of the Frontier tradition consists not only in its own vigor in shaping the worship of churches originating on the frontier but also in its history of reshaping many other traditions in its own image. Yet the Frontier tradition has been almost totally ignored in liturgical scholarship, as if such an omnipresent American phenomenon did not deserve description, still less interpretation.

Paradoxically, the essential discovery of the frontier churches was a form of worship for the unchurched, a need none of the other traditions had yet dealt with seriously. Not until 1662 did the Anglican tradition even have a rite for "Baptism of such as are of Riper Years" (adults). Although several traditions practiced evangelistic preaching outside the church, none of them developed a whole system of worship that led *to* baptism rather than leading *from* it. Even for Methodism in England, there were few adults to be baptized except for occasional Quaker converts. Thus Protestant worship was still operating within a world of Christendom when it reached the American frontier.

Some definitions are in order. By the Frontier tradition, we mean worship practices that acquired their distinctive characteristics on the American frontier. These practices, in turn, influenced the worship of churches and sects that never came near the frontier but adopted what had become dominant characteristics of American Protestant worship. We can speak of denominations such as Southern Baptists, Disciples of Christ, and Churches of Christ as within the Frontier tradition. It is not too much to speak of the results of the frontier experience as "the Americanization of Protestant worship," even though many of the consequences of this experience lay far in time and space from the woods and plains of the West.

The frontier itself is a nebulous concept, since it kept moving and changing. Essentially, the frontier extends in time for a century after the Revolution and in space from the Appalachians to the West Coast. Kentucky, Tennessee, and western New York were the key areas in shaping the Frontier tradition in worship. By the time of President Andrew Jackson (1829–1837), a third of the population was west of the Appalachians. The country that at first seemed limitless kept leading people farther west, across mountains, woods, and plains. Even Daniel Boone of Kentucky eventually ended up in Missouri as the frontier moved westward.

Our third encounter with Free Church worship is in the Frontier tradition. Certainly this new tradition has several roots in other traditions but enough distinctive growth of its own to enable us to call it a separate entity. It inherited from the Separatist and Puritan tradition two important characteristics: biblicism and local autonomy. Biblicism was largely superseded by pragmatism, but autonomy remained prevalent. From the Reformed tradition came the camp meeting plus the leadership of individuals as varied as James McGready, Richard McNemar, Barton W. Stone, Thomas Campbell, Alexander Campbell, and Charles G. Finney, although only McGready remained a Presbyterian. The Methodist tradition contributed the passion for making converts through evangelistic preaching, the emphasis on congregational song, and a direct link to the Great Awakening of the previous century.

Yet from about 1800 on, the special circumstance of ministering on the frontier to a people largely unchurched led to the development of a distinctive new tradition of worship, the first to originate in America. Its two staples are a pragmatic bent to do whatever is needed in worship and the freedom to do this uninhibited by canons or service books. In a sense, it is a tradition of no tradition, but that attitude soon became a tradition in its own right. True to its origins, the Frontier tradition flourishes today not only in church buildings but also at large in radio and television evangelism. As the dominant tradition in American Protestantism, it continues to expand rapidly, not only in familiar territory such as North America but also in almost every other part of the world—the Soviet Union, Central America, Asia, and Africa.

The Frontier tradition is more radical in its departure from late-medieval worship than the Puritan tradition. Accordingly, we locate the Frontier tradition farther left of center on the scheme of Protestant worship (see Diagram 2 in chapter 1).

We shall look at the origins of Protestant worship on the American frontier, survey its characteristics, consider the Frontier tradition as the most readily available model for new religious movements, and then examine the present character of this tradition.

Origins of the Frontier Tradition

The Frontier tradition in Protestant worship came about as a response to a practical pastoral problem: how to minister to a largely unchurched population scattered over enormous distances of thinly settled country. The method that eventually proved most workable derived from sacramental worship rather than from preaching services. The Scottish Presbyterian practice of sacramental seasons three or four times a year had been transplanted to this country by Scotch and Scotch-Irish immigrants in western Pennsylvania and western North Carolina. This involved an intensive period of examination of conscience and preparation for the Lord's Supper, concluding with celebration of the sacrament itself, all over the course of several days.

In 1796, James McGready (ca.1758–1817) left his church in western North Carolina to serve three small churches in Logan County, Kentucky. In the summer of 1800, he staged what is sometimes called the first camp meeting as an outdoor communion season at Gaspar River, Kentucky. This is as convenient a date as any for the origin of the Frontier tradition, although there certainly are historical connections to the Great Awakening of 1725–1760.

In 1801, a mammoth camp meeting was held at Cane Ridge, Bourbon County, Kentucky, with Barton W. Stone (1772–1844), another Presbyterian minister, as a leading participant. The extraordinary success of this meeting despite its isolated location (10,000 to 25,000 were in attendance) guaranteed the continuation of the camp meeting as a form of both mission and worship. Camp meetings became important social events long before county fairs and agricultural expositions were popular. People came to meet their neighbors, to eat something different (Cane Ridge ended when the food ran out), to break the monotony of frontier life by finding some excitement, and occasionally to get religion. It was not a particularly pious crowd that arrived, but a more pious one departed.

Several things are liturgically important about these gatherings. Having originated in preparations for the Lord's Supper, camp meetings gave the sacraments a major role and always ended with the baptism of converts and the eucharist. Camp meetings were genuinely ecumenical events, with Methodists, Presbyterians, Baptists, and Disciples collaborating in sponsoring the meeting and preaching at different places on the same grounds; for the closing sacramental services, however, the faithful and the new converts regrouped along denominational lines. Camp meetings also brought together whites and blacks and occasionally native Americans, all sharing in one another's music and preaching.[1]

It is significant that worship was specifically designed to make converts. Music that was easy to learn was developed and set to choruses often taken from Isaac Watts hymns, with repetitive texts and tunes. New techniques were introduced: a mourners' bench for those who desired prayer for their conversion, the sawdust trail for converts to come forward, and a series of bizarre physical expressions, which some leaders opposed and others relished as signs of true conversion. Camp-meeting leaders agreed that in order to move people spiritually it was also necessary to move them physically.

Gradually, it was observed that four-day meetings thrived best and should conclude with the sacraments on Sunday. Even obdurate and unrepentant sinners might be worn down by four days of incessant singing, praying, and preaching. Indeed, many did catch religion through these strange new forms of worship, and those who were converted were sure to return the next year and bring their friends. Thus worship came to build up the body of Christ by bringing in fresh converts. The circumstances of their conversion explain why baptism and reception into the church came to be conceptually and actually separate occasions. One was baptized upon conversion at the camp meeting, but one was received into the church by being united to a specific local congregation of faithful people, usually after a period of ethical scrutiny. Thus the role of the settled congregation was at least as important as that of the amorphous group of strangers at camp meeting who might witness the baptism of converts. As a result, most Protestant churches in America still provide rites for joining a congregation, an act quite distinct from joining the universal church through baptism.

One of the most important frontier developments in the first third of the nineteenth century was the formation of what came to be known as the Christian Church (Disciples of Christ) and the Churches of Christ. Barton W. Stone, Thomas Campbell (1763–1854), and Alexander Campbell (1788–1866) were Presbyterian ministers who found themselves diverging from Reformed practices to agree about a new form of biblical restorationism. This new biblicism formed the basis for a union, consummated in 1832, with formation of the Christian Church (Disciples of Christ). Their motto became "Where the Scriptures speak, we speak; where they are silent, we are silent." Thomas Campbell applied it to worship: "Nothing ought to be received into the faith or worship of the Church, or to be made a term of communion among Christians, that is not as old as the New Testament."[2]

The most radical form of the new biblicism was the assertion that, since the New Testament church met for the eucharist each Sunday, so should the contemporary church. And so, on the American frontier, a lasting practice of the whole Christian community communicating each Sunday was finally achieved. Methodists had lost weekly communion after the death of Wesley, Roman Catholics were not to achieve it as general practice for most laity until the twentieth century, and Anglicans were only slowly to restore the practice after 1833. But within a year or two after 1830, the Christian Church and the Mormons in America, and the Plymouth Brethren in England, achieved and retained weekly communion for everyone.

For all three of these groups, however, it was a eucharist unlike what any other churches had known. The celebrant was a layman (except for Mormonism—Church of Jesus Christ of Latter-day Saints—in which most men could be priests). The liberal position on ministry for the eucharist had been chosen; laity were to preside. Senior members of the congregation took turns as "president of the meeting" and were expected "to preside with Christian dignity." When clergy did preside among Disciples (and their role in the whole movement seems ambiguous), it was to preach, often after a layman had conducted the ordinance of the Lord's Supper. Jacksonian democracy had finally reached even the eucharist in this radical form of liturgical equality.

For the lay leader, no liturgical texts were provided, but each person was to offer "thanksgivings to the best of his ability." Something close to the second-century practice was recovered in this new freedom to improvise all liturgical texts.[3]

Stone and Alexander Campbell both moved to a Baptist position on initiation with baptism for believers only and immersion as the normal mode. They agreed that repentance often followed baptism. In accord with scripture (they believed), no creeds were to be used in worship because creeds were a later development. (Perhaps in reaction, Methodists flaunted the Apostles' Creed at the very beginning of their 1905 order of worship.)

It is difficult, as we have seen among the English Puritans, to arrive at a consensus of just what are the biblical norms for worship. The introduction late in the nineteenth century of such unscriptural items as pipe organs led to schisms. The result was a coalition of noninstrument churches, which after 1906 were simply counted separately as the Churches of Christ. These persist in prohibiting musical instruments in worship but keep the Campbellite practices of weekly communion and believers' baptism. In the 1920s, some "one-cup" churches developed in parts of Oklahoma and Texas when the individual communion glasses, then becoming current for sanitary reasons, were opposed as unscriptural.[4] The Churches of Christ resolutely continue to apply biblicism to the ordering of worship.

The gradual acceptance by other Disciples of such nonbiblical innovations as missionary boards, national denominational organizations, instrumental music, and many of the worship practices of other traditions shows how difficult a consistent biblicism was to maintain. Yet weekly communion and lay leadership of the eucharist have survived undiminished.[5]

The frontier was not permanent, and long before it vanished its worship patterns began to infiltrate the more staid and settled parts of this country. No person promoted this process as much as Charles G. Finney (1792–1875), who may be the most influential liturgical reformer in American history. The result was the domestication of frontier practices, as the revival system, despite strenuous opposition, soon spread to all parts of the United States and much of Canada.

Finney's parents were among the "go-outers" who had left Connecticut to move to the wilder regions of upstate New York beyond the Appalachians early in the nineteenth century. A practicing lawyer, Finney was converted in 1821. Years later, he recounted his own conversion experience: "No words can express the wonderful love that was shed abroad in my heart. I wept aloud with joy and love; and I do not know but I should say, I literally bellowed out the unutterable gushings of my heart. These waves came over me, and over me, and over me, one after the other."[6] He was ordained by Presbyterians in 1824 and started preaching revivals in such towns of upstate New York as Utica and Troy. After great successes there, Finney set his sights on the big cities of the East Coast where opponents to his worship practices lurked. The big cities soon capitulated, and in 1832 Finney became pastor of Second Presbyterian Church in New York City. Partly because of continuing opposition from other Presbyterians, especially at Princeton, Finney became a Congregationalist and pastor of Broadway Tabernacle in New York City. In a short time (1837), he moved to the Midwest as pastor of the Oberlin (Ohio) Congregational Church and professor, theologian, and president at Oberlin College. His writings, especially *Lectures on Revivals of Religion* (1835), were almost as influential as his own example in preaching revivals around the country.

In essence, what Finney called "new measures" were simply practices that had proven effective on the frontier; protracted meetings lasting several days replaced camp meetings, and an anxious seat took the place of the mourners' bench. Anxious meetings gathered those uncertain of their spiritual state for urgent counseling, an old practice in new style. What was "new" was not the measures themselves—they had long been honed to perfection—but their newfound locale in the mainstream of East Coast Protestant worship.

Finney's rationale for adopting new measures in worship is significant. In contrast to the liturgical biblicism of his contemporaries, Finney argued in the *Lectures* that "God has established no particular measures to be used" in worship. Rather, "we are left in the dark as to the measures which were pursued by the apostles and primitive preachers," for the apostles' only commission was "Do it—the best way you can—ask wisdom from God—use the faculties he has given you."[7] Furthermore, existing forms of worship are surveyed and rejected. None is normative because they have all changed over time and often conflict: Choirs have been introduced in recent years amid controversy; Congregationalists stand up for prayer whereas Methodists kneel.[8] Therefore a minister need not be constrained by historical practice. Where Puritans rejected the authority of tradition as based on human invention, Finney discarded traditions when they did not prove as effective as newer methods. The essential test, then, is a pragmatic one: Does it work? If so, keep it; if not, discard it. Finney and his associates represent a liturgical revolution based on pure pragmatism. It is a new and distinctive American voice not unlike Walt Whitman's rejection of European cultural dominance: "Come, Muse, migrate from Greece and Ionia."

We find articulated in Finney a decisive departure from an important premise of Free Church worship. He was quite clear that the Bible does not prescribe specific forms for worship, only that "there should be *decency and order*" (1 Cor. 14:40).[9] Pragmatism has triumphed over biblicism. The meaning of freedom has shifted from being free to follow scripture to being free to do what works.

The test for worship is its effectiveness in producing converts in a largely unchurched nation. Despite current belief, the majority of the founding fathers and mothers of America were not "godly, righteous, and sober"; only about 5 percent were church members. In 1960, that figure peaked at 70 percent.[10] Although not the sole reason for such an increase, revivalism was (and continues to be) a most significant factor.

Revivalism developed an order of worship that came to dominate American Protestant worship. Characteristically, its normal Sunday service had three parts: a song service or praise service sometimes caricatured as "preliminaries," a sermon, and a harvest of new converts. The result of nineteenth-century developments is clear in the 1905 *Methodist Hymnal.*[11] The "Order of Public Worship" began with a voluntary, hymn, Apostles' Creed, prayer, Lord's Prayer, anthem, Old Testament lesson, Gloria Patri, New Testament lesson, notices, offering, and a hymn. Then came the sermon, and the service ended with an invitation "to come to Christ or to unite with the church." Those so persuaded were to come forward during the singing of a final hymn. It is basically the order of worship still used in thousands of United Methodist churches in the South. Sunday after

Sunday, Southern Baptists, Presbyterians, Disciples (with the addition of the Lord's Supper), and many other denominations make this three-part form their basic order of worship. While it is sometimes lampooned as the "hymn sandwich" because the threefold components are marked off by hymnody, the order reflects revivalism's basic technique of warming up, calling to conversion, and reaping the results in calling those converted to come forward for baptism.

Effectively merchandized today by radio and television, the basic structure has not changed much except to become still more polished. Recent attempts to move the sermon back to a place earlier in the service are often resisted because the expectation is still strong that the sermon should lead to immediate results. Among Disciples and Churches of Christ, the sermon often comes after the Lord's Supper so it can produce obvious fruit. Americans respect success, and here is a form of worship that has proven itself thoroughly successful in reaching the unchurched who happen to be present or have turned on the radio or television.

Characteristics of the Frontier Tradition

The development of a tradition of worship is never simple, and we can only survey here some of the main characteristics of the Frontier tradition. The main context of frontier worship was people, largely unchurched, who could be reached only through the adoption of new measures. The fact that worship should be the primary form of mission rather than education, social action, or charitable service is significant. It meant discovery of a new function for worship, although one foreshadowed in the first Great Awakening and Wesleyan movement. For conversion itself to become a main function of worship was a major historical shift.

Most of the traditions of Protestant worship assimilated some frontier patterns, with the exception of the Anabaptists and Anglicans. Lutherans, Reformed, Puritans, Quakers, and Methodists all went through a process of Americanization that involved adoption of a pragmatic approach and many of the techniques that had worked on the frontier. Samuel Simon Schmucker (1799–1873), who dominated eastern Lutheranism during much of his lifetime, believed that Lutherans could adapt frontier practices profitably. Others, such as Charles Porterfield Krauth (1823–1883), found such "American Lutheranism" repugnant.[12] Similar controversies racked Presbyterianism, with the Cumberland Presbyterian Church emerging in 1810 to satisfy the worship and theological needs of frontier regions and Princeton Theological Seminary representing the opposition to such innovations.

Frontier Christianity provided a "black hole" that tended to swallow up many of the distinctive characteristics of previous traditions. For some, sporadic episodes of restorationism helped recover earlier patterns; for others, they were simply lost. Thus the idea of a service book for all services is certainly foreign today to Presbyterians and Methodists even though Knox and Wesley had provided just such books.

We must look at the human dimensions of such a shift away from European patterns of worship to a distinctive Americanization of worship. First of all, the people on the frontier were different, even from those on the East Coast. The process of westward migration tended to attract fiercely independent persons who exemplified American self-reliance. Jacksonian democracy reflected the era of the common man as the requirement of owning land in order to vote was broken down and a new kind of equality achieved. Many of the frontier churches did quite well without ordained clergy. Baptists relied on local farmer-preachers, and Mormons basically assumed most white male adults into one of several priesthoods. Even the more clerical Methodists depended heavily on lay preachers. One of the greatest revivalists, Dwight L. Moody (1837–1899), remained a layman.

Frequently uneducated and often illiterate, frontier people were not about to adopt a prayer-book tradition for their worship, and even their hymns had to be simple so as to be readily memorized. Emotionalism was not repugnant, and sometimes "rousements" were deliberately sought by worship leaders; Barton Stone listed such phenomena as "the jerks," "the dancing exercise," "the barking exercise," "the laughing exercise," "the running exercise," and "the singing exercise."[13] A high level of active participation was achieved, including vigorous singing and demonstrative shouts during sermons. Bodily movement down the sawdust trail was encouraged for converts while others demonstrated their enthusiasm by clapping, raising their hands "for Jesus," and more bizarre forms in outdoor meetings. Inhibitions were greatly relaxed on the frontier, and a whole new vocabulary of active participation developed.

Women were important in the new developments. Although some groups insisted (as some still do) that women and men sit apart, this was soon forgotten as women's roles expanded. One of the frequent criticisms of Finney was that he allowed women to pray aloud in "promiscuous assemblies"—that is, mixed gatherings—certainly an unbiblical act (1 Cor. 14:34–35). As he says, "Serious apprehensions were entertained for the safety of Zion, if women should be allowed to get together to pray."[14] From this, it was only a short step to women playing public roles in reform crusades and finally entering the political arena.[15] The political consequences of the midweek prayer meeting were enormous.

Children were less fortunate. The prevailing tendency was to ignore them until they were old enough for conversion and then hope they would get religion at a revival. Bushnell pointed out that this was a deficient approach to Christian nurture. The growing Sunday school movement eventually developed its own opening exercises that were often planned as children's worship.

Black communities often participated in camp meetings and revivals. They both gave to and received a great deal from this tradition. Much of the vigorous active participation of the frontier worship and revivals had African antecedents. Even today, revivalism provides the general format for worship in many black churches. The frontier saw new developments in piety. For the people of the frontier, religion was a highly individual matter in which the church meant very little other than as an organization to continue revivals. Much of the effort of those converted was directed to a whole series of reform crusades at that time not directly related to churches: prison reform, home and foreign missions, Sunday schools, abolition of slavery, women's rights, and temperance.[16] Thus, like worship, piety took very active forms. Good causes abounded, and the energies of the converted were directed to supporting them. The same methods of worship that could produce converts proved effective in enlisting supporters for social reform. With suitable songs and fervent preaching, one could harvest a crop of volunteers from the converted. The temperance movement was reflected in such hymns as "Mourn for the Thousands Slain" or "The Sparkling Rill." This worship often engendered crusades.[17]

In so doing, it was easier to paint the opposition in stark terms: demon rum, Simon Legree, heathens beneath palm trees. Revivalism had always operated in terms of absolutes: saved or damned, converted or unconverted. The gradualism of Christian nurture was foreign to its ethos. Thus the converted could relish the joys of their salvation as they sang lines such as "A wonderful joy and salvation has come to my soul."[18] It brought a determination to reach those outside the fold, echoed in Fanny Crosby's "Rescue the Perishing" and a quiet confidence radiated in hymns such as "Blessed Assurance, Jesus Is Mine," or "Sweet Hour of Prayer."[19] Many of these now seem smug and simplistic but are a good index to a piety cast in terms of absolutes.

Much of the hymnic imagery was biblical, and Bible reading was expected of all who were to enter the kingdom. Efforts made at education were chiefly centered on knowledge of the Bible. The Sunday school opening exercise almost always involved Bible readings, and memorization of verses was a favorite class assignment. The ability to quote biblical passages from memory was a favorite means of dealing with life's vagaries.

Sacramental piety was largely shaped by the rationalism of the Enlightenment. Wesley's insistence that the sacraments were divinely ordained means of grace seemed strangely quaint on the frontier. Baptism was a means of identifying the converted but there was little emphasis, even among the Methodists who stoutly defended infant baptism, on baptism itself as the new birth through which God regenerated people. Most of the groups originating on the frontier preferred believers' baptism, certainly more in keeping with rationalism. The Disciples and Mormons, who celebrated the Lord's Supper weekly, saw it more as a reference to Christ's past saving acts rather than present intrusion into history. For most Christians on the frontier, the enlightenment attitude to the sacraments was the only available option. They did not go out of their way to refute the traditional approach found in Calvin or Wesley; they simply no longer lived in a sacral universe.

Thus the prevalent attitude to the eucharist that survives even today in many Protestant churches is a Garden of Gethsemane piety: Christ died for you, so cannot you at least do a bit better? The message of the Lord's Supper tends to be simply "Be good." This moralizing fits in very well with the pragmatic approach to worship. Sacraments really do nothing more than reinforce preaching with visual aids. Like preaching, they are mandated by Christ's own words and therefore cannot be discarded. But it is hard to find many exceptions among the frontier churches to an enlightenment piety of the sacraments.

Throughout the nineteenth century, we see an evolution in the typical place for worship of the Frontier tradition. Even the early camp meeting went through a series of refinements, ending in three standard forms: rectangular, circular (most popular), and horseshoe shaped.[20] Within these confines, marked by the wagons of campers, covered platforms were erected for several preachers, with mourners' benches at the front. In time, these gave way to permanent campgrounds with cottages for the campers and large wooden tabernacles, seating a thousand or more, for services. Some of these tabernacles remain as marvels of Victorian woodwork, often in "carpenter Gothic." Usually the forms are rectangular or oval (Winona Lake, Indiana; Lake Junaluska, North Carolina; Chautauqua, New York) or octagonal (Waxahatchie, Texas).

At the same time, small wooden chapels were built as soon as there was sufficient local population. At first, Baptists and Disciples located by streams for outdoor baptisms; Methodists and Presbyterians needed less water. A variety of architectural styles might be used to adorn what essentially were very functional buildings. The interiors varied little except for the Methodist communion rail and the Presbyterian communion pew (in the first third of the century). The chief liturgical center was the pulpit. As the century evolved, the pulpit became a desk upon a platform and the platform sprouted three formidable chairs for presider, visiting preacher, and song leader. Built primarily for preaching, such a worship space was often appropriately called the "auditorium."

The changing role of music came to have visible consequences. Gilt or gaudily painted ranks of organ pipes increasingly became the most visible element in most Protestant churches. Groups of singers blossomed into full choirs. Almost always the most functional arrangement in terms of sound was chosen, the concert-stage arrangement with choir elevated and facing the congregation.

If a pragmatic organization of space developed, the same was even more true of the organization of time. A weekly schedule of services was followed throughout the year. Sunday morning was the high point, with a less formal service Sunday evening. Midweek prayer services gave laity a chance to voice prayers.

The Christian year was replaced by a pragmatic one, uninterrupted by traditional seasons and feasts except for Christmas (celebrated with a children's pageant) and Easter. New events blossomed, reflecting the needs of church life: Memorial Day, Mother's Day, Children's Day, Rally Day (Sunday school promotions), World Communion Sunday, and Loyalty (fund-raising) Sunday. There was always a week-long revival that served much the same purpose as Lent. Usually this centered on a visiting preacher and often concluded with the Lord's Supper. Nearby camp meetings might be attended en masse.

The annual homecoming service in warm weather still featured a commemorative service and dinner on the grounds, a sort of "religious familism" as kinship events and communion of the saints.[21] Essentially it was All Saints' Day, but that term was never used. From the secular world, July Fourth, Labor Sunday, Thanksgiving Day, and New Year's Eve were observed with special services. Church suppers provided a form of agape at frequent intervals. Depending on the denomination, frequency of celebrations of the Lord's Supper varied anywhere from weekly to quarterly.

The key event of the life cycle was one's conversion. For antipedobaptists (those not baptizing infants), conversion led to baptism. Owning the covenant of the local church—that is, accepting a local statement of Christian faith—might be a separate occasion. Wedding and funeral rites were improvised locally. Ordinations were performed in the congregation to which one had been called with nearby ministers or laymen doing the laying on of hands.

Set forms of prayer seem to have been and continue to be suspect throughout the history of the Frontier tradition. Perhaps the most graphic instance is the willingness to have even the eucharistic prayer composed by a different lay elder each week in the Christian Church (Disciples of Christ).[22] This removes both personal continuity and printed consistency. Yet the content of such eucharistic prayers varies little, for they follow familiar patterns of remembrance and thanksgiving. Such a practice affirms the role of the laity and may increase devotion as people listen to hear their neighbors pray.

On the other hand, prayer on Sunday morning in most churches of the Frontier tradition was monopolized by the pastoral prayer. The use of unison prayer, prominent in the Episcopal Church (confession, postcommunion) was rare aside from the Lord's Prayer. With no service books, there was neither means nor felt need for unison prayer. The pastoral prayer (which had been prescribed in detail by the *Westminster Directory* as "Public Prayer before the Sermon") swallowed up most other forms of prayer; it came to include confession, praise, thanksgiving, offering, intercession, petition and, not infrequently, announcements.

If the minister dominated prayer on Sunday morning, the situation was otherwise in the evening. On Sunday evening, altar prayers gave individuals a chance to kneel at the altar rail (called "the altar") for simultaneous silent prayers. Sometimes soft music accompanied them. At the midweek service, laity expressed their prayers aloud one after another. And family prayers, led by the father, often encouraged each family member to offer spontaneous prayer.

A frequent practice was to pray in public for an unconverted or unrepentant individual by name. This was encouraged in anxious meetings whenever perturbed individuals invited such action, but it also occurred often in unsolicited form in revival services and even normal worship. Such pleas, directed to the Almighty, often proved effective with the most hardened sinner, almost as salvation by embarrassment!

As might be expected, preaching was the chief item in the Sunday services, usually taking up half or more of the actual time. The protracted meetings, borrowed from the camp meeting, gave the preacher an opportunity to work with the same congregation over a period of several days on days and at hours on which they were unaccustomed to worship. Thus the preacher could concentrate on the unconverted. Visiting preachers might vary the Sunday rhetoric, but the message of call to repentance and conversion would be familiar. Abundant manuals gave meticulous instructions on revival preaching, such as "the style most suitable for revival preaching" (clear) or "Can there be too much preaching in a revival?" (yes, of some kinds).[23]

In the usual service shaped by revivalism, the sermon as the second and dominant part of the service could invite fervent response through shouts of "Amen" and other positive exclamations. Thus the level of participation was not confined to hearing but included a limited amount of dialogue. The preliminaries produced a feeling of expectancy, and the sermon was the climax of the service. Such a situation could encourage exhibitionism and a tendency to do the spectacular. Despite this temptation, great "princes of the pulpit" flourished and were emulated by countless others. The results could be measured concretely by the number of converts who presented themselves during the singing of the hymn of invitation.

In small churches, there might not be many unchurched people present, but it was always necessary to call the converted to further repentance. As a system of church life, revivalism became as polished as the medieval sacramental system. From birth to conversion to death it took care of all of life's exigencies. And preaching was an essential part of each event.

Church music that works may seem a strange concept for those who look at music as an offering to God, but the function of church music has never been that simple. Music played a very significant role on the frontier and in revivalism, but it was not the same role it had played in the past. Essentially, the function of evangelistic music was to prepare people for preaching that was to bring them to repentance and conversion. This was definitely not music for its own sake but music with a specific function beyond itself.[24]

Music was used, first of all, to unite a congregation to act as one body. By singing with others, one acknowledges common feelings, beliefs, and hopes. Even though much of the language was first person singular, everyone tried to sing to the same tune and tempo. Thus revival music functioned to create a sense of unity among worshipers. Such music tended to be a powerful emotional stimulant. At its worst it was sentimental and trivial, but this could make it all the more effective. When exploited, such music could be used as a softening-up technique for what was to come.

Creating the sense of expectancy was another pragmatic use of music in revival worship. By using a form more elevated and participatory than ordinary speech, it heightened the sense of expectancy that made the suitable matrix for the sermon. Except for the final hymn of invitation, the musical portion of the service was all before the sermon.

A whole repertoire of music was developed during the century. The white and black spirituals eventually gave way to the gospel hymns of Ira Sankey and later to the gospel songs of Charles A. Tindley and Thomas A. Dorsey. The musical heritage of the early period has been rediscovered in recent years, drawing from such volumes as *Kentucky Harmony* (ca.1816), *Southern Harmony* (1835), and *The Sacred Harp* (1844). Charles Ives (1874–1954) drew heavily on this literature in his Third Symphony, sonatas for violin and piano, and choral works. Most of the revival texts are personal, introspective reflections, recounting the state of one's own soul. Certainly it was heartfelt music. Despite the efforts of Lowell Mason (1792–1872) to upgrade the quality of American church music by imposing sophisticated European standards, a lush growth of indigenous American music sprang up in the nineteenth century.

As a rule, the music was not clearly integrated into the service in any particular fashion, nor did it follow a pattern through the church year as Lutherans tended to do. It was used to embellish, and the actual sequence during the first minutes did not seem of great importance. Sometimes soft organ music hummed during prayer. Music also played a role in Sunday school opening exercises although often the songs sung there were different from those sung in church services. Service music was rare except for the omnipresent doxology of Bishop Thomas Ken (1637–1711) and an occasional *Gloria Patri*. Bishop Ken's doxological stanza, "Praise God from Whom All Blessings Flow," usually sung at the offering, is probably the most widely used bit of service music across English-speaking Protestantism.

The choir was a new feature in American frontier worship but proved its worth by creating an atmosphere that could soften hearts.[25] At worst, it could be used as a form of entertainment, and churches frequently vied with each other for musical appeal. Each of the great revivalists, from Finney on, used a music leader—Thomas Hastings (1784–1872) in Finney's case. Many of these leaders introduced choirs and wrote revival songbooks. When one realizes how new these choirs were to most congregations in the nineteenth century outside of English cathedrals and Lutheran parishes, it is amazing how soon they became common everywhere. If solos, duets, quartets, and octets could be effective in bringing souls to Christ, then choirs could do so even better. And it was just such a pragmatic judgment that won the day, as in so much of the worship tradition originating on the frontier.

The Frontier Tradition as a Model

The frontier-revival approach to worship came to dominate the American scene so completely that, as new groups arose in the American religious spectrum, the Frontier tradition provided the natural model by which to fashion their worship life. From the 1820s on, America has been a place of religious free enterprise, with new movements appearing in every decade since. Many were schisms, rarely occasioned by worship, in which familiar patterns of worship simply continued. Indeed, worship often provided a stabilizing influence by giving a continuity that splinter groups otherwise lacked.

Fresh movements often began with founders whose familiar worship territory was located in the Frontier tradition. And since the reasons for founding new movements were usually matters of belief, ethics, or polity rather than worship, the founders often continued frontier-revival worship, gradually imposing their own distinctive characteristics on it.

The Mormons, or more correctly the Church of Jesus Christ of Latter-day Saints and the Reorganized Church of Jesus Christ of Latter Day Saints, represent this procedure in action. A resident of the "burned-over district" of upstate New York, Joseph Smith (1805–1844) had been converted in a revival or by visions in 1820.[26] During the 1820s, he discovered and translated golden plates which established the standard Mormon mythology as *The Book of Mormon* (1830). In 1830, he organized a new church. Despite the extraordinary history in their sacred books, Mormon worship reveals much of its frontier origins, 1826–1834.

There is a democratization of leadership so that virtually all males can be ordained to various levels of priesthood, either of the Aaronic or Melchizedekian orders. Baptism is for believers only and by immersion, as was common among most new movements on the frontier. But children are considered ready for baptism at age eight. Furthermore, baptism is practiced for the dead on the basis of 1 Peter 4:6. This retroactive form of baptism is done with someone standing in for the dead. Marriage for eternity (celestial marriage) is provided by marriage in Mormon temples, whereas non-Mormon marriages are for time only.

Aside from these peculiarities, Mormon worship does not differ remarkably from that of other frontier churches, such as the Disciples, perhaps because of Sidney Rigdon (1793–1896), an early convert. The Lord's Supper is celebrated each week, but water is used instead of wine (there were no grapes in the Utah Territory when the Mormons first settled it). The service consists of the same elements of hymnody, scripture reading, preaching, and the Lord's Supper as one might find, say, in a Church of Christ congregation. Basically it is the familiar three-part pattern with a very brief Lord's Supper as part of the opening portion and the sermon preached by local members of the priesthood. The Reorganized Church has shown interest in developments among the liturgically central and right-wing churches in recent years.

Visitors to a Seventh-day Adventist Church will be disappointed if they arrive on Sunday, but on Saturday they will find much that is familiar from the Frontier tradition. The Adventist movement originated from the book *Evidence from Scripture and History of the Second Coming of Christ, About the Year 1843* (1836) published by the Baptist lay preacher William Miller (1782–1849), of Low Hampton, New York. When the world failed to end on October 22, 1844, as expected by many of his followers, other leaders picked up the message, eventually Ellen G. White (1827–1915), a Methodist-turned-Adventist from Maine. She and others confirmed (by visions) that God's intent was that people worship on the Sabbath, resulting in a change of the day of worship.

The normal sabbath service differs little from that of most churches of frontier-revival background. Baptism is for believers only and celebrated through immersion. The Lord's Supper is celebrated "on the next to last Sabbath of the quarter," always with foot washing preceding it. It is announced in advance so members can "prepare their hearts."[27] Sabbath rest is carefully observed between Friday and Saturday sundowns, the hours usually noted in service bulletins. Liturgical texts and fixed forms are not deemed necessary, and the actual ordering of worship is left to individual congregations. However, the orders of worship fall commonly in the prevalent tripartite frontier pattern.[28]

We move farther afield to look at Christian Science. Its founder, Mary Baker Eddy (1821–1910), was reared as a Congregationalist. She won fame with her book *Science and Health with Key to the Scriptures,* first published in 1875. In Christian Science worship, the frontier sequence of preliminaries and sermon is followed but the harvest is omitted. In place of a sermon, two readers, usually a man and a woman, read in alternate fashion from the Bible and *Science and Health.* Except for the choice of hymns, every word of the service is decreed in advance at Boston Church headquarters, making it more regulated than Tridentine Roman Catholic worship. In the midweek service, one of the readers presides and people give testimonies of healing and rescue from sin and sickness. There is no outward service of baptism, although it is accepted as inward experience. Twice a year, "Communion" is celebrated but without bread and wine. Its model is not the Last Supper but the resurrection meal on the shore of the Sea of Tiberias (John 21:9–13). Christian Science worship seems largely a modified form of frontier patterns but focused on health more than on salvation.

Newer groups, such as the Unification Church ("Moonies"), have found the prevailing American Frontier tradition a readily available pattern for melding their distinctive styles of worship with whatever innovations they care to bring. Thus the Frontier tradition reaches far beyond those churches that originated on the American frontier and probably has more offspring, legitimate and not, than any other Protestant tradition.

The Frontier Tradition Today

With so many adaptations in nearly two centuries, the Frontier tradition has thrived. In secular terms, marketing worship for the unchurched has prospered by reaching the largest audience and has enabled this tradition to garner the largest market share of any Protestant worship tradition in America. Whatever the limitations may be in the pragmatic approach to worship, by its own standard of effectiveness it has worked.

However, no tradition remains completely static; all undergo changes as they travel through history even in so short a span as less than two hundred years. In this case, much of the change is directly related to the upward social mobility of the people involved, especially in terms of education and cultural tastes. Shouting is only one way to express enthusiasm, and it may be less natural to a college graduate than to an illiterate. At any rate, as members become more affluent and educated, changes are observable in how they worship, usually in more subdued ways. Many changes are obvious in the fourth half-century of this tradition.

A good index to this in America is often the advent of architect-designed churches. In the early stages of the frontier, almost any builder could frame and finish a wooden church building. Then, when more money became available, a local designer would sketch a brick or stone building that a local contractor could build. A crucial time came when congregations employed professional architects to design buildings specifically for their needs, not just copy-book architecture from some builder's companion but designs that were unique and original. And eventually, a few churches were designed by architects with national reputations: H. H. Richardson, Ralph Adams Cram, Eliel Saarinen, Pietro Belluschi. Few congregations reached these levels, very few from the Frontier tradition, partly because big-name architects were more inclined to break molds than fit them.

One can trace the movement of Southern Baptist churches from large Greek temples built in the early part of this century to neo-Georgian structures with porticoes and towers built in recent decades. The leap to contemporary architectural forms still seems too great for many congregations unless they can catch up with postmodern architecture. But the very fact that these buildings rehash a period style shows a basic conservatism and nostalgia for a past that never was theirs. They are aping the images of the power groups of the late colonial and federal periods, a time when established Anglicans and Puritans held sway.

The interiors of these buildings reflect change too. They are commodious and elegant, with fiberglass sunken baptisteries. No longer (as once was common) is local talent enlisted to paint scenes of the River Jordan flowing into the baptismal pool. The pool is now discreetly hid behind curtains except when in use. Spacious provision is made for the choir, and organ pipes fill the front of the church. The pulpit dominates, appropriately, for most of the service focuses on it. As befits its occasional use, the altar-table is a minor appurtenance.

The advances in church music show how important music is for this tradition. Five schools of sacred music are sponsored by the Southern Baptist churches and have done much to raise the quality of music in terms of performance and professional standards.[29] One authority claims that "of all evangelical groups, Southern Baptists have made the most progress in church music in recent years"[30] and now employ 3500 full-time ministers of music. At the same time, a lively industry of supplying music of an evangelical bent flourishes. The Bill Gaither group in Nashville has found a large market for its *Hymns for the Family of God,*[31] and Gaither's hymns are widely popular.

Most of these groups now have seminary-educated clergy. In seminary and elsewhere, clergy have been exposed to other worship traditions and a certain amount of cross-fertilization has occurred. At one large Southern Baptist seminary, preaching is now taught on the basis of the common lectionary. That involves changes in the whole focus of preaching, the church year, and the structure of the Sunday service.

Not all groups have moved at the same speed. Howard Dorgan, in *Giving Glory to God in Appalachia,* studied ten congregations of various types of Baptists in western North Carolina and nearby states. He documents the persistence of distinctive styles of preaching and ways of celebrating foot washing and the Lord's Supper. Recordings have been made of "sacred speech, chant, and song in an Appalachian Baptist church" and of unaccompanied hymn singing.[32]

The Frontier tradition has had great appeal to blacks although rivaled in popularity in the twentieth century by the Pentecostal tradition. Blacks have often developed styles of their own.[33] One of the key features of this tradition is that it is based on local autonomy so congregations that might otherwise resent authority imposed from beyond are free to be themselves. The pastor is supreme in the ordering of worship. Paradoxically, this type of worship magnifies the importance of the minister in relegating so much of the service to his or her discretion and personality. Yet, at the same time, the congregation plays a very active role in black churches of this tradition. There are apt to be a multitude of officers in the local church with various roles, and everyone participates in the preaching and other parts of the service through exclamations of agreement or applause.

Frequently, black preaching becomes a highly specialized form of rhetoric. Sometimes it can become chantlike in its repeated speech pattern: a, b, c, *d;* a, b, c, *d.* The whole congregation is pulled into this performance and it essentially is dialogic with a competent minister listening as well as speaking and listeners speaking in dialogic form. Preaching reaches its most active form of participation under such circumstances.

How has the Frontier tradition related to other Protestant traditions, especially in America where it has become so dominant? As we have seen, other traditions were often pulled into its orbit. But there were also opposing signs such as restorationism among nineteenth-century Lutherans and Presbyterians. Other traditions moved in directions of theological liberalism, which resisted the sharp distinctions revivalism tended to make between those saved and those not. Major segments of the Reformed, Methodist, and Puritan traditions moved in that direction, and to increased preoccupation with social concerns rather than with individual salvation.

In the period since Vatican II, the gap has widened even more. By and large, the groups from the liturgical right and center traditions have accepted much of the new Roman Catholic agenda for liturgical reform. This has tended to blur the distinctions between these groups so that it is possible to go to a Methodist eucharist that is no different from an Episcopal one except that Methodists use real bread and Episcopalians real wine! Most of these groups are involved in widespread use of the common lectionary and the commitment to the church year that usually brings. Some are experiencing the gradual emergence of a new sacramental piety and practice. Of the frontier churches, the Disciples of Christ are probably the most affected by these reforms; the Churches of Christ may be among the least.

The frontier churches have not been insulated from these changes but many have chosen to ignore them. The lectionary has had some appeal, but lectionary preaching demands a whole new approach, unfamiliar in a tradition that began by preaching to the unchurched. Contemporary language in prayers and hymns has attracted some. And the melodies and rhythms of the church music of the sixties has had some popularity, especially among younger people.

Of course, many of the post-Vatican II reforms have consisted of revision of liturgical books. For groups that have never used any set forms, this has not been particularly useful. Thus where the eucharistic prayer is improvised for each celebration, it does not much matter how many or what types of these Roman Catholics or United Methodists have in print when an infinite variety already occurs. Even the publication of liturgical texts, were there an agency to do so, would probably be resisted as violating the independence of local congregations.

Development of a eucharistic piety and more frequent celebration of the Lord's Supper do not seem to have much appeal either, although these have made inroads in other traditions. The enlightenment type of sacramental piety continues to dominate. Baptism is taken with great seriousness but more as a sign of individual decision for God than as God's claim of an individual within community.

By and large, the Frontier tradition seems to have resisted most of the post-Vatican II reforms which other traditions have found inviting. It may be a tribute to the vitality of this tradition that it is able to avoid being influenced much by others.

It is characteristic of the Frontier tradition that it should show so much concern for the unchurched. From the camp meeting onward, much of its locale has not been in churches but in the outdoors, in temporary tabernacles, in sports arenas, and all manner of unecclesiastical environments. A whole succession of great revivalists have preached whenever and wherever they could gain an audience.

The modern television evangelists have done the same, reaching out to the unchurched in the privacy of their homes. Robert Schuller comes from the Reformed tradition; Jerry Falwell is of the Baptist Bible Fellowship International within the Frontier tradition; and Oral Roberts, Jimmy Swaggart, Jim Bakker, and Pat Robertson represent the Pentecostal tradition. Yet all use basically the same worship format, although in a more ecclesiastical style for Schuller. Their programs usually are worship, and for most of them it is the threefold pattern of the revival services: preliminaries (heavy on the music), fervent sermon, and harvest (via mail for those not physically present).

These are all broadcast services yet the pattern varies little. Finney would recognize it and certainly approve of its pragmatic stress on effectiveness; he preached that "a revival is the result of the *right* use of the appropriate means."[34] The Frontier tradition is the only one that has adapted itself to the electronic media. A mass on television becomes simply a spectacle because one is not there to touch and be touched by others. Other traditions have not found ways of inviting worship through the airwaves. But the Frontier tradition began by reaching out to the unchurched and is still doing it by offering them worship with the aid of the latest electronic technology.

11

Pentecostal Worship

The Pentecostal tradition is the newest Protestant worship tradition, one that was born with the twentieth century itself. As the most recent, it has had less time for development than the others. This fact places us closer to its origins, although already we are several generations removed from its founders.

The chief characteristic of the Pentecostal tradition is its unstructured approach to worship in which the Holy Spirit is trusted to prompt not only the contents of the service but also its sequence. Unlike the Frontier tradition, which relies on a carefully prepared and familiar structure, the Pentecostal tradition is strangely free from the compulsion to get from A to Z in any service and may meander from Z to F and then on to O and T. In the process, a variety of gifts may be shared by the congregation: speaking in tongues, interpretation, prophecy, and ecstatic singing or dancing. Thus the Spirit blows where it wills and uses whom it chooses. Although familiar patterns soon establish themselves, the Pentecostal tradition knows fewer constraints than any of the others with the exception of the Quakers.

Like the Quakers, the real emphasis in worship is on the immediacy of the Spirit, and not on scripture. No conflict is seen between the two but the focus is on the Spirit present in people, not in printed pages. Biblicism is not a prime concern, although selected passages of scripture are frequently cited to justify the practices that have developed. And it cannot be denied that reflection on scriptural passages about glossolalia (speaking in tongues), healing, or baptism with the Spirit helped inspire the founders of Pentecostalism. In this sense, there is restoration, but it often seems ex post facto.

We shall discuss a wide variety of diverse denominational expressions of Pentecostal worship. As the movement rapidly spread around the world, it interacted with a wide variety of cultures. Yet despite worldwide diversity, enough features are common to make the Pentecostal a distinct and identifiable tradition.

The relationship of the Pentecostal tradition to the others we have surveyed is complex. Many Pentecostal churches derive from Holiness churches, which in turn stemmed from nineteenth-century Methodism. A few Pentecostals came from Baptist backgrounds. Congregational autonomy in the ordering of worship and much of the preaching and hymnody relate to the prevailing turn-of-the-century frontier revival patterns. On the other hand, many of the original leaders came from Methodist backgrounds (such as C. F. Parham) or had been members of groups derived from Methodism via the Holiness movements (such as the Church of the Nazarene). Much of the favorite hymnody comes from Methodist sources from Wesley to Crosby. It is difficult to say which tradition is more prominent in the ancestry, Frontier or Methodist.

There are other traditions to which it is tempting to look for historical connections, but they seem to be slight. The Quaker tradition, too, is based on Spirit-filled worship in which the Spirit calls people to speak. A. J. Tomlinson was reared as a Quaker, and some of Parham's students in Topeka were Quakers, but these do not seem to be determinative influences. There are also overlaps from several nineteenth-century movements but with no clear historical connections. The Shakers frequently practiced speaking in tongues, especially during the period of Mother Ann's work in the 1840s. In the early years of the Catholic Apostolic Church, the 1830s, speaking in tongues was a common experience, and it occurred occasionally among some early Mormons and Adventists. From none of these, however, can we trace any historical relationship to twentieth-century Pentecostalism.

We consider the Pentecostals slightly farther to the right on the scheme of Protestant worship than the Quakers on the grounds that Pentecostals have preserved such elements of late-medieval worship as outward and visible sacraments, much use of music, roles for ordained clergy, and scripture lessons and sermons. Traditional Quakerism cast off even these remnants of late-medieval worship. Yet we would place Pentecostalism left of all traditions except the Quakers, because it moves farther away from the received tradition than the others.

Pentecostal worship made an important contact with other traditions in the 1960s, and today hardly any of the mainline churches are exempt from such contacts. Thousands of Episcopal, Methodist, Presbyterian, Lutheran, and Roman Catholic congregations have experienced elements of Pentecostal worship. We shall speak of "classical Pentecostal" worship as that belonging to the groups origi-

nating earlier in this century. Those groups coming after 1960 will
be referred to as "neo-Pentecostal." We shall look first at the chief
events in the origins of Pentecostal worship and at the distinctive
characteristics of its early evolution. Then we shall briefly survey
recent developments.

Origins of the Pentecostal Tradition

The initial appearance of the Pentecostal tradition is said to have
come in the first hours of the twentieth century, on New Year's Day,
January 1, 1901. It occurred in the person of a student at the Bethel
Bible College in Topeka, Kansas, Agnes N. Ozman. The director of
the school, Charles Fox Parham (1873–1929), had advised the students to search the scriptures for evidence of a person's baptism with
the Holy Spirit. Such evidence, they found, was always signaled by
speaking in tongues. As Miss Ozman later related it, "Near eleven
o'clock on this first day of January . . . I began to speak in tongues
glorifying God, bless HIM! I talked several languages."[1] Her experience was soon shared by the rest of the college, and the students
spread out to share the marvelous news.

Parham continued to be a key figure for a few more years, although his first efforts in Kansas flickered and went out. Persistent,
he finally had some success in preaching a message touted as "full
gospel" or "Pentecostal," with emphasis on healing. In 1905, he
began a campaign in Houston, Texas, complete with a Bible school.
As it turned out, he was about to be John the Baptist to another
Holiness preacher, William J. Seymour.

Both men were involved in the Holiness movement, which came
out of late-nineteenth-century Methodism. John Wesley, moving
beyond the controversies of the Reformation era over good works,
had regained an emphasis on the importance of sanctification in the
Christian life. Following the Greek fathers, he insisted that the
Christian life is lived with perfection as its goal, although Wesley
never claimed to have achieved it himself. These aspects of Wesley's
theology came to the forefront in various movements after the Civil
War, culminating in the eventual formation of such churches as the
present-day Wesleyan Church, or the Church of the Nazarene.
Liturgically, they seem to be little different from the Methodist
tradition from which they evolved. Members experienced the "second blessing," assurance that they had received the indwelling presence of the Holy Spirit. Sanctification, baptism with the Holy Spirit,
and second blessing are synonymous terms for these Holiness
churches, describing an experience after and distinct from conversion or justification. The so-called right-wing Holiness churches have
never seen the need for any observable manifestation of sanctification

such as speaking in tongues. The Topeka events were a significant move away from the Holiness churches in that "for the first time the concept of being baptized (or filled) with the Holy Spirit was linked to an outward sign—speaking in tongues."[2]

Images of perfectionism following conversion were also voiced by Finney in his theology of Christian perfection, a theology closer to Wesley than to Calvin. Many of the revival techniques were used to spread the Holiness and Pentecostal messages, including camp meetings, revivals, and preaching services. But the Pentecostals distinguished themselves from other Holiness churches by their insistence that speaking in tongues is the requisite evidence of reception of the Spirit. The "gift of tongues" is a highly prized ability to speak in tongues in public or private given to most Christians; the "sign of tongues" is considered requisite for all Christians as evidence of baptism with the Holy Spirit. The question asked by much of nineteenth-century introspective hymnody is basically, "Can I have assurance that I am saved?" Speaking in tongues provided the definitive and concrete sign for Pentecostals of redemption, a kind of divine stamp of approval. In this sense, Pentecostalism provided the logical reassurance that the Holiness churches had been seeking, the evidence of salvation.

It was this Holiness background from which William J. Seymour (1870–1922), a black preacher, blind in one eye, came when he went as associate pastor to a Nazarene church in Los Angeles. Conflict ensued immediately because the pastor believed she had received baptism of the Spirit and had no need for the evidence of speaking in tongues. Seymour was forced to conduct services in a private home. From there, he moved to a former Methodist Church on Azusa Street, and the great Pentecostal explosion of 1906 began.[3] Known as the Apostolic Faith Gospel Mission and well publicized by the press, it came to be the focus of an international movement as "fire descended upon the earth." Hundreds received baptism of the Spirit as evidenced by speaking in tongues; hundreds were healed; and thousands came to observe the spectacle and remained to praise God for the work they saw before their eyes.

Seymour's services at Azusa Street in 1906–1907 attracted a swarm of ministers and laity of various traditions, many of whom became prophets of Pentecostalism, spreading the tradition around the world. Florence Louise Crawford went to Portland, Oregon, to found the Apostolic Faith; William H. Durham carried the message to Chicago; and G. B. Cashwell conducted revivals in the Southeast, converting A. J. Tomlinson. Charles H. Mason returned to Memphis to launch what became the largest of all Pentecostal churches, the largely black Church of God in Christ. An Englishman, Thomas Ball Barratt, minister of a Methodist church in Oslo, Norway, experi-

enced a Pentecostal service in New York (and may have visited
Azusa Street) and took the spark back to Norway. And an Anglican
priest, Alexander A. Boddy (1854–1930), brought the flame to England in 1907.[4] The fire of Azusa Street soon spread around the
world. (In 1966, Sweden had the highest per-capita percentage of
Pentecostals of any country in the world.[5])

Within a short time, a great number of Pentecostal churches
evolved, developing their own worship practices but with many common features. Over three hundred Pentecostal denominations
evolved in the United States alone; we can mention only a few of
them. The Assemblies of God was founded in 1914 and has headquarters in Springfield, Missouri. Several of its members have
become superstars of modern television evangelism. The Church of
God in Christ practices baptism by immersion, foot washing, and the
Lord's Supper. The Church of God (Cleveland, Tennessee) was directed for many years by A. J. Tomlinson (1865–1943) as general
overseer, but eventually he was rejected. This church practices baptism, the Lord's Supper, foot washing, speaking in tongues, and
healing. Aimee Semple McPherson (1890–1944) founded the International Church of the Foursquare Gospel in 1927 on four positions:
salvation, Holy Spirit baptism, healing, and the second coming. Her
style of leadership was spectacular, but ordinary worship included
baptism with water, baptism of the Spirit as evidenced by tongues,
the Lord's Supper, and a great emphasis on healing.

Pentecostalism spread quickly to much of the Third World, where
it quickly developed indigenous forms. In Chile, as early as 1907, it
sprang up under the leadership of Methodist pastor Willis C.
Hoover, who had been inspired by reading of an outpouring of the
Spirit in a mission in Mukti, India, an event that had involved
tongues as early as 1906.[6] Pentecostalism in Brazil was to see fantas-
tic growth beginning in 1910.[7] In Africa, a great variety of Pentecostal churches have evolved, combining various native religions with
apostolic Christianity.[8]

As if there could be no stranger or more foreign a mission field,
in the 1960s Pentecostal worship erupted in mainline American
churches. In 1960 an Episcopal priest, Dennis Barrett, announced
that he enjoyed Pentecostal gifts including the gift of tongues.[9] Various Methodists, Lutherans, and Presbyterians soon gave evidence of
similar gifts. Two thirds of the way through the twentieth century,
these works of the Spirit made an unexpected advent among Roman
Catholic college students, beginning in 1966 at Duquesne University
in Pittsburgh, springing shortly to the University of Notre Dame,
and thence to such unlikely spots as the University of Michigan.
Similar evidences of the Spirit soon became common in many Roman
Catholic parish churches.

The churches reacted in shocked amazement. Although many were hostile and defensive at first, most came to accept and welcome neo-Pentecostals in their midst,[10] so that many neo-Pentecostals have become valuable members of local churches. Not all cases have been so happy. Missouri Synod Lutherans and some Southern Baptists have proved more resistant, and occasionally the new Spirit movement has been divisive when people resent those who profess to have more spiritual gifts than others enjoy.

Characteristics of Pentecostal Worship

It is difficult to generalize about Pentecostal worship because there are so many varieties of churches which, though they have much in common, also have their individual characteristics. Most baptize believers only and practice immersion, but some baptize infants and may sprinkle. As we try to characterize the features most Pentecostals hold in common, we must realize that there are exceptions to almost any blanket statement. Our concern is to delineate the central portion of the tradition, not its fringe elements.

Before 1960, it would have been easy to make sweeping generalizations about the people who worshiped according to this tradition. In the first half century of the movement, it appealed almost entirely to the "disinherited," as H. Richard Niebuhr described that class.[11] Pentecostals were those who were on the lowest rung of the social and economic order; they were oppressed and impecunious, and many outsiders thought that their worship provided an escape from deprivation. Early Pentecostalists were about as different from the people who were Quakers as they could be.

These statements could be made with accuracy only for certain segments of classical Pentecostals today. These groups abound in storefront churches and slowly move up the social scale, buying buildings other denominations have given up. Yet there have always been exceptions. The businessmen's breakfasts of the Full Gospel Businessmen's Fellowship International from 1951 onward pointed toward upward mobility. And the usual process of better-educated congregations demanding seminary-educated clergy has functioned as elsewhere. Still, Pentecostals seem to have more contact with the entry level of American society than other groups, and many congregations still remain the place where the poorly dressed and obviously destitute are most warmly made welcome.

From the very start, it has been clear that the Spirit is no respecter of persons. One of the most marked characteristics of Pentecostal worship is its ability to cut across social distinctions. People are valued not for themselves but for the gifts they contribute to worship: speaking in tongues, interpretation, prophecy, testimonies, and healing. And these gifts are distributed quite regardless of sex or race. Frequent claims are made that people speaking in tongues, although ignorant of the language, have spoken Chinese, Kefonti, Hebrew, or some other recognizable language. These claims are widely disputed.[12] Certainly the gifts create a radical equality among all present, since no one knows who will speak, interpret, or prophesy on any occasion.

Quite clearly, this demands new roles for ordained clergy. It is usually made mandatory that persons have had the sign of tongues before being considered for ordination. The minister must also have an innate willingness to follow the Spirit where it may lead during a service. Hence a programed order of worship is often alien, although familiar patterns develop and predictability is rather high. Still, the agenda is the Spirit's, not the presider's; he or she simply coordinates the sequence. This calls for sensitive leadership, the willingness to go with the flow and sense the movement of events. The minister must preside rather than dominate. Even during preaching, outbursts of the Spirit are not considered interruptions but, rather, gifts in which to rejoice. Such leadership invites the highest degree of active participation yet known in a major tradition and enhances, rather than competes with, participation by all. Clergy function best by making full participation possible for everyone.

The backgrounds of Pentecostal worshipers are marvelously varied. As we have indicated, the early leadership included both whites (Parham, Tomlinson) and blacks (Seymour, Mason). The earliest Pentecostal worship drew people from all races, worshiping together regardless of color. But before long this dissipated into separate denominations: for example, Church of God (Cleveland, Tennessee), largely white, and Church of God in Christ, mostly black. The Pentecostal is the only tradition that blacks have helped to shape from its very beginnings. Blacks have been active in influencing the Methodist and Frontier traditions, but only in Pentecostal groups have they helped create the whole tradition. Indeed, although Seymour had been a student of Parham, it was Seymour's Azusa Street mission to which future leaders, white and black, flocked from America and abroad.

Women also shaped this tradition from its origins. The first publicized speaker in tongues was Agnes N. Ozman (later Mrs. Agnes LaBerge), and the Spirit first fell on Jennie Moore at Azusa Street. Seymour had two black women elders at Azusa Street after he had been locked out by the woman pastor of the Nazarene Church where he had been called. Florence Louise Crawford, one of his first disciples, soon took the Apostolic Faith movement to Portland and the Pacific Northwest. And one of the most spectacular leaders was Aimee Semple McPherson of Foursquare Gospel fame. Women made and continue to make major contributions in developing this tradition despite the general conservatism and fundamentalism of most of the groups. Paul's injunctions (1 Cor. 14:34–35) about women keeping silent in church have not been a deterrent as they have in some other conservative bodies.

The neo-Pentecostals bring even more diversity to the tradition. Kilian McDonnell has documented thoroughly in *Charismatic Renewal and the Churches*[13] just how completely the neo-Pentecostals replicate the population as a whole in sociological, psychological, educational, and economic terms. Far from being sociological deviants or psychological aberrants, they are as normal as their non-Pentecostal peers. Their chief characteristic is that they have no distinctive character. Typically, most are middle class and college educated. (The presider in one Roman Catholic neo-Pentecostal community was a leading stockbroker.) These people simply represent a cross section of American society itself.

Given such a diverse assortment of humanity, it is difficult, though not impossible, to delineate any characteristic piety. We can note some common features among classical Pentecostals. An important ingredient of their piety is the millennial hope that resonates in most Pentecostal worship. Since the early days of the tradition, the various signs of the Spirit's presence have been indicators of the near end of the age. The prophet Joel's prophecy, "Thereafter the day shall come when I will pour out my spirit on all mankind" (2:28), was taken in a literal sense to mean that the advent of modern Spirit gifts was a sign of the imminent reign of Christ. Worship itself is both a foretaste of the kingdom and a means of advancing its coming. Depending upon which system of millenarianism is followed, the making of converts who receive the Spirit advances the work of Christ whether before or after the millennium. Such worship is always future-oriented (as in the early church) because it participates in the future events and helps to advance the return of Christ.

This eschatological hope is manifest in much Pentecostal hymnody. Typical hymn titles include "He's Coming Soon," "The Wedding Feast Draws Near," and "When the Saints Go Marching In."[14] Classical Pentecostals have usually been fundamentalists in interpretation of scripture, and the Bible plays an enormously important part in life and worship. Only short selections may be read in worship, often rather esoteric passages used as texts for the sermon. But biblical piety permeates the movement, and the standard names and slogans are largely drawn from the Acts of the Apostles. Pentecostals see themselves as modern exponents of the type of Christianity to which the book of Acts is a witness, and the names of Pentecostal denominations and congregations often include the adjective "apostolic." It is no accident that the witness of Acts to speaking in tongues as the normal sign of the presence of the Spirit (such as Acts 10:45–47) is taken so seriously or that healing is often expected in worship. Foot washing is a considered an ordinance in the Church of God in imitation of John 13. Quite frequently, Pentecostals focus on passages that center on works of the Spirit and may be neglected in other traditions.

Pentecostals have transcended the enlightenment approach to the sacraments so common in American Protestantism. In this sense, they are the first postenlightenment tradition. Far from being scandalized by the thought of God making direct intervention in worship, that very concept is a basic premise of Pentecostal worship. The difference from traditional preenlightenment Christianity is a transferral, so that baptism of the Spirit is a higher gift than baptism with water. Water baptism and the Lord's Supper are frequently referred to as scriptural ordinances, often along with foot washing and healing. God is seen as acting in these, as in all Pentecostal worship.[15] In some groups, the eucharist is not very frequent because God's gracious acts abound in other ways; in others it is a weekly occurrence. But even then, it is often only a minor part of the service. If the Holy Spirit is present in tongues, then the washing of baptism is hardly a unique experience of grace (although a necessary one in most churches). If the Holy Spirit acts visibly in the healing of individuals, then the Lord's Supper does not convey a greater presence, although one commanded by Christ and therefore celebrated at least occasionally. In another sense, all Pentecostal worship is sacramental in manifesting visibly and audibly within the gathered community the action and presence of the Holy Spirit.

A strong communal sense permeates Pentecostal piety, reminding one of 1 Corinthians 12:12–13. Gifts are given to individuals, but they are given for the benefit of all. Some roles are complementary: Speaking in tongues demands an interpreter; those giving testimony must listen to the testimony of others. All gifts work together for building up the body of Christ rather than serving as private possessions. And this means that every individual can at times perform distinctive functions in the community's worship according to whatever gifts he or she is given. Active participation in worship reaches one of its broadest degrees of inclusiveness. If one is not personally acting in the Spirit, those nearby may be, so there is much about which to rejoice and shout because of the proximity of the Spirit in one's neighbor. Since the Spirit can alight anywhere, the level of expectancy remains high.

Some sense of the Pentecostal feeling about space may be indicated in the indifference to preserving the site of the Azusa Street mission (torn down in 1931), an opportunity offered and declined. Many Pentecostals have worshiped in storefront churches. The storefront has many advantages: It is immediately accessible to the street and lacks the physical and emotional barriers of climbing steps into a public building. Storefronts are familiar spaces, welcoming even to the most shy person. These buildings make a statement of mission and acceptance that formal church buildings cannot. There is also the financial advantage for such churches in low-rent districts. Since many of them operate on a "faith basis," without budget or fixed income but only with trust in the Lord, expenses are kept low. Studies have shown that the groups most affected by urban renewal have often been storefront churches, which cannot afford to rent elsewhere.[16]

With upward social mobility, Pentecostals began to buy disused churches or build their own, eventually employing architects. The usual space often has a platform and pulpit, which may have a concert-stage-choir arrangement behind it. A sunken baptistery is usually necessary, since most groups practice baptism by immersion. In short, little is different from the buildings characteristic of the Frontier tradition.

For most Pentecostal congregations, the weekly organization of time is divided among the main Sunday morning service, an evening service on Sunday, and a midweek prayer service. Some congregations relish "tarrying time" after the Sunday morning service. In a more leisurely way, various gifts may be manifested in this time. The tight constriction of an hour-long service is an obstacle frequently ignored. Evening services tend to be somewhat more relaxed than morning services, and the midweek services probably derive from a Methodist prototype.

Many Pentecostals do not sense a need for frequent eucharistic celebrations, although among the British Assemblies of God there is a weekly eucharist. Celebrations range from one to four times a year to monthly or weekly. In some groups, it is linked to foot washing out of a sense of obedience to Jesus' example in John 13.[17] The traditional church year is not treated with much seriousness other than Christmas and Easter. More attention is given to yearly revivals, usually with a visiting speaker. Pentecostals and Holiness groups have been the last to give up camp meetings, and in some parts of the country these still occur regularly at permanent campgrounds.

The most important lifetime event comes in receiving the Holy Spirit, an act made manifest by some gift, usually speaking in tongues. Some groups would accept other gifts as evidence. Pentecostals are divided as to whether the process of salvation involves two stages or three. All agree that the first stage is conversion, justification, and baptism with water. Some would say the next stage is baptism of the Spirit leading to a lifetime of sanctification. Others argue that sanctification is a second stage, leading eventually to a third stage, marked after sufficient time by baptism of the Spirit, which will not inhabit an unclean temple. The constituents of the Christian life are the same; the sequence and number of stages are debated.[18]

Most groups practice baptism of believers by immersion. However, some baptize infants, usually by sprinkling, and the Pentecostal Holiness Church allows choice of age and mode.[19] Clearly water baptism is less important, although a divine command, than Spirit baptism. A major debate has revolved around baptism in the name of Jesus only. An early schism rent Pentecostal groups over the biblical evidence for baptism in the name of Jesus (Acts 2:38; 10:48; and others).[20] For some groups, this led to assertions that the Trinity consisted of but one person, Jesus. This "Oneness" movement is reflected in the United Pentecostal Church International, which practices Jesus-only baptism.

Baptism of the Spirit is more important. When one can testify to receiving this gift, there is rejoicing and frequently applause at the announcement. There do not seem to be specific ceremonies for recognition of this moment in an individual's life, but the good news is usually announced in the context of worship.

A frequent part of worship is the healing of those who seek it. They often kneel before the congregation and the minister and others who have the gift of healing participate in the laying on of hands and in prayer. Often, those seeking health announce the nature of their maladies and are prayed for specifically. In some cases, the biblical practice (James 5:14) of anointing with oil is followed. Healing is considered a normal component of Sunday worship and not a special event. The history of the movement is filled with evidence that such healing practice has had the desired effect.

An important part of every service is prayer. So, too, usually are congregational hymnody, choral music, scripture lessons, preaching, an offering, and various forms of altar calls (for conversion, healing, or prayer). Prayer may be voiced by the minister or anyone else. The sources are oral rather than written, except for the Lord's Prayer. Quite frequently, individuals may voice concerns, and the whole community prays for them or those they designate. Prayer is fully democratic in that all participate in voicing it with no distinction of roles. This frequently interrupts the minister's prayers or sermon. He or she simply pauses and resumes later.

By its very nature, Spirit-filled worship abounds in prayer. This is not limited to ordinary speech; presumably much glossolalia is addressed to the Deity. Some may pray in tongues while others pray in ordinary speech. Kilian McDonnell says that "tongues is to prayer what abstract painting is to art."[21] As an abstract form of speech, speaking in tongues may be a means of expressing the ineffable in a way that satisfies deep human instincts. As Paul says, "We do not even know how we ought to pray, but through our inarticulate groans the Spirit himself in pleading for us" (Rom. 8:26, NEB). Speaking in tongues is usually expressed in a vehement and urgent fashion; the speaker or someone else often interprets in a less passionate style.

In some congregations, prayer is spoken aloud by everyone at the same time, whether in normal speech or tongues. This babble of voices often becomes almost a musical form, with voices rising and falling and frequent repetition of phrases: "Yes, Jesus," "Praise the Lord," "Hallelujah," "We love you, Jesus." The possibility of blending one's spoken prayers with those of others tends to release inhibitions about speaking out and encourages fervent active participation by most of those present, all self-consciousness having fled. This practice of prayer has a distinct beauty to those accustomed only to solo or unison prayer.

Prayer is also a physical action, and usually those praying raise one or both arms to heaven. The practice is biblical—"and in thy name lift my hands in prayer" (Psalm 63:4, NEB; also 88:9) and known in the earliest days of the church. It underscores that prayer is far more than a matter of words, an act that involves the totality of one's being. This act has come almost to be a sign of Pentecostal worship, especially of neo-Pentecostals who worship within their own tradition.

Testimonies of God's saving actions in one's life or the life of a close friend or relative are frequently voiced. Often these are expressed in language of prayer, thanking God for what God has done by narrating the acts of God and maybe asking for more help. Testimony is often considered a special gift. Its nature is *eucharistia anamnesis* (thanksgiving memorial), often expressed as prayer.

Fixed prayers rarely appear even in sacraments. Prayer may be made before a person is immersed or before bread is broken, but it is always spontaneous and usually brief. The contents vary little even though not written. Supplication for those being baptized and narration of the Last Supper are common ingredients expressed in somewhat fresh wording each time.

It is difficult to generalize about Pentecostal preaching since it can take so many forms, from careful exegetical preaching to highly emotional chantlike repetitiousness. Especially in the black churches, it elicits frequent responses from the congregation in a dialogic relationship between preacher and people. The preacher realizes that interpolations are not interruptions and rolls with the responses to make such preaching a constant matter of relating to the hearers. Early Puritans gave the people the last word on sermons; Pentecostals may intervene all the way through with shouts, applause, song, tongues, and comments. The result is a highly participatory form of preaching in which dead silence is not looked on as rapt attention but as dead preaching. The preacher has no monopoly of the people's time, although he or she does most of the speaking. In line with much revival preaching, calls to conversion and to new life in the Spirit are frequent themes. But the styles in which such concerns are expressed are quite diverse.

Music is no less varied. In most congregations, there is considerable congregational singing from the denominational hymnal or some other. Much of the hymnody consists of introspective hymns of personal experience as in the later Methodist and the Frontier traditions. Fanny Crosby is a favorite in Pentecostal hymnals. But there are distinctive Pentecostal hymns, especially those dealing with the joys from baptism of the Spirit: "Pentecostal Fire Is Falling," "They Were in the Upper Chamber," or "The Comforter Has Come."[22] Standard hymns are present too, especially Watts and Wesley. Most of the hymns labeled "Communion" are hymns about Calvary, not Easter.

Neo-Pentecostals have already developed a repertoire of hymnody. "God and Man at Table Are Sat Down" is a favorite among United Methodist neo-Pentecostals, springing from the eucharistic emphasis at Oral Roberts University.[23]

The ways of singing hymns differ from most central or right-wing traditions. Choruses are popular, and verses or entire hymns are often repeated. Frequently, the minister or song leader may pick up key phrases from the hymn and repeat them over and over. Without using the term, antiphons are widely used in this fashion on an ad lib basis.

Solo and choral music are often present as "special" music. This frequently occurs during the offering but can happen at almost any time. The solos or anthems are often introspective hymns about personal religious experience. Occasionally, spontaneous dancing may break out.

A wide assortment of instruments is often used. Sometimes, people in the congregation use tambourines to accentuate exclamations. Saxophones, accordions, guitars, and all manner of instruments may be used during the service or while the congregation gathers. The level of sophistication simply depends on the people present; among neo-Pentecostals all the instrumental music may be from pipe organs.

But such worship is always open to unexpected possibilities with the realization that the Spirit moves as it wills. Spontaneity has been the great Pentecostal witness; it is now being passed on to churches of other traditions.

Recent Developments

Worship traditions are never static, especially when dominated by the Holy Spirit! Recent decades have brought some major changes in Pentecostal worship in addition to the sudden interest shown in it by those of other western traditions. Some indications of the general direction of these shifts can be delineated.

A major direction of change has been away from the isolation of Pentecostal churches toward more sharing of contacts with one another and with different traditions. This has moved many Pentecostals to closer affinity with evangelicals, especially those who worship in the Frontier tradition. Other traditions have become eager to learn from Pentecostals.[24] Wider ecumenical relations have been established, especially with the admission of two Pentecostal churches from Chile into the World Council of Churches in 1961. With the advent of neo-Pentecostalism, contacts have accelerated as the mainline churches become more familiar for Pentecostals. Television evangelism has brought several Pentecostal leaders (Oral Roberts, Jim Bakker, Jimmy Swaggart) into the living rooms of all Americans.

The process has brought some assimilation from other traditions, most notably in the area of music. Professional musicians and trained choirs have become more and more common. Still, it is questionable whether much of the post-Vatican II liturgical agenda of the Roman Catholic Church, which has made such a heavy impact on traditions from Lutheran through Methodist, has had much effect here. Since printed texts and set forms (other than hymns) are alien to this tradition, those components have not had any appeal. Sacraments still seem to be secondary, with other means of immediate access to the Spirit taking priority. Overall, more seems to have been borrowed *from* the Pentecostals than *by* them in recent years.

Significant changes have occurred in the Third World, where Pentecostal worship has spread enormously. A very significant development in Chile and Brazil has been a closer connection of worship and justice. Pentecostals in these countries have increasingly been identified with the struggle for justice, and worship has become a form of empowerment. Oppressive regimes have often found worshiping assemblies a chief source of resistance. Those whose human dignity is affirmed by the ability to participate so fully and so equally in worship find their own self-image is enhanced. The Pentecostal churches have made major contributions to literacy, to overcoming poverty, and to resisting unjust governments.[25]

Africa has seen a wild proliferation of independent churches, mostly Pentecostal, many of them originating in missions from the

United States and Europe. The mission efforts of Pentecostals make those of the mainline churches seem meager by comparison. Enormous numbers of missionaries are supported by churches whose members' per capita income is not great but whose giving is. Pentecostal missionaries are found all over Latin America, Africa, and in many parts of Asia. In Africa, indigenous groups have sprung up in their wake, often incorporating elements of local culture. Native leaders have often acquired wide popularity and made their own personal imprint on worship. The result has been an amazing variety of churches which seem to vie with one another to resemble most closely the Christianity of the book of Acts. Healing in worship seems to be particularly prominent in addition to other Spirit gifts. The African Pentecostals have led in successful efforts at indigenization in worship, although some would question how much acculturation is permissible.

Inevitably, the upward social mobility of Pentecostals in America and Europe has brought changes in worship. A sign of such progression is changing educational standards for ministry. In 1949, the Assemblies of God decreed that a college degree would never be required for ordination. Yet as more and more of the American population attends college, so do Pentecostals, and eventually they began to establish colleges and seminaries. The early leaders had all been self-educated men and women whose chief studies were the Bible. Now the churches are responding to new educational realities. Ordination once followed active ministry and exercise of gifts; now it often follows a seminary education.

At the same time, Pentecostals began building architect-designed churches, many of them beautifully furnished and sometimes of enormous size. Robed choirs and large pipe organs became frequent accoutrements of Pentecostal churches. These congregations hardly reflect a people disinherited.

Yet such manifestations of material progress have brought some serious soul-searching among Pentecostals. There has been active resistance to denominational organization of Pentecostals. One protest, the New Order of Latter Rain movement, originated in 1947 in Canada and flourished as a protest against the growing respectability of Pentecostal worship. It advocated restoration and return, not so much to the New Testament itself as to the heroic days of early twentieth-century Pentecostal worship, barely half a century old. Nichols says, "The meetings were publicized as a new outpouring (i.e., Latter Rain) of the Holy Spirit upon a movement that had become dry and barren."[26] Other groups continue to spring up when they feel the original Pentecostal impetus is being lost.

Behind this is a very real fear, expressed occasionally by Pentecostals, that the gifts of the Spirit may actually be drying up among them. There is concern lest speaking in tongues becomes less frequent as the emotional intensity of meetings slackens. And the frequency and intensity of other gifts of the Spirit seem to dissipate. Whether this reality is true or not, the fear of its being so is certainly genuine.

On this point, the advent of neo-Pentecostals has been reassuring. There does not seem to be a lack of the Spirit's presence in gatherings of Episcopal, Methodist, Lutheran, Presbyterian, or Roman Catholic neo-Pentecostals. Since the Spirit is no respecter of persons, it breaks across social barriers to speak through stockbrokers and lawyers. Staid, respectable people have proved to be suitable vehicles for the Spirit's witness. At the same time, at the lowest socioeconomic levels, new groups continually form among the poor. Frequently, although not always, these groups adopt Pentecostal worship as their natural medium.

We have said that the Pentecostals were not greatly affected by post-Vatican II reforms but that they have influenced the mainline churches. We may cite some of these influences. Chief among them is new realization of the value of spontaneity. As we have defined the Pentecostal tradition, the chief factor is openness to unexpected possibilities in worship. Most other worship (except Quaker) has been refined to the point of excluding anything random. But now many non-Pentecostals have learned the value of randomness, and consequently spontaneity is valued. This is provided for even in the *Book of Common Prayer* (1979) in the intercessions, where any and all may speak out. Intercessory prayer is probably the place at which spontaneity has become most common in other traditions too. Sometimes spontaneity also occurs as response to the sermon.

At the same time, other churches are beginning to take more seriously their responsibilities for healing the body and mind. In most traditions, healing services have developed in recent years where there had been none or they had been strictly private sickroom rites. Now, public services of healing are no longer rarities. Even speaking in tongues is not as frightening an experience as once thought. It is quietly tolerated or even welcomed in many congregations that once would have been wary of such a mysterious phenomenon.

The value of such a large degree of active participation has been difficult for other traditions to accept, especially those with a hierarchical concept of ministry. Pentecostal worship represents full democratization of participation. It shows that it is quite possible, even feasible, for Christians to worship without benefit of clergy or even of fixed structures. In Pentecostal worship, all are called to express their worship spontaneously in the context of a worshiping community. It is still a radical concept for most Christians, but it has thrived and matured for nearly a century and will doubtless continue to develop for much longer. Perhaps a sign of maturity is the willingness of Pentecostals to share their riches with others.

12

The Future
of Protestant Worship

It is time to draw some conclusions from our survey of Protestant worship. In these pages, we have covered the developments of 470 years in various movements ranging across Europe and North America and extending into all parts of the globe. I shall make some concluding observations in hope of stimulating others to reflect further on the meaning of the evidence presented here.

First we need to ask, "What have we learned about Protestant worship beyond the assemblage of various facts?" We need to detect some patterns beneath this evidence, to see what coherent lessons may be present. Without forcing the facts, are there insights we can derive from the array of information assembled here? We also need to review some common features in matters of current concern at the end of the 1980s. Since most of these relate to several traditions, we can note them briefly here.

Where does all this lead? Being a prophet is always a dangerous profession because the only thing we know about the future is that it will be different from both past and present, and that may change! But this never prevents people from hazarding some observations about what is likely to happen. So we shall speculate about what seems to lie just ahead as Protestant worship continues to develop. Finally, what can we now say about the place of Protestant worship in the total panorama of Christian worship? Where does it takes its place alongside Roman Catholic, Orthodox, and Oriental worship?

What Has Been Learned?

We have seen the origins of a variety of worship traditions as people and the needs of people have changed. Within a period of fifty years, five significantly different traditions were formed to meet the varying needs of diverse kinds of sixteenth-century people. Between 1520 and 1570, the Lutheran, Reformed, Anabaptist, Anglican, and

Puritan traditions achieved substantially their lasting forms and agendas. In this short space of time, a wide variety of possibilities appeared to minister to the different people and pieties spawned by the late Middle Ages.

In the centuries since, the process has been slower but no less definite. It has averaged one new tradition per century: Quaker in the seventeenth, Methodist in the eighteenth, Frontier in the nineteenth, and Pentecostal in the twentieth. Within each of the nine traditions, various styles have developed to accommodate the tradition to a variety of ethnic and cultural groups. It is significant that each century has found new possibilities of worship necessary, resulting in the origination of a new tradition. Perhaps this reflects a slow process of liberation as new peoples successively achieve power to worship in ways they find natural.

In other words, we see a growing awakening of concern for the needs of varieties of peoples with differing pieties as times change. In modern terms, inculturation seems to take care of itself when people are free to structure their own Christian worship. It is only when this freedom is denied to them that inculturation becomes a problem. They may have to be subversive, as were the Puritans in England, or break away geographically, as on the frontier in America, to achieve true inculturation. But the process of shaping Christian worship according to the needs of Christian people seems a normal and natural one unless inhibited by the arbitrary authority of political or ecclesiastical forces. Two factors seem to inhibit inculturation: the power realities of enforcing a national political consensus using worship as a medium of conformity and those of centralized ecclesiastical control of worship. The former was tried by Charlemagne to suppress local rites; the latter effectively terminated Roman Catholic missions in China by insisting on the use of Latin. Both forms of centralization discourage inculturation by enforcing artificial and unnatural circumstances.

Over the period of nearly five centuries, changes have occurred within each tradition, although they have been more subtle in some, such as the Quaker tradition, than in others. Each generation has made its own contribution to an inherited tradition. Sometimes there have been mammoth changes, as in the middle third of nineteenth-century Anglicanism; sometimes only minor adjustments, as in the middle third of twentieth-century Frontier tradition. In some cases, the changes have been in the direction of restorationism, such as the medieval revival in Anglicanism or neo-Lutheranism, recovering what was central for previous generations.

Yet, despite such changes, each tradition has retained its own individual identity. Methodist worship today is still as distinct as in the days of Wesley, though quite changed. Each generation has contributed its own memories of how things are done and, in so doing, altered the way many things are done. Methodist people still know who they are despite ten generations of change. Change, then, does not seem to lessen a tradition's sense of identity as long as it is change that comes from within that tradition.

Even change from external sources does not necessarily threaten identity within a tradition. Indeed, the ability to borrow from other sources may be a sign of self-confidence within a tradition. Many of the exchanges have been mutual, with a tradition giving as it receives. It is a sign of health within a tradition that it is not intimidated by the prospect of being affected by others. Methodists originally were frightened by the changes taking place in nineteenth-century Anglicanism and then accepted many of them for themselves. In so doing, they eventually incorporated some of these changes into their own tradition.

Thus although there has been much borrowing over the course of time, most traditions remain as distinct as ever. Just because Anglicanism accepted the Methodist use of hymnody or because Presbyterians accepted the Puritan practice of pew communion does not mean these traditions are any less distinct than they were.

The value of liturgical scholarship is that it helps identify the distinctive characteristics of the different traditions. A tradition is most vulnerable when its origins and developments remain undocumented. After this scholarly work has been done, a tradition can be more secure, for it will know what is its own distinctive identity. Only when a certain security is found can a tradition feel free to borrow from others without being threatened by loss of identity. Scholarship is necessary to this security, to know who one is. Borrowing is usually a sign of health because it is not likely until a certain sense of knowing and respecting one's own tradition has been achieved. Fear of borrowing is a sign of lack of confidence.

One of the things we have learned is that lack of a strong sacramental life does not seem to vitiate the vigor or intensity of a worship tradition. By a strong sacramental life, I mean the frequent celebration of the Lord's Supper plus the belief that God uses the sacraments as means of grace, in traditional terms, or as divine self giving, in modern terms. As we have seen, a strong sacramental life is relatively recent and still sporadic in Lutheran and Anglican traditions. All the sixteenth-century traditions, within a few decades of their founding, lost the observance of weekly celebrations of the eucharist except within certain restricted geographic areas or small groups. Others, which tried to establish a strong sacramental life, such as some Separatists or Methodists, subsequently lost it. Yet each of these groups thrived.

Thus we are forced to admit that sacraments are certainly not essential to Christian worship, as the Quakers show full well. Even a moderate sacramental life seems quite acceptable to most Presbyterians and Methodists. And many Episcopalians and Lutherans still seem content with the eucharist one Sunday a month. Christian worship for these groups is strong and vital but not primarily sacramental. Jesus Christ alone remains the first and enduring sacrament, the only permanent encounter of God and humanity for all groups of Christian worshipers.

One feature of our journey through time that we cannot overlook is the broadening of the possibilities for active participation by the whole congregation. The first changes in the sixteenth century not only made hearing and seeing more important but brought new forms of active participation such as congregational hymnody among Lutherans and sung psalmody among the Reformed. Subsequent traditions brought congregational discussion of the sermon (among Puritans) or speaking from the Spirit among Quakers. New forms of spontaneous prayer and testimony, as well as renewed hymnody, characterized Methodism. The Frontier gained new active forms such as physical movement and shouted exclamations while Pentecostals experienced the scattering of a variety of spiritual gifts throughout the congregation. In short, the general direction has been to more possibilities for active participation and to greater amounts of it. Even the medieval revival in Anglicanism was accompanied by congregational hymnody. Regressions seem few and progress abundant in this area. One cannot but wonder what new forms of active participation lie ahead as the laity are more and more enfranchised.

What Should Be Avoided?

The present day seems to be a time of convergence in western worship both Protestant and Roman Catholic. Never before has there been such widespread sharing of the riches of the various traditions. The value of silence is gradually being treasured by others than Quakers; hymnody is nearly universal; spontaneity is cherished and sometimes even organized by non-Pentecostals. An elaborate church year is gradually making its way where it was never observed before, and celebrations of the eucharist are more frequent. Yet there may be certain dangers in convergence, and gains have to be balanced against losses. If convergence becomes too prominent, we must ask whether some of the richness of the variety of Protestant worship will suffer. *The richness of Protestant worship consists in its diversity and its consequent ability to serve a wide variety of peoples.* Too much convergence may bring an inability to serve some people. If we have learned one thing, it is that there are many adequate ways to worship the trinitarian God of Christianity. The continuing existence of a variety of peoples is the best argument for a pluralistic approach to Christian worship. It seems unlikely that a tradition could commence and thrive unless it served some people and served them better than the other options. The durability of so many varied traditions indicates that too much convergence is not an end to be sought. Certainly, identical forms of worship for all western Christians would be a deplorable achievement.

There are implicit dangers in making any forms of worship definitive. Even the best-intentioned effort of the World Council of Churches consensus document, *Baptism, Eucharist and Ministry,* [1] in suggesting normative patterns is subject to question. The last thing we would wish to see accomplished is the elimination of some of the diversity of Protestant worship. It accomplishes nothing to reconcile pedobaptists and antipedobaptists, although both probably need to reform the casualness that often creeps into their practice. Nor is there any point to trying to unite those who observe the seventh day for worship and those who prefer the first day of the week. The desire to make normative judgments leads to highly arbitrary assumptions that could undercut the worship forms natural to many people. If we profess that the way people worship establishes the way they believe, we have to accept the consequences. The purpose of worship reform is not the elimination of multiplicity or the achievement of administrative efficiency. It is simply to enable people to worship with deeper commitment and participation—which may require more denominations and traditions rather than fewer ones.

What Lies Ahead?

It is risky to write anything about the future because we know next to nothing about it. Still, it may be worthwhile to speculate about what the future may bring for Protestant worship. Part of dealing with the past is recognizing what may be the likely consequences of the events we have surveyed. Much of the future may already be upon us, but we have not yet recognized the signs of our times, as we live amid them.

One can reasonably assume that the origination of new traditions of worship has not come to an end. As we have seen, traditions often arise unexpectedly without much warning. It is quite likely that a tenth tradition or even an eleventh is already developing in our midst. This may occur even more readily as the center of gravity of world Christianity moves into the southern hemisphere, with its immense variety of non-European cultures. African, Asian, and South American cultures and peoples will be major forces in shaping new Protestant traditions of worship. Indeed, there is a high probability that new traditions are taking shape in those areas in our time, although they may not yet be apparent. On the other hand, a new tradition, perhaps feminism, may currently be developing in the midst of European and North American Protestantism.

A very real possibility is the development of worship traditions that are more or less syncretic with other world religions. We have seen in recent decades a reappropriation within Christianity of its own Jewish roots. Although one can argue a lineal inheritance here, modern Christianity operated oblivious to much of its Jewish heritage so that when these roots were finally recalled they had almost as much strangeness about them as an unrelated religion. Yet the discovery of the Jewish meaning of giving thanks to God, or the significance of observing calendric commemorations, or the various meanings of sacrifice have all enabled Christians to be more faithful to their own tradition.

It is likely that Christian worship will be enriched by contact with non-Christian worship. At least such contacts can make us realize how culturally contingent the practices are that Christians regard as normative. Why cannot the eucharistic vessels be carried atop the head as in some cultures or the celebrants squat before a low table instead of standing to pray? Exposure to other cultures makes us realize what a limited segment of human experience Europeans and North Americans have chosen to employ in worship.

This is especially true when it comes to art forms. The world religions have been no less diligent in creating art forms to glorify their vision of God. The use of drums and dances in worship would seem unnatural to most Christians outside of Africa; to many Africans, worship without them seems unspeakably dull. We are content to represent Christ and the saints with only one head, two legs, and two arms, but maybe more attributes can be expressed in multiple appendages as in some Hindu art. The artistic experiences of other religions can teach us much.

What Is the Distinctive Role of Protestant Worship?

For four centuries, the best case for Protestant worship has frequently, although unwittingly, been made by an unlikely source, the Roman Catholic Congregation of Rites, established in 1588, and its modern successor, the Congregation for Divine Worship. After centuries of excessive centralism, a period of liberation ensued after Vatican II, for the *Constitution on the Sacred Liturgy* had urged that liturgy "foster the genius and talents of the various races and peoples."[2]

Yet the euphoria that greeted this era proved to be short-lived, and the habit of liturgical uniformity showed itself to be unbreakable. As recently as March 21, 1988, the Congregation for Divine Worship issued a "Declaration on Eucharistic Prayers and Liturgical Experimentation" that reads, "Any liturgical experimentation that may seem necessary or advantageous receives authorization from this Congregation alone, in writing, with norms clearly set out, and subject to the responsibility of the competent local authority."[3] Petitions for change must be submitted to Rome, and "while awaiting the response of the Apostolic See, no one, not even a priest, may put the petitioned adaptations into use or on his own add, remove, or change anything in the liturgy." A full quarter of a century after the *Constitution* mandated inculturation, this document promises that the "Congregation for Divine Worship is going to publish guidelines on the adaptations to the cultures and traditions of peoples" eventually—hardly a high priority if it must wait so long.

Such a declaration makes the role of Protestant worship appear all the more vital to Christianity. In many areas besides liturgy, Protestantism has had to play the role of pioneer for western Christianity, often investigating the future fifty years ahead of others. Protestant biblical studies, until recently, were half a century in advance. When theological investigations were saddled with the ahistorical yoke of neo-scholasticism, Protestant theologians could work untrammeled by such restraints and explore areas that are now common property. Protestantism sometimes seems Catholicism half a century ahead of itself. Much of the role of risk taker in worship has devolved upon Protestants too. Few of the changes accepted in Roman Catholicism after Vatican II in worship were really new; they were new only to Roman Catholics. Most had been pioneered by various Protestant groups; some, such as using the vernacular, for centuries.

Pioneering is dangerous business. Often it involves making mistakes that can only be recognized after the territory has been settled. But after risks have been taken, usually much has been learned, if nothing more than not to do it again. Shaker dance died out because it could not be kept fully communal with an aging community. No one knew that would happen; now we all know. So all Christianity is indebted to those who ventured and learned something new about the nature of Christian worship.

The role of Protestant worship in the general context of all Christian worship is that of pioneer. One cannot praise too highly the insistence of the Orthodox and Oriental churches on preserving the values and practices of the past. But equally significant is the need for exploring new possibilities that relate to a human species that is both always the same but also always changing. It is the peculiar vocation of Protestant worship to adapt Christian worship in terms of peoples as their social contexts and very beings change. Protestant worship has reflected these shifts with notable success in the past; it is best equipped to do so in the future. That is its special historical responsibility in the totality of Christian worship.

The future of Protestant worship, then, is open. We cannot foretell it except to predict that it will be different. It is most likely that new traditions will develop. And it is almost certain that the existing nine traditions will continue to evolve as they have already for generations. Beyond that, nothing is certain.

But we can assert with confidence that, when more study and research are given to understanding the process, all the churches will benefit. Very little has been done to conceptualize the process of transmission of the various traditions down to the present, especially the Americanization of worship. With more research comes greater consciousness of how traditions evolve. Such new consciousness is likely to feed into the process itself, preventing the repetition of blind alleys and opening new possibilities by revealing past strengths and weaknesses. Such study is greatly needed and will give important benefits to each and every tradition.

Apparently our Creator relishes diversity; we are created with an enormous variety of gifts. The whole point of Protestant worship is that these various gifts be used in the praise of their Creator. May all peoples in their own diverse ways continue to give praise to God now and forever!

Notes

CHAPTER 1: THE STUDY OF PROTESTANT WORSHIP

1. Maxwell's book is now titled *History of Christian Worship* (Grand Rapids: Baker Book House, 1982); see Select Bibliography listing for all books for which the full facts of publication are not given in the Notes.
2. See Davies's monumental five volumes, *Worship and Theology in England.*
3. *Constitution on the Sacred Liturgy* (Collegeville, Minn.: Liturgical Press, 1963), pp. 12–13.
4. Margaret R. Miles, *Image as Insight* (Boston: Beacon Press, 1985), pp. 95–125.
5. Regis A. Duffy, *Real Presence* (New York: Harper & Row, 1982), p. 23.
6. Cheslyn Jones, Geoffrey Wainwright, and Edward Yarnold, eds., *The Study of Spirituality* (London: S.P.C.K., 1986).
7. See James F. White and Susan J. White, *Church Architecture* (Nashville: Abingdon Press, 1988), pp. 18–37.
8. Geoffrey Wainwright, *Doxology, passim.*

CHAPTER 2: LATE MEDIEVAL WORSHIP AND ROMAN CATHOLIC WORSHIP

1. Joseph Jungmann, "The State of Liturgical Life on the Eve of the Reformation," *Pastoral Liturgy* (New York: Herder & Herder, 1962), pp. 67–68.
2. Theodor Klauser, *A Short History of the Western Liturgy,* 2nd ed. (Oxford: Oxford University Press, 1979), p. 117.
3. Herman Wegman, *Christian Worship in East and West* (New York: Pueblo Publishing Co., 1985), p. 217.
4. Bernd Moeller, "Religious Life in Germany on the Eve of the Reformation," in *Pre-Reformation Germany,* ed. Gerald Strauss (London: Macmillan Co., 1972), p. 25.
5. Carlos M. N. Eire, *The War Against the Idols,* p. 17.
6. Steven E. Ozment, *The Reformation in the Cities* (New Haven, Conn.: Yale University Press, 1975), p. 44.
7. Yngve Brilioth, *Eucharistic Faith and Practice,* p. 93.
8. Joseph Jungmann, *The Mass of the Roman Rite* (New York: Benziger Brothers, 1951), I, 142.

9. Frederick S. West, "Anton Baumstark's Comparative Liturgy in Its Intellectual Context" (unpublished Ph.D. dissertation, University of Notre Dame, 1988), pp. 274–275.

10. Klauser, *Short History,* p. 119.

11. George Dunne, quoted by George Minamiki, *The Chinese Rites Controversy* (Chicago: Loyola University Press, 1985), p. 220.

12. Jungmann, *Pastoral Liturgy,* p. 87.

13. Klauser, *Short History,* p. 119.

14. F. Ellen Weaver, "The Neo-Gallican Liturgies Revisited," *Studia Liturgica* 16 (1986/1987), 54–72.

15. Susan J. White, *Art, Architecture, and Liturgical Reform: The Liturgical Arts Society, 1928–1972* (New York: Pueblo Publishing Co., 1989).

16. Thomas F. O'Meara, "Modern Art and the Sacred: The Prophetic Ministry of Alain Couturier, O.P.," *Spirituality Today* 38 (1986), 31–40.

CHAPTER 3: LUTHERAN WORSHIP

1. *Luther's Works,* XXXVI, 11–126.

2. Thomas S. Kuhn, *The Structure of Scientific Revolutions* (Chicago: University of Chicago Press, 1962).

3. "Concerning the Order of Public Worship," *Luther's Works,* LIII, 11.

4. "The German Mass" (Deutsche Messe), *Luther's Works,* LIII, 61–90.

5. "Large Catechism," *The Book of Concord,* p. 444.

6. "The Sacrament of Penance," "The Holy and Blessed Sacrament of Baptism," and "The Blessed Sacrament of the Holy and True Body of Christ, and the Brotherhoods," *Luther's Works,* XXXV, 9–23.

7. *Luther's Works,* XXXV, 49–73.

8. *Luther's Works,* XXXVI, 124.

9. *Luther's Works,* XXXVI, 62.

10. Geoffrey Wainwright, *Doxology,* has a fine discussion of the priority of theological resolutions over liturgical statements for Protestant theologians. Luther inaugurates this tendency.

11. For a contrary view, see Francis Clark, *Eucharistic Sacrifice and the Reformation* (London: Darton, Longman & Todd, 1960).

12. For a careful study see Gustaf Aulén, *Eucharist and Sacrifice,* pp. 65–101.

13. Cf. Vilmos Vajta, *Luther on Worship,* pp. 27–63.

14. Peter Brunner, *Worship in the Name of Jesus* (St. Louis: Concordia Publishing House, 1968), pp. 126–213.

15. "The Misuse of the Mass," *Luther's Works,* XXXVI, 133–230.

16. "Der Abendmahlsteil der Gottesdienstordnung Karlstadts 1521" in *Coena Domini I,* p. 13.

17. Ibid., pp. 14–24.

18. "To the Christian Nobility of the German Nation," *Luther's Works,* XLIV, 128.

19. "Concerning the Ministry," *Luther's Works,* XL, 11.

20. "Christian Nobility," *Luther's Works,* XLIV, 129.

21. "Greater Catechism," *Book of Concord,* p. 444.

22. "Concerning the Order of Public Worship," *Luther's Works,* LIII, 11.

23. *Luther's Works,* LIII, 19–40.

24. *Luther's Works,* LIII, 61–90.

25. "The German Mass," *Luther's Works,* LIII, 63–64.

26. See Robert D. Hawkins, "The Liturgical Expression of Sanctification: The Hymnic Complement to the Lutheran *Concordia"* (unpublished Ph.D. dissertation, University of Notre Dame, 1988).

27. *Book of Concord,* pp. 337–461.

28. See Beverly A. Nitschke, "Confession and Forgiveness in the *Lutheran Book of Worship,* " (unpublished Ph.D. dissertation, University of Notre Dame, 1988), ch. 1.

29. "Holy and Blessed Sacrament of Baptism," *Luther's Works,* XXXV, 34.

30. "Large Catechism," *Book of Concord,* p. 446.

31. Geoffrey Cuming, *The Godly Order,* pp. 23–25.

32. "Formula Missae," *Luther's Works,* LIII, 23.

33. "The Order of Baptism," *Luther's Works,* LIII, 97.

34. "The Order of Baptism Newly Revised," *Luther's Works,* LIII, 107–109.

35. Quoted by Arthur C. Repp, *Confirmation in the Lutheran Church* (St. Louis: Concordia Publishing House, 1964), p. 17.

36. *Luther's Works,* LIII, 111–115.

37. *Luther's Works,* LIIII, 125. See Ralph F. Smith, "Ordering Ministry: The Liturgical Witness of Sixteenth-Century German Ordination Rites" (unpublished Ph.D. dissertation, University of Notre Dame, 1988), ch. 2.

38. *Luther's Works,* LIII, 326.

39. Margaret R. Miles, *Image as Insight* (Boston: Beacon Press, 1985), Plate 19; K. E. O. Fritsch, *Der Kirchenbau des Protestantismus von der Reformation bis zur Gegenwart* (Berlin, 1893), pp. 31–33; *Leiturgia* (Kassel: Johannes Stauda Verlag, 1954), I, 392.

40. "The German Mass," *Luther's Works,* LIII, 68–69.

41. Yngve Brilioth, *A Brief History of Preaching* (Philadelphia: Fortress Press, 1965), p. 103.

42. "The German Mass," *Luther's Works,* LIII, 68.

43. *Luther's Works,* LIII, 214–309. Note especially a literal translation of his most popular hymn, here rendered as "Our God He Is a Castle Strong," pp. 284–285.

44. See Emil Sehling, ed., *Die evangelischen Kirchenordnungen des XVI Jahrhunderts* (Leipzig: O. R. Reigland, 1902–1905, vols. 1–5; Tübingen: J. C. B. Mohr, 1955–1977, vols. 6–15).

45. Luther D. Reed, *The Lutheran Liturgy* (Philadelphia, Fortress Press, 1947), pp. 89–91.

46. "Against the Heavenly Prophets," *Luther's Works,* XL, 130.

47. See Yngve Brilioth, *Eucharistic Faith and Practice,* ch. 7; also, Frank C. Senn, "Liturgia svecanae ecclesiae: An Attempt at Eucharistic Restoration During the Swedish Reformation" (unpublished Ph.D. dissertation, University of Notre Dame, 1979).

48. See *Coena Domini I,* pp. 275–284.

49. Thomas F. O'Meara, "Lutheranism: A School of Spirituality," *Dialog* 23 (Spring 1984), 126–134.

50. See Fritsch, *Der Kirchenbau des Protestantismus,* pp. 41–152. Also, *Leiturgia,* I, 391–395.

51. See Friedrich Kalb, *Theology of Worship in Seventeenth-Century Lutheranism,* pp. 104–137.

52. See Friederich Blume, *Protestant Church Music,* pp. 127–250.

53. Philipp Wackernagel, *Das deutsche Kirchenlied von der ältesten Zeit bis zu des XVII Jahrhunderts* (Leipzig, 1864–1877), 5 vols.

54. See Erik Routley, *Church Music and the Christian Faith* (Carol Stream, Ill.: Agape, 1978), pp. 54–58; also Günther Stiller, *Johann Sebastian Bach and Liturgical Life in Leipzig,* ed. by Robin A. Leaver (St. Louis: Concordia Publishing House, 1984).

55. Remark in lecture to seminary students, Union Theological Seminary, 1954.

56. George Muenich, "The Victory of Restorationism: 'The Common Service,' 1888–1958" (unpublished paper, 1985).

57. Luther D. Reed, *The Lutheran Liturgy* (Philadelphia: Fortress Press, 1947), pp. 170–171.

58. Fritsch, *Der Kirchenbau des Protestantismus,* pp. 160–180.

59. Ernest D. Nielsen, *N. F. S. Grundtvig* (Rock Island, Ill.: Augustana College Library, 1955), pp. 98–112.

60. Volumes 1 to 10, published jointly in Minneapolis, St. Louis, and Philadelphia by Augsburg, Concordia, and Fortress, 1969–1976.

61. *Occasional Services* (Minneapolis: Augsburg Publishing House; Philadelphia: Board of Publication, 1982). See Paul Nelson, "Lutheran Ordination in North America: The 1982 Rite" (unpublished Ph.D. dissertation, University of Notre Dame, 1987).

62. *Lutheran Book of Worship* (Minneapolis: Augsburg Publishing House; Philadelphia: Board of Publication, 1978).

63. *Lutheran Worship* (St. Louis: Concordia Publishing House, 1982).

CHAPTER 4: REFORMED WORSHIP

1. *Constitution on the Sacred Liturgy* (Collegeville, Minn.: Liturgical Press, 1963), p. 25.

2. See the record of the debates in *Luther's Works,* XXXVIII, 15–89; also, Hermann Sasse, *This Is My Body,* pp. 180–220.

3. See, from 1526, "The Sacrament of the Body and Blood of Christ—Against the Fanatics," *Luther's Works,* XXXVI, 335–361; from 1527, "That These Words of Christ 'This Is My Body,' etc., Still Stand Firm Against the Fanatics," *Luther's Works,* XXXVII, 5–150; from 1528, "Confession Concerning Christ's Supper," *Luther's Works,* XXXVII, 161–372.

4. Bruno Bürki, in *Coena Domini I,* p. 181. Latin text, pp. 185–188. See also R. C. D. Jasper and G. J. Cuming, *Prayers of the Eucharist,* 3rd ed. (New York: Pueblo Publishing Co., 1987), pp. 181–186.

5. Howard G. Hageman, *Pulpit and Table,* p. 17.

6. "Of Baptism," *Zwingli and Bullinger,* ed. by G. W. Bromiley, Library of Christian Classics (Philadelphia: Westminster Press, 1953), p. 156.

7. Charles Garside, Jr. *Zwingli and the Arts* (New Haven, Conn.: Yale University Press, 1966), pp. 7–26.

8. *Coena Domini I,* pp. 189–198; Jasper and Cuming, pp. 187–188.

9. Bürki, in *Coena Domini I,* p. 340.

10. *Institutes of the Christian Religion,* Library of Christian Classics (Philadelphia: Westminster Press, 1960), II, 1:9, p. 253.

11. *Institutes,* IV.14.3, p. 1278.

12. *Institutes,* IV.1.1, p. 1012.

13. *Calvin: Theological Treatises,* Library of Christian Classics (Philadelphia: Westminster Press, 1954), p. 63.

14. Bard Thompson, *Liturgies of the Western Church,* p. 197.

15. *Coena Domini I,* p. 357.

16. "Draft Ecclesiastical Ordinances," *Calvin: Theological Treatises,* p. 59.

17. Hughes Oliphant Old, *The Patristic Roots of Reformed Worship,* pp. 141–155.

18. William D. Maxwell, *The Liturgical Portions of the Genevan Service Book* (London: Faith Press, 1965), pp. 144–159.

19. *Institutes* IV.19.34, p. 1481.

20. *Institutes,* IV.19.21, p. 1468.

21. *Institutes,* IV.14.20, p. 1296.

22. See privately published paper by Hughes Oliphant Old, "Matthew Henry and the Puritan Discipline of Family Prayer," 1978.

23. See B. A. Gerrish, *The Old Protestantism and the New* (Chicago: University of Chicago Press, 1982), pp. 106–117.

24. William D. Maxwell, *Liturgical Portions.*

25. Hageman, *Pulpit and Table,* p. 37.

26. Jasper and Cuming, *Prayers of the Eucharist,* pp. 283–289.

27. *Coena Domini I,* pp. 481–486.

28. *Coena Domini I,* pp. 409–413.

29. Thompson, *Liturgies of the Western Church,* pp. 322–341.

30. *Institutes,* IV.10.30, p. 1208.

31. *The Westminster Directory* (Bramcote, Beeston, Nottingham: Grove Books, 1980).

32. Ibid., p. 9.

33. Thompson, *Liturgies of the Western Church,* pp. 385–405.

34. Richard Baxter, *The Reformed Pastor* (New York: American Tract Society, n.d.), pp. 156–159.

35. *Directory for Family-Worship: For Piety and Uniformity in Secret and Private Worship, and Mutual Edification* (Philadelphia: 1829).

36. *Presbyterian Liturgies* (Grand Rapids: Baker Book House, 1960), p. 226.

37. Hageman, *Pulpit and Table,* pp. 70–75.

38. John W. Nevin, *The Anxious Bench: The Mystical Presence* (New York: Garland Publishing, 1987).

39. Lancaster Series on the Mercersburg Theology, (Philadelphia: United Church Press, 1966).

40. See Old, "Matthew Henry and the Puritan Discipline of Family Prayer."

41. Philip Schaff, ed., *Creeds of Christendom* (Grand Rapids: Baker Book House, 1969), III, 467–468.

42. *Coena Domini I,* p. 490.

43. See Wilfred B. W. Whitaker, *Sunday in Tudor and Stuart Times* (London: Houghton Publishing Co., 1933).

44. See Gwen Kennedy Neville, *Kinship and Pilgrimage: Rituals of Reunion in American Protestant Culture* (New York: Oxford University Press, 1987).

45. *Psalter Hymnal* (Grand Rapids: Board of Publication, 1976).

46. See James F. White, *Protestant Worship and Church Architecture* (New York: Oxford University Press, 1964), pp. 89–94, for details about a variety of these

experiments. See also George Hay, *The Architecture of Scottish Post-Reformation Churches* (Oxford: Clarendon Press, 1957).

47. *The Book of Psalms for Singing* (Pittsburgh: Board of Education and Publication, 1973).

48. Horace T. Allen, in *Worship* 48 (Dec. 1974), 580–594.

49. Hughes Oliphant Old, *Worship That Is Reformed According to Scripture.*

50. These were all published in Philadelphia by The Westminster Press.

51. Ibid.

52. *The Book of Common Order* (Edinburgh: Saint Andrew Press, 1979).

53. *Rejoice in the Lord* (Grand Rapids: Wm. B. Eerdmans Publishing Co., 1985).

54. *Psalter Hymnal* (Grand Rapids: C.R.C. Publications, 1987).

55. *A Book of Services* (Edinburgh: Saint Andrew Press, 1980).

56. *The Book of Worship* (New York: United Church of Christ, 1986).

CHAPTER 5: ANABAPTIST WORSHIP

1. *Coena Domini I,* pp. 21–24.

2. George H. Williams, *The Radical Reformation,* pp. xxiii–xxxi.

3. "Christian Baptism," *The Complete Writings of Menno Simons,* p. 237.

4. "Of Baptism," *Zwingli and Bullinger,* Library of Christian Classics (Philadelphia: Westminster Press, 1953), p. 138.

5. Ibid., p. 156.

6. "The Large Catechism," *Book of Concord* (Philadelphia: Fortress Press, 1959), p. 444.

7. Menno Simons, "Foundation of Christian Doctrine," *Complete Writings,* p. 120.

8. John Leith, ed., *Creeds of the Churches* (Atlanta: John Knox Press, 1973), p. 285.

9. Peter Riedeman, "Account," in *Anabaptism in Outline,* ed. Walter Klaassen, p. 221.

10. Rolin S. Armour, *Anabaptist Baptism,* p. 54.

11. Harold Bender, "The Hymnology of the Anabaptists," and N. van der Zijpp, "The Hymnology of the Mennonites in the Netherlands," *Mennonite Quarterly Review* XXXI (Jan. 1957), 5–15.

12. *Mennonite Hymnal* (Newton, Kans: Faith and Life; and Scottdale, Pa.: Herald Press, 1969).

13. Thieleman van Braght, *The Bloody Theater, or Martyrs' Mirror* (Scottdale, Pa.: Herald Press, 1977).

14. Hans Schlaffer, "A Pleasant Letter of Comfort" (1527); Klaassen, *Anabaptism in Outline,* p. 196.

15. Cyril Richardson, *Early Christian Fathers,* Library of Christian Classics (Philadelphia: Westminster Press, 1953), p. 175.

16. "Schleitheim Confession," Leith, *Creeds,* p. 285.

17. *Balthasar Hübmaier, Theologian of Anabaptism,* tr. and ed. H.W. Pidkin and John Howard Yoder.

18. Williams, *The Radical Reformation,* p. 705.

19. Leith, *Creeds,* p. 287.

20. Williams, *The Radical Reformation,* p. 506.

21. Armour, *Anabaptist Baptism,* pp. 19–57.

22. Ibid., pp. 76–96.

23. Ibid., p. 134.

24. *Book of Worship* (Elgin, Ill.: Brethren Press, 1964), pp. 196–230.

25. *Mennonite Hymnal,* no. 344.

26. John A. Hostetler and Gertrude Enders Huntington, *The Hutterites in North America* (New York: Holt, Rinehart & Winston, 1967), pp. 26–27, 80–82. Also Victor Peters, *All Things Common: The Hutterian Way of Life* (New York: Harper & Row, 1971), pp. 124–126.

27. See Walter Klaassen, *Biblical and Theological Bases for Worship in the Believers' Church* (Newton, Kans.: Faith and Life, 1978), pp. 16–24.

CHAPTER 6: ANGLICAN WORSHIP

1. See the second edition (1982).

2. See *The First and Second Prayer Books of Edward VI* (London: J. M. Dent & Sons, 1952), p. 4. Spelling modernized in most quotations.

3. G. Stella Brook, *The Language of The Book of Common Prayer,* p. 89.

4. 1549 *BCP, First and Second Prayer Books,* pp. 21–22.

5. Ibid., pp. 223–224.

6. Ibid., pp. 348, 354.

7. Ibid., p. 225.

8. Ibid., p. 216.

9. Ibid., p. 392.

10. Ibid., p. 230.

11. Ibid.

12. Ibid., p. 392.

13. Ibid.

14. Frank Streatfeild, *The State Prayers* (London: A. R. Mowbray, 1950).

15. Letter bound with *The Sunday Service of the Methodists in North America* (London, 1784).

16. *First and Second Prayer Books,* p. 323.

17. J. D. C. Fisher, *Christian Initiation: Baptism in the Medieval West* (London: S.P.C.K., 1965), pp. 120–140.

18. *First and Second Prayer Books,* p. 408.

19. Ibid., p. 236.

20. Ibid., p. 266.

21. G. W. O. Addleshaw and Frederick Etchells, *The Architectural Setting of Anglican Worship,* pp. 43–45.

22. *First and Second Prayer Books,* p. 219.

23. Ibid., p. 347.

24. J. G. Davies, *The Architectural Setting of Baptism* (London: Barrie & Rockliff, 1962), pp. 96–100.

25. *First and Second Prayer Books,* p. 3.

26. Ibid., p. 6.

27. Ibid., p. 4.

28. Friedrich Blume et al., *Protestant Church Music* (London: Victor Gollancz, 1975), pp. 691–708.

29. See "The British Church," in *The Works of George Herbert* (Oxford: Clarendon Press, 1964), pp. 109–110.

30. "Canons of 1604," in J. V. Bullard, ed., *Constitutions and Canons Ecclesiastical* 1604 (London: Faith Press, 1934).

31. Addleshaw and Etchells, *Architectural Setting,* pp. 124–145.

32. Ibid., p. 249.

33. W. Jardine Grisbrooke, *Anglican Liturgies of the Seventeenth and Eighteenth Centuries* (London: S.P.C.K., 1958), pp. 56–135.

34. G. W. O. Addleshaw, *The High Church Tradition* (London: Faber & Faber, 1941).

35. Benjamin Hoadly, *A Plain Account of the Nature and End of the Sacrament of the Lord's-Supper* (London, 1735), p. 24.

36. See Marion J. Hatchett, *The Making of the First American Book of Common Prayer.*

37. Yngre Brilioth, *The Anglican Revival* (London: Longmans, Green, 1925).

38. See Horton Davies, *Worship and Theology in England* (Princeton: Princeton University Press, 1965), V, 287–290.

39. See Marvin R. O'Connell, *The Oxford Conspirators* (London: Macmillan Co., 1969). For a later phase, see James Bentley, *Ritualism and Politics in Victorian Britain* (London: Oxford University Press, 1978).

40. See James F. White, *The Cambridge Movement.*

41. Horton Davies, *Varieties of English Preaching 1900–1960* (London: SCM Press, 1963).

42. Letter of Benjamin Webb to John Mason Neale, *Letters of John Mason Neale* (London: Longmans, Green, 1910), p. 126.

43. Peter J. Jagger, *A History of the Parish and People Movement* (London: Faith Press, 1978). See also Donald Gray, *Earth and Altar* (London: Alcuin, 1986).

44. A. G. Hebert, *Liturgy and Society* (London: Faber & Faber, 1935).

45. *The Calendar and Lectionary* (London: Oxford University Press, 1967).

46. *The Book of Occasional Services* (New York: Church Hymnal Corporation, 1979), pp. 115–130.

CHAPTER 7: SEPARATIST AND PURITAN WORSHIP

1. Calvin, *Institutes,* IV.x.30, p. 1208.

2. Horton Davies, *The Worship of the English Puritans,* pp. 49–56.

3. Philip Schaff, *Creeds of Christendom* (Grand Rapids: Baker Book House, 1969), III, 646.

4. Stephen Mayor, *The Lord's Supper in Early English Dissent,* p. 47.

5. Quoted by Bryan D. Spinks, *From the Lord and "The Best Reformed Churches,"* p. 32.

6. See Christina Hallowell Garrett, *The Marian Exiles* (Cambridge: Cambridge University Press, 1938).

7. John Booty, ed., *The Book of Common Prayer 1559* (Charlottesville, Va.: University Press of Virginia, 1976), p. 48.

8. Henry Gee and W. J. Hardy, eds., *Documents Illustrative of English Church History* (London: Macmillan Co., 1910), p. 471.

9. See John H. Primus, *The Vestments Controversy* (Kampen: J. H. Koh, 1960).

10. W. H. Frere and C. E. Douglas, eds., *Puritan Manifestoes,* p. 8.

11. Wilfred B. Whitaker, *Sunday in Tudor and Stuart Times* (London: Houghton Publishing Co., 1933), pp. 48–66.

12. Perry Miller and Thomas H. Johnson, *The Puritans* (New York: Harper & Row, 1963), I, 281.

13. Horton Davies, *Worship and Theology in England* (Princeton, N.J.: Princeton University Press, 1970), I, 264.

14. Peter Hall, ed., *Reliquiae Liturgicae,* I: *The Middleburgh Prayer-Book* (Bath, 1847).

15. See Davies, *Worship of the English Puritans,* pp. 98–114, for the respective arguments.

16. Quoted in Perry Miller, *Orthodoxy in Massachusetts, 1630–1650* (Boston: Beacon Press, 1959), p. 137.

17. Alexander Whitaker, quoted in *American Christianity,* ed. H. Shelton Smith, Robert T. Handy, and Lefferts A. Loetscher (New York: Charles Scribner's Sons, 1960), I, 48.

18. John Cotton, *The Way of the Churches of Christ in New England* (London, 1645).

19. See Bryan D. Spinks, *Freedom or Order?* p. 47.

20. J. Franklin Jameson, ed., *Johnson's Wonder-Working Providence* (New York: Barnes & Noble, 1967), p. 253.

21. Samuel Willard, *A Compleate Body of Divinity* (Boston, 1726).

22. Quoted by Doug Adams, *Meeting House to Camp Meeting,* p. 31.

23. Smith, Handy, and Loetscher, *American Christianity,* I, 202–204.

24. Cf. James F. White, "A Good Word for William Dowsing," *Theology Today* 18 (July 1961), 180–184.

25. Marian Card Donnelly, *The New England Meeting House of the Seventeenth Century* (Middletown, Conn.: Wesleyan University Press, 1961).

26. *The Westminster Directory* (Bramcote, Beeston, Nottingham: Grove Books, 1980), p. 18.

27. Adams, *Meeting House,* pp. 28–29.

28. Cf. Betty Bandel, *Sing the Lord's Song in a Strange Land* (London and Toronto: Associated University Presses, 1981).

29. Adams, *Meeting House,* pp. 82–83.

30. Jonathan Edwards, *The Religious Affections* (New Haven, Conn.: Yale University Press, 1959).

31. Adams, *Meeting House,* pp. 90–97.

32. Davies, *Worship and Theology,* IV, 271–281.

33. Horace Bushnell, *Christian Nurture* (New Haven, Conn.: Yale University Press, 1967), p. 4.

34. Von Ogden Vogt, *Art and Religion* (New Haven, Conn.: Yale University Press, 1921, 1929; republished [Boston: Beacon Press], 1948, 1960).

35. Horton Davies, "The Expression of the Social Gospel in Worship," *Studia Liturgica* II (Sept. 1963), 174–192.

36. P.T. Forsyth, *The Church and the Sacraments* (London: Independent Press, 1955).

37. P.T. Forsyth, *Positive Preaching and the Modern Mind* (London: Independent Press, 1964).

38. William E. Orchard, *The Order of Divine Service* (London: Oxford University Press, 1921).

39. William E. Orchard, *The Temple* (New York: E. P. Dutton Co., 1918).

40. *A Book of Worship for Free Churches* (New York: Oxford University Press, 1948).

41. *Book of Worship: The United Church of Christ* (New York: U.C.C. Office for Church Life and Leadership, 1986).

42. *A Book of Services* (Edinburgh: Saint Andrew Press, 1980).

CHAPTER 8: QUAKER WORSHIP

1. Evelyn Underhill, *Worship* (New York: Harper & Brothers, 1937), pp. 307–312.

2. Robert Barclay, *An Apology for the True Christian Divinity,* p. 320.

3. Ibid., p. 328.

4. John Woolman, *The Journal and Major Essays of John Woolman,* ed. Phillips P. Moulton (New York: Oxford University Press, 1971).

5. Barclay, *Apology,* p. 348.

6. Ibid., p. 408.

7. Ibid., p. 445.

8. Ibid., p. 427.

9. Ibid., p. 446.

10. *Rules of Discipline of the Yearly Meeting, Held on Rhode Island for New England* (New Bedford, Mass.: Edward Anthony, 1856), p. 27.

11. Ibid., pp. 23–24.

12. Barclay, *Apology,* p. 408.

13. *Rules,* p. 107.

14. Ibid., p. 27.

15. See Edward D. Andrews, *The People Called Shakers,* pp. 3–53.

16. See Marjorie Procter-Smith, *Women in Shaker Community and Worship,* pp. 84–97

17. *A Summary View of the Millennial Church, or United Society of Believers, Commonly Called Shakers,* 2nd ed. (Albany, N.Y.: Van Benthuysen, 1848), p. 92.

18. Bertha Lindsay and Lillian Phelps, *Shaker Music* (Canterbury, N.H.: Canterbury Shakers, n.d.), n.p.

19. Edward and Faith Andrews, *Visions of the Heavenly Sphere: Shaker Spirit Drawings* (Charlottesville, Va.: University Press of Virginia, 1969).

20. *A Summary View,* p. 265.

21. Andrews, *People Called Shakers,* pp. 251–289.

22. Procter-Smith, *Women,* pp. 59–60.

23. Ibid., pp. 141–158.

24. Edward D. Andrews, *A Shaker Meeting House and Its Builder* (Hancock, Mass.: Shaker Community, 1962).

25. *A Summary View,* p. 287.

26. See Edward D. Andrews, *The Gift to Be Simple: Songs, Dances and Rituals of the American Shakers* (New York: Dover Books, 1940); also, Daniel Patterson, *The Shaker Spiritual* (Princeton, N.J.: Princeton University Press, 1979).

27 Francis B. Hall, ed., *Quaker Worship in North America,* pp. 53–74.

28. Thomas D. Hamm, *The Transformation of American Quakerism: Orthodox Friends, 1800–1907,* pp. 130–137.

CHAPTER 9: METHODIST WORSHIP

1. Leslie Church, *The Early Methodist People* (London: Epworth, Press, 1948), pp. 222–262.

2. See *John Wesley's Sunday Service for the Methodists in North America,* Bicentennial Edition (Nashville: United Methodist Publishing House, 1984).

3. "Minutes of the Conferences," in *John Wesley,* ed. Albert C. Outler (New York: Oxford University Press, 1964), p. 144.

4. *Works of John Wesley,* ed. Albert C. Outler (Nashville: Abingdon Press, 1984), I, 381.

5. "The Rules of the United Societies," *John Wesley,* p. 179.

6. *Works of John Wesley,* III, 428–429.

7 John C. Bowmer, *The Sacrament of the Lord's Supper in Early Methodism,* p. 55.

8. Church, *Early Methodist People,* pp. 155–160.

9. John Bishop, *Methodist Worship in Relation to Free Church Worship,* pp. 92–94.

10. Frank Baker, *Methodism and the Love-Feast* (London: Epworth Press, 1957).

11. See excerpts for these by Laurence H. Stookey in *Seasons of the Gospel* (Nashville: Abingdon Press, 1979), p. 109.

12. David Tripp, *The Renewal of the Covenant in the Methodist Tradition,* pp. 12–15.

13. *John Wesley's Sunday Service,* pp. 139–161.

14. See John D. Grabner, "A Commentary on the Rites of 'An Ordinal,' The United Methodist Church" (unpublished Ph.D. dissertation, University of Notre Dame, 1983), pp. 1–40.

15. George W. Dolbey, *The Architectural Expression of Methodism,* and Paul N. Garber, *The Methodist Meeting House* (New York: Board of Missions, 1941).

16. Outler, *Works of John Wesley,* I, 13–29.

17. *John Wesley's Sunday Service,* p. 138.

18. *John Wesley's Sunday Service,* letter appended and dated Sept. 10, 1784.

19. See J. Ernest Rattenbury, *The Eucharistic Hymns of John and Charles Wesley,* pp. 14–19.

20. Ibid., pp. 195–249.

21. William N. Wade, "A History of Public Worship in the Methodist Episcopal Church," pp. 146–152.

22. Jesse Lee, *A Short History of the Methodists,* facsimile of 1810 ed. (Rutland, Vt.: Academy Books, 1974), p. 107.

23. William Chazanoff, *Welch's Grape Juice* (Syracuse, N.Y.: Syracuse University Press, 1977).

24. Thomas O. Summers, *The Golden Censer* (Nashville, 1859).

25. Andrew Trimen, *Church and Chapel Architecture* (London, 1849).

26. See the demographics in Whitney R. Cross, *The Burned-Over District* (New York: Harper & Row, 1965), pp. 55–77.

27. See Peter Cartwright, *Fifty Years as a Presiding Elder* (Cincinnati, 1871), also *Autobiography,* intro. by Charles L. Wallis (Nashville: Abingdon Press, 1956).

28. Melva Wilson Costen and Darius Leander Swann, eds., "The Black Christian Worship Experience: A Consultation."

29. Mechal Sobel, *The World They Made Together* (Princeton, N.J.: Princeton University Press, 1987), pp. 204–213.

30. *The Wesleyan Camp Meeting Hymn Book* (Wendell, Mass., 1829), nos. 12 and 86.

31. See William T. Ward, *Variety in the Prayer Meeting* (Cincinnati: Methodist Book Concern, 1915).

32. Joseph E. Gould, *The Chautauqua Movement: An Episode in the Continuing American Revolution* (Albany, N.Y.: State University of New York Press, 1961).

33. Charles Johnson, *The Frontier Campmeeting* (Dallas: S.M.U. Press, 1955), pp. 41–48.

34. Bernard Ruffin, *Fanny Crosby* (Philadelphia: United Church Press, 1976).

35. J. Jefferson Cleveland, "A Historical Account of the Hymn in the Black Worship Experience," *Songs of Zion* (Nashville: Abingdon Press, 1981), pp. 1–4.

36. See Elbert Conover, *The Church Builder* (New York: Interdenominational Bureau, n.d.), *Building the House of God* (New York: Methodist Book Concern, 1928), and *The Church Building Guide* (New York: Interdenominational Bureau, 1946).

37. *The Christian Year* (New York: Federal Council of Churches, 1937 and 1940).

38. Nolan B. Harmon, *The Rites and Ritual of Episcopal Methodism* (Nashville: Publishing House of the M. E. Church, South, 1926).

39. Wilbur P. Thirkield and Oliver Huckel, *Book of Common Worship* (New York: E. P. Dutton & Co., 1932).

40. Johnston Ross, *Christian Worship and Its Future* (Nashville: Abingdon Press, 1927).

41. Fitzgerald Parker, *The Practice and Experience of Christian Worship* (Nashville: Cokesbury Press, 1929).

42. David L. Taylor, "The Order of St. Luke and the *Versicle,*" *Doxology* III (1986), 48–56.

43. Stephen W. McNierney, *Underground Mass Book* (Baltimore: Helicon Press, 1968).

44. These were all published in Nashville by United Methodist Publishing House or Abingdon Press, 1972–1988.

45. *The United Methodist Hymnal* (Nashville: United Methodist Publishing House, 1989).

46. *An Ordinal* (Nashville: United Methodist Publishing House, 1980).

47. *Common Lectionary* (New York: Church Hymnal Corp., 1983).

48. *The Methodist Service Book* (London: Methodist Publishing House, 1975).

49. *Hymns and Psalms* (London: Methodist Publishing House, 1983).

CHAPTER 10: FRONTIER WORSHIP

1. Charles A. Johnson, *The Frontier Camp Meeting,* pp. 113–120.

2. "Declaration and Address," in *American Christianity,* ed. H. Shelton Smith, Robert T. Handy, and Lefferts A. Loetscher (New York: Charles Scribner's Sons, 1960), I, 584.

3. Allan Bouley, *From Freedom to Formula* (Washington, D.C.: Catholic University Press, 1981), pp. 111–113.

4. David Edwin Harrell, Jr., "Restorationism and the Stone-Campbell Tradi-

tion," *Encyclopedia of the American Religious Experience* (New York: Charles Scribner's Sons, 1988), II, 855.

5. Keith Watkins, *The Breaking of Bread,* pp. 48–67.

6. *Memoirs of Charles G. Finney* (Louisville, Ky.: Pentecostal Publishing Co., 1908), p. 20.

7. Charles G. Finney, *Lectures on Revivals of Religion,* ed. William G. McLoughlin, p. 251.

8. Ibid., p. 257.

9. Ibid., p. 276.

10. Franklin H. Littell, *From State Church to Pluralism* (Garden City, N.Y.: Doubleday & Co., 1962), p. 32.

11. *Methodist Hymnal* (New York: Eaton & Mains, 1905), p. ii.

12. Matthias Loy, "The Lutheran Cultus," and Sigmund Fritschel, "A Proper Understanding of Freedom in Worship," make the case for a traditional Lutheran cultus against excessive freedom, in *Lutheran Confessional Theology in America 1840–1880,* ed. Theodore G. Tappert (New York: Oxford University Press, 1972), pp. 301–339.

13. *Biography of Eld. Barton Warren Stone Written by Himself,* reprinted in *The Cane Ridge Reader,* ed. Hoke S. Dickinson, (n.p., n.d.), pp. 40–41.

14. Finney, *Lectures,* p. 259.

15. Whitney R. Cross, *The Burned-over District,* pp. 177–178, 237.

16. Timothy L. Smith, *Revivalism and Social Reform.*

17. Sandra S. Sizer, *Gospel Hymns and Social Religion* (Philadelphia: Temple University Press, 1978), pp. 138–159.

18. *The Epworth Hymnal* (New York, 1885), no. 158.

19. Ibid., nos. 253, 177, and 199.

20. See Johnson, *Frontier Camp Meeting,* pp. 42–48.

21. Cf. Gwen Kennedy Neville and John H. Westerhoff III, *Learning Through Liturgy* (New York: Seabury Press, 1978), pp. 7–57.

22. Watkins, *The Breaking of Bread,* pp. 101–107.

23. G. W. Hervey, *Manual of Revivals* (New York: Funk & Wagnalls, 1884), chs. 4 and 6.

24. See "Church Music as a Functional Act," Donald P. Hustad, *Jubilate! Church Music in the Evangelical Tradition,* pp. 14–25.

25. Ibid., p. 47.

26. Cross, *The Burned-over District,* pp. 138–150, and Fawn M. Brodie, *No Man Knows My History* (New York: Alfred A. Knopf, 1946).

27. *Church Manual* (n.p.: General Conference of Seventh-day Adventists, 1963), p. 111.

28. Ibid., p. 105. See also Norval F. Pease, *And Worship Him* (Nashville: Southern Publishing Association, 1967).

29. Cf. Melva R. W. Costen, "A Comparative Description of Curricular Offerings in Church Music Degree Programs at Accredited Protestant Theological Seminaries in the United States" (unpublished Ph.D. dissertation, Georgia State University, 1978).

30. Hustad, *Jubilate!,* p. ix.

31. Bill Gaither, *Hymns for the Family of God* (Nashville: John T. Benson Publishing Co., 1976).

32. *Powerhouse for God,* recorded by Jeff Todd Titon and Kenneth M. George

(Chapel Hill, N.C.: University of North Carolina, 1982), and *Primitive Baptist Hymns of the Blue Ridge,* recorded by Brett Sutton and Pete Hartman (Chapel Hill, N.C.: University of North Carolina, 1982).

33. Melva Wilson Costen and Darius Leander Swann, eds., "The Black Christian Worship Experience," *Journal of the Interdenominational Theological Center* 14 (Fall 1986–Spring 1987).

34. Finney, *Lectures,* p. 13.

CHAPTER 11: PENTECOSTAL WORSHIP

1. Quoted by Robert Mapes Anderson, *Vision of the Disinherited,* p. 53.
2. John T. Nichol, *The Pentecostals,* p. 28.
3. Anderson, *Vision,* pp. 65–78.
4. Walter J. Hollenweger, *The Pentecostals,* pp. 184–185.
5. Nichol, *Pentecostals,* p. 180.
6. Ibid., p. 52.
7. Hollenweger, *Pentecostals,* pp. 75–93.
8. Ibid., pp. 111–175.
9. Morton Kelsey, *Tongue Speaking,* pp. 98–104.
10. See the early responses of the churches in Kilian McDonnell, *Charismatic Renewal and the Churches,* pp. 41–78.
11. H. Richard Niebuhr, *The Social Sources of Denominationalism* (New York: Meridian Books, 1957), pp. 26–76.
12. William J. Samarin, *Tongues of Men and Angels,* pp. 2, 103–128, 227.
13. McDonnell, *Charismatic Renewal,* pp. 111–144.
14. *Pentecostal Hymnal Revised* (St. Louis: Pentecostal Publishing House, 1953), nos. 155, 81, 297.
15. Hollenweger, *Pentecostals,* pp. 385–398.
16. Jane Jacobs, *The Death and Life of Great American Cities* (New York: Random House, 1961), pp. 187–199.
17. Hollenweger, *Pentecostals,* pp. 395–396.
18. Ibid., p. 25.
19. Nichol, *Pentecostals,* pp. 106–107.
20. Grant Wacker, "Pentecostalism," *Encyclopedia of the American Religious Experience* (New York: Charles Scribner's Sons, 1988), III, 941.
21. McDonnell, *Charismatic Renewal,* p. 9.
22. *Pentecostal Hymnal Revised,* nos. 1, 42, 93.
23. *Supplement to the Book of Hymns* (Nashville: United Methodist Publishing House, 1982), no. 940.
24. See John Root, *Encountering Westindian Pentecostalism* (Bramcote, Beeston, Nottingham: Grove Books, 1979).
25. Hollenweger, *Pentecostals,* pp. 149–175.
26. Nichol, *Pentecostals,* p. 238.

CHAPTER 12: THE FUTURE OF PROTESTANT WORSHIP

1. *Baptism, Eucharist and Ministry* (Geneva: World Council of Churches, 1982), pp. 6–7, 15–16, 30–31.
2. *Constitution on the Sacred Liturgy* (Collegeville, Minn.: Liturgical Press, 1963), p. 25.
3. *Bishops' Committee on the Liturgy Newsletter* 24 (April 1988), 14–15.

Glossary

a cappella   singing without musical accompaniment.

altar call   an invitation to come forward to kneel at the communion rail for those newly converted or wishing to renew their commitment to Jesus Christ.

altar prayers   prayers in which individuals come forward to kneel at the communion rail in silent prayer.

altar   table on which the Lord's Supper is celebrated. The term is also used for the communion rail (Protestant) or space about the altar (Roman Catholic). Equivalent terms: altar-table, communion table, Lord's table, holy table.

Annunciation   March 25, the feast commemorating the visit of the angel Gabriel to the Virgin Mary and the conception of Christ (Luke 1:26–38).

Ante-communion   the first part of the Lord's Supper, service of the Word, fore-mass, syntaxis, pro-anaphora.

anthems   choral music, often of scriptural texts, usually of greater technical difficulty than congregational song.

Athanasian Creed   a lengthy creedal statement of unknown origin but probably from the late fourth or early fifth centuries, occasionally used in worship in the West.

Ausbund   the selection of hymns used by some Anabaptists since the sixteenth century.

Ave Maria   "Hail Mary," a short prayer dating from the eleventh century and coming into wide use in the sixteenth century, based on Luke 1:28, 42.

Baptism, Eucharist, and Ministry   an attempt to find ecumenical agreement on these three items, produced by the World Council of Churches in 1982 after many years of preparation.

baptistery   building or space within a building housing the pool or font that contains the water used for baptism.

breviary the book containing the texts for the daily services of prayer and praise, a compilation of several previous books.

canon liturgically the main portion of the eucharistic prayer, great thanksgiving, or anaphora (after the *Sanctus*), in the Lord's Supper.

canticles various hymnic materials from both Testaments other than the psalms, often said or sung, for example, the Magnificat (Luke 1:46–55).

catechism the basic doctrines of Christian faith for the study of young or new Christians, often in question-and-answer form.

chancel the portion of a church building designed for the use of the persons presiding, usually clergy or singers.

chantry chapels chapels erected for saying memorial masses for deceased benefactors, becoming numerous in parish churches and cathedrals from the fourteenth century.

chasuble long garment worn by priests at the Lord's Supper, dating from secular poncho worn by Romans of both sexes.

Collect for Illumination prayer of invocation for the Holy Spirit to act through the reading of scripture and preaching.

Collectio Rituum a ritual or collection of pastoral services: marriage, baptism, for example.

compline the last of the daily services said before retiring in the late evening.

confessional documents statements of the faith of a specific tradition such as the Augsburg Confession of 1530 (Lutheran) or Westminster Confession of 1646 (Presbyterian).

Congregation of Rites since 1588, the official Roman Catholic bureau in charge of the standardization of worship and of canonization of saints.

congregationalism the principle that each local Christian community is self-governing and hence competent to order worship for itself.

consecration the setting apart of a thing or person for holy uses. This can refer to the bread and wine in the Lord's Supper, religious workers, buildings, or furnishings.

Consensus Tigurinus "Zurich Agreement," on the doctrine of the Lord's Supper agreed to by Swiss Protestants in 1549.

cope cloak worn by clergy on important ceremonial occasions other than the Lord's Supper.

cultus a general term for all the forms and practices of worship of a specific tradition at a given time.

daily office a daily cycle of services of prayer and praise. The number of services vary according to the church concerned; the contents are basically psalmody, scripture, hymns, and prayers.

Deutsche Messe Luther's second revision of the mass, published in German in 1526, including detailed instruction about the order of service and music.

Deutsche Evangelische Messe German Evangelical Mass published by Balthasar Hübmaier about 1526.

Didache "The Teaching of the Twelve Apostles," a church order dating from the late first or early second century.

dominical injunctions commands from Jesus Christ to "do this" (1 Cor. 11:24–25) and "make disciples . . . baptizing" (Matt. 28:19), interpreted as warrants for sacraments.

elevation the lifting of the consecrated bread and wine in the Lord's Supper after the words of institution, as offering and for adoration.

ephphatha word of Jesus (Mark 7:34), meaning, in Aramaic, "be opened," at various times reenacted in baptismal rites.

epiclesis prayer of invocation for the Father to send the Holy Spirit to the people and gifts present in the eucharist, part of the eucharistic prayer.

Epiphany January 6, the feast variously commemorating the birth of Christ, the visit of the Magi, or the first sign at Cana (John 2:11).

epistle the lesson read in the Sunday service and other occasions, often today as the second lesson, from the New Testament epistles or (occasionally) Revelation.

extreme unction a sacrament among Roman Catholics, originally and most recently of healing but long regarded as preparation for death.

Formula Missae Luther's first revision of the mass, published in Latin in 1523, generally conservative.

fraction the act of breaking of the bread in the Lord's Supper (Matt. 26:26).

Gallican liturgies the liturgies other than the Roman rite in use in the West in the early Middle Ages, largely replaced from the ninth century onward but known for variety and poetical expression.

Gallicanism the relative independence of the Roman Catholic Church in France from interference from Rome, particularly from the seventeenth to the nineteenth centuries although with earlier precedents.

Gloria in excelsis a musical part of the eucharist, beginning with the words "Glory to God in the highest"; the Great Doxology as contrasted to the Lesser Doxology, the *Gloria Patri,* "Glory to the Father."

Gospel the lesson read from the canonical Gospels in public worship, usually read last and sometimes with ceremony.

Hampton Court Conference conference in 1604 between Puritan leaders and the new King James I of England, resulting in the King James Bible.

homily a sermon, particularly one published and read as a sermon.

iconoclasm the destruction of images because of concern that they detract from the true worship of God or teach false doctrine.

images representations by painting, sculpture, or glazing of members of .he Trinity and holy persons from all ages, sometimes venerated.

incense a smoke from burning gum or wood that produces a fragrant odor, recognized as symbolic of prayer ascending (Ps. 141:2).

inclusive language language structured so as not to detract from the full human worth of all persons by sexual, racial, ethnic, or handicapping differentiations; a linguistic manifestation of equality.

introit   essentially a sung entrance hymn at the beginning of the Lord's Supper, usually based on a psalm.

invitatories   verses at the beginning of a prayer service, usually leading to Psalm 95.

kirk   the Scottish word for church, often used for the Church of Scotland.

lauds   the ancient morning service of prayer and praise, part of the daily cycle.

libation   the act of pouring the wine in the Lord's Supper from a flagon into a chalice or chalices.

litany   a form of public prayer in which a refrain is repeated by the congregation in response to a series of petitions or thanksgivings spoken by an individual.

matins   originally a nighttime service but, since the Reformation, the morning service of prayer and praise, often said or sung daily.

Mediator Dei   encyclical letter of Pope Pius XII issued in 1947 with a view to regulating the developing liturgical movement.

Mennonites   the largest body of Anabaptists, which grew rapidly in the Netherlands in the sixteenth century and is now worldwide.

missal   the book containing the texts and rubrics for saying mass, a compilation of several books previously in use.

modern devotion   a renewed spiritual life which spread from Holland after the late fourteenth century.

Mormons   the Church of Jesus Christ of Latter-day Saints or the Reorganized Church of Jesus Christ of Latter Day Saints.

motet   a choral piece of music sung in various parts, often unaccompanied, usually based on a sacred text.

nave   the portion of a church building usually occupied by the congregation; the main portion.

offertory   the moment in worship when offerings of gifts such as money, bread and wine, or music are offered for holy use.

ordinary time   a term used since 1969 for the seasons after Epiphany and Pentecost by Roman Catholics.

ordination   the rite of setting aside certain persons for distinctive functions in the Christian community as lay officers or clergy.

penance   a sacrament among Roman Catholics for the forgiveness of sins and reconciliation of repentant Christians with God and one another.

pontifical   the book containing services performed by a bishop such as ordinations and consecrations of persons, buildings, and objects.

postils   books of sermons, often published to help other preachers.

Preces Privatae   collection of private prayers by the saintly Anglican bishop Lancelot Andrewes (1555–1626), published after his death.

predestination   the belief that God has predetermined the identity of all to be saved or damned (Rom. 8:28–30).

prime   a short daily service at the first hour of the day, mostly obsolete.

private pew   a church pew owned and occupied by private individuals, in the eighteenth and nineteenth centuries. The selling of pews often financed church building but is now almost universally repudiated as a practice.

prone   an unofficial service, often added to the mass in the late medieval period before, during, or after mass, usually in the vernacular and including a sermon.

propers   texts in worship that change from date to date as contrasted to those that do not. Includes prayers, hymns, lessons, and psalms.

psalmody   the psalms of the Old Testament used in worship, either said or sung.

relics   sacred objects, especially parts of the bodies of holy persons or items in close contact with their bodies.

reliquaries   vessels to contain and (sometimes) display relics.

requiem mass   a celebration of the eucharist in commemoration of the life of someone deceased.

responsories   short dialogical verses and responses, usually between the leader of worship and the congregation.

ritual   the handbook of services such as baptismal, marriage, and burial rites performed by a pastor; hence, pastorale or manual.

rood screen   a screen in medieval churches separating the nave from the chancel with a cross (rood) over it.

rubric   directions as to what to do in a service, often printed in red.

rubricism   the mentality that worship must be carried out strictly according to prescribed rules, or rubrics.

Sanctus   part of the eucharistic prayer "Holy, holy, holy," usually sung.

Sarum Use   the late-medieval version of Roman Catholic rites in general use throughout the southern province of England.

Savoy Conference   meeting in 1661 of Puritans and Anglicans as a last attempt of reconciliation of liturgical agenda, proving fruitless.

Small Catechism   Luther's small book for the instruction of Christians in the basics of the faith, published in 1529.

Thirty-nine Articles   the original official doctrinal statement of the Church of England, issued first in 1563.

transubstantiation   doctrine that the substances (but not the appearances) of bread and wine become the body and blood of Christ in the eucharist; official teaching of Roman Catholics since 1215.

Trent, Council of   council for the reform of the Roman Catholic Church, convened in three periods between 1545 and 1563.

Unification Church   a recent denomination, popularly known as "Moonies" from their leader the Rev. Sun Myung Moon.

Vatican II   Roman Catholic council from 1962 to 1965, instrumental in opening Roman Catholicism to much of the thought and practices of the modern world.

vespers   the evening daily office of prayer and praise, also known as evening prayer or evensong.

vestments   garb worn by clergy for the eucharist and other services, originating as secular clothing but long hallowed by ecclesiastical custom.

vigils   nighttime services of prayer and praise, eventually becoming part of the daily cycle of services.

Westminster Directory   document replacing the *Book of Common Prayer* from 1645 to 1660 with detailed instructions for the ordering of worship.

Select Bibliography

GENERAL

Barclay, Alexander. *The Protestant Doctrine of the Lord's Supper*. Glasgow: Jackson, Wylie & Co., 1927.

Blume, Friedrich. *Protestant Church Music:* London: Victor Gollancz, 1975.

Coena Domini I. Ed. Irmgard Pahl. Freiburg, Switzerland: Universitätsverlag, 1983.

Davies, Horton. *Worship and Theology in England*. 5 vols. London: Oxford University Press; Princeton, N.J.: Princeton University Press, 1961–1975.

Davies, J. G., ed. *The New Westminster Dictionary of Liturgy and Worship*. Philadelphia: Westminster Press, 1986.

Jones, Cheslyn, Geoffrey Wainwright, and Edward Yarnold, eds. *The Study of Liturgy*. New York: Oxford University Press, 1978.

Maxwell, William D. *An Outline of Christian Worship*. London: Oxford University Press, 1936; reissued as *History of Christian Worship* (Grand Rapids: Baker Book House, 1982).

Micklem, Nathaniel, ed. *Christian Worship*. Oxford: Oxford University Press, 1936.

Senn, Frank, ed. *Protestant Spiritual Traditions*. Mahwah, N.J.: Paulist Press, 1986.

Thompson, Bard. *Liturgies of the Western Church*. Cleveland: Meridian Books, 1961; Philadelphia: Fortress Press, 1980.

Wainwright, Geoffrey. *Doxology: The Praise of God in Worship, Doctrine, and Life* New York: Oxford University Press, 1980.

White, James F. *Introduction to Christian Worship*. Nashville: Abingdon Press, 1980.

———. *Protestant Worship and Church Architecture*. New York: Oxford University Press, 1964.

LUTHERAN

Aulén, Gustaf. *Eucharist and Sacrifice*. Edinburgh: Oliver & Boyd, 1958.

The Book of Concord. Ed. Theodore G. Tappert. Philadelphia: Fortress Press, 1959.

Brilioth, Yngve. *Eucharistic Faith and Practice: Evangelical and Catholic*. London: S.P.C.K., 1953.

Kalb, Friedrich. *Theology of Worship in Seventeenth-Century Lutheranism* St. Louis: Concordia Publishing House, 1965.

Leiturgia: Handbuch des evangelischen Gottesdienstes. 5 vols. Kassel: Johannes Stauda Verlag, 1954–1970.

Luther's Works. 55 vols. Philadelphia: Fortress Press, 1960– .

Nelson, Clifford, ed. *The Lutherans in North America.* Rev. Ed. Philadelphia: Fortress Press, 1980.

Sasse, Hermann. *This Is My Body.* Adelaide: Lutheran Publishing House, 1977.

Vajta, Vilmos. *Luther on Worship.* Philadelphia: Muhlenberg Press, 1958.

REFORMED

Calvin, John. *Institutes of the Christian Religion.* 2 vols. Ed. John T. McNeill and tr. Ford Lewis Battles. Philadelphia: Westminster Press, 1960.

Eire, Carlos M. N. *The War Against the Idols.* Cambridge: Cambridge University Press, 1986.

Forrester, Duncan, and Douglas Murray. *Studies in the History of Worship in Scotland.* Edinburgh: T. & T. Clark, 1984.

Hageman, Howard G. *Pulpit and Table.* Richmond: John Knox Press, 1962.

Macleod, Donald. *Presbyterian Worship.* New rev. ed. Atlanta: John Knox Press, 1980.

Melton, Julius. *Presbyterian Worship in America.* Richmond: John Knox Press, 1967.

Nichols, James Hastings. *Corporate Worship in the Reformed Tradition.* Philadelphia: Westminster Press, 1968.

Old, Hughes Oliphant. *The Patristic Roots of Reformed Worship.* Zurich: Theologischer Verlag, 1975.

———. *Worship That Is Reformed According to Scripture.* Atlanta: John Knox Press, 1984.

Schmidt-Clausing, Fritz. *Zwingli als Liturgiker.* Göttingen: Vandenhoeck & Ruprecht, 1952.

Wallace, Ronald S. *Calvin's Doctrine of the Word and Sacrament.* Edinburgh: Oliver & Boyd, 1953.

Zwingli, Ulrich. *Commentary on True and False Religion.* Durham, N.C.: Labyrinth Press, 1981.

ANABAPTIST

Armour, Rollin Stely. *Anabaptist Baptism: A Representative Study.* Scottdale, Pa.: Herald Press, 1966.

Durnbaugh, Donald. *The Believers' Church.* London: Macmillan Co., 1968.

Estep, William R. *The Anabaptist Story.* Grand Rapids: Wm. B. Eerdmans Publishing Co., 1975.

Friedmann, Robert. *The Theology of Anabaptism.* Scottdale, Pa.: Herald Press, 1973.

Klaassen, Walter. *Anabaptism: Neither Catholic Nor Protestant.* Waterloo, Iowa: Conrad Press, 1973.

———, ed. *Anabaptism in Outline.* Scottdale, Pa.: Herald Press, 1981.

Menno Simons. *The Complete Writings of Menno Simons.* Scottdale, Pa.: Herald Press, 1974.

Pidkin, H.W., and John Howard Yoder, trs. and eds. *Balthasar Hübmaier, Theologian of Anabaptism.* Scottdale, Pa.: Herald Press, 1989.

Williams, George H. *The Radical Reformation.* Philadelphia: Westminster Press, 1962.

ANGLICAN

Addleshaw, G. W. O., and Frederick Etchells. *The Architectural Setting of Anglican Worship.* London: Faber & Faber, 1948.

Bradshaw, Paul F. *The Anglican Ordinal.* London: S.P.C.K., 1971.

Brook, Stella. *The Language of the Book of Common Prayer.* London: André Deutsch, 1965.

Cardwell, E. *A History of Conferences on the Book of Common Prayer.* Oxford: Oxford University Press, 1849.

Cuming, Geoffrey. *The Godly Order.* London: Alcuin Club/S.P.C.K., 1983.

———. *A History of Anglican Liturgy.* 2nd ed. London: Macmillan Co., 1982.

Hatchett, Marion J. *The Making of the First American Book of Common Prayer.* New York: Seabury Press, 1982.

Ratcliff, E. C. *Liturgical Studies.* London: S.P.C.K., 1976.

Shepherd, Massey H., Jr. *The Oxford American Prayer Book Commentary.* New York: Oxford University Press, 1950.

White, James F. *The Cambridge Movement.* Cambridge: Cambridge University Press, 1979.

SEPARATIST AND PURITAN

Adams, Doug. *Meeting House to Camp Meeting: Toward a History of American Free Church Worship from 1620 to 1835.* Saratoga, Calif.: Modern Liturgy-Resource Publications, 1981.

Davies, Horton. *The Worship of the English Puritans.* Westminster, Md.: Dacre Press, 1948.

Frere, W. H., and C. E. Douglas, eds. *Puritan Manifestoes.* London: S.P.C.K., 1954.

Hambrick-Stove, Charles E. *The Practice of Piety.* Chapel Hill, N.C.: University of North Carolina Press, 1982.

Mayor, Stephen. *The Lord's Supper in Early English Dissent.* London: Epworth Press, 1972.

Skoglund, John E. *Worship in the Free Churches.* Valley Forge, Pa.: Judson Press, 1965.

Spinks, Bryan D. *Freedom or Order? The Eucharistic Liturgy in English Congregationalism, 1645–1980.* Allison Park, Pa.: Pickwick Publications, 1984.

———. *From the Lord and "The Best Reformed Churches."* Rome: C.L.V. Edizioni Liturgiche, 1984.

Stout, Harry S. *The New England Soul.* New York: Oxford University Press, 1986.

QUAKER

Andrews, Edward D. *The People Called Shakers: A Search for the Perfect Society.* New enl. ed. New York: Dover Publications, 1963.

Barclay, Robert. *An Apology for the True Christian Divinity as the Same Is Held Forth and Preached by the People, in Scorn, Called Quakers.* London, 1678.

Comfort, William Wistar. *Just Among Friends: The Quaker Way of Life.* Philadelphia: American Friends Service Committee, 1959.

Hall, Francis B., ed. *Quaker Worship in North America.* Richmond, Ind.: Friends United Press, 1979.

Hamm, Thomas D. *The Transformation of American Quakerism: Orthodox Friends, 1800–1907.* Bloomington, Ind.: Indiana University Press, 1988.

Lucas, Sidney. *The Quaker Story.* New York: Harper & Brothers, 1949.

Procter-Smith, Marjorie. *Women in Shaker Community and Worship: A Feminist Analysis of Religious Symbolism.* Lewiston, N.Y.: Edwin Mellen Press, 1985.

Steere, Douglas V. *On Speaking Out of the Silence.* Wallingford, Pa.: Pendle Hill Pamphlets, 1972.

————. *Prayer and Worship.* New York: Association Press, 1938.

Trueblood, Elton. *The People Called Quakers.* New York: Harper & Row, 1966.

METHODIST

Baker, Frank. *From Wesley to Asbury.* Durham, N.C.: Duke University Press, 1976.

Bishop, John. *Methodist Worship in Relation to Free Church Worship.* New York: Scholars Studies Press, 1975.

Borgen, Ole E. *John Wesley on the Sacraments: A Theological Study.* Nashville: Abingdon Press, 1972.

Bowmer, John C. *The Sacrament of the Lord's Supper in Early Methodism.* Westminster, Md.: Dacre Press, 1951.

Costen, Melva Wilson, and Darius Leander Swann, eds. "The Black Christian Worship Experience." *Journal of the Interdenominational Theological Center* 14 (Fall 1986–Spring 1987).

Dolbey, George W. *The Architectural Expression of Methodism.* London: Epworth Press, 1964.

Rattenbury, J. Ernest. *The Eucharistic Hymns of John and Charles Wesley.* London: Epworth Press, 1948.

Routley, Erik. *The Musical Wesleys.* New York: Oxford University Press, 1968.

Tripp, David. *The Renewal of the Covenant in the Methodist Tradition.* London: Epworth Press, 1969.

Wade, William N. "A History of Public Worship in the Methodist Episcopal Church," unpublished Ph.D. dissertation, University of Notre Dame, 1981.

FRONTIER

Cross, Whitney R. *The Burned-over District.* New York: Harper & Row, 1965.

Dorgan, Howard. *Giving Glory to God in Appalachia.* Knoxville, Tenn.: University of Tennessee Press, 1987.

Finney, Charles G. *Lectures on Revivals of Religion.* Ed. William G. McLoughlin. Cambridge, Mass.: Harvard University Press, 1960.

Gilmore, Alec, ed. *Christian Baptism.* Philadelphia: Judson Press, 1959.

Hustad, Donald P. *Jubilate! Church Music in the Evangelical Tradition.* Carol Stream, Ill.: Hope Publishing Co., 1981.

Johnson, Charles A. *The Frontier Camp Meeting.* Dallas: S.M.U. Press, 1955.

McLoughlin, William G. *Revivals, Awakenings, and Reform.* Chicago: University of Chicago Press, 1978.

Smith, Timothy L. *Revivalism and Social Reform.* Nashville: Abingdon Press, 1957.

Watkins, Keith. *The Breaking of Bread.* St. Louis: Bethany Press, 1966.

Weisberger, Bernard A. *They Gathered at the River.* Boston: Little, Brown & Co., 1958.

PENTECOSTAL

Anderson, Robert Mapes. *Vision of the Disinherited.* New York: Oxford University Press, 1979.

Bloch-Hoell, Nils. *The Pentecostal Movement.* London: Allen & Unwin, 1964.

Bruner, Frederick Dale. *A Theology of the Holy Spirit: The Pentecostal Experience and the New Testament Witness.* Grand Rapids: Wm. B. Eerdmans Publishing Co., 1970.

Hollenweger, Walter J. *The Pentecostals.* Minneapolis: Augsburg Publishing House, 1972.

Kelsey, Morton. *Tongue Speaking.* New York: Crossroad Publishing Co., 1981.

McDonnell, Kilian. *Charismatic Renewal and the Churches.* New York: Seabury Press, 1976.

Nichol, John Thomas. *The Pentecostals.* Plainfield, N.J.: Logos International, 1971.

O'Connor, Edward D. *The Pentecostal Movement in the Catholic Church.* Notre Dame, Ind.: Ave Maria Press, 1971.

Samarin, William J. *Tongues of Men and Angels: The Religious Language of Pentecostalism.* New York: Macmillan Co., 1972.

Synan, Vinson. *The Holiness-Pentecostal Movement in the United States.* Grand Rapids: Wm. B. Eerdmans Publishing Co., 1971.

Index of Persons

Index of Subjects